Japan's Comfort Women

This groundbreaking and highly controversial book reveals how sex is used and abused to maintain military morale and discipline. It reveals the story of the "comfort women" who were forced to enter prostitution as sexual slaves of the Japanese Imperial Army in the period immediately before and during World War II.

Using previously untapped personal testimonies and an unprecedented range of archival and documentary research, Yuki Tanaka exposes Japanese military and political leaders who ordered and controlled this regime of sexual exploitation, and movingly describes its devastating effects on the lives of scores of thousands of Asian women victims.

Controversially, *Japan's Comfort Women* also examines the sexual conduct of the Allied forces in this period and the nature of the postwar "comfort women" system that Japan created to service US soldiers during the Occupation. The author's exhaustive research in Japanese, American and Australian archives reveals how the US government, for reasons of political expediency, failed to prosecute as war criminals those responsible for the "comfort women" system.

This book offers unique insights into this terrible episode in Japanese, Asian and American history and the broader dimensions of military violence against women.

Yuki Tanaka is a Professor at the Hiroshima Peace Institute, Hiroshima City University, Japan. He is the author of the provocative, bestselling book *Hidden Horrors: Japanese War Crimes in World War II*, and was the historical advisor on a recent BBC TV documentary film series, *Horror in the East*.

Asia's Transformations
Edited by Mark Selden
Binghamton University and Cornell University, USA

The books in this series explore the political, social, economic and cultural consequences of Asia's twentieth-century transformations. The series emphasizes the tumultuous interplay of local, national, regional and global forces as Asia bids to become the hub of the world economy. While focusing on the contemporary, it also looks back to analyze the antecedents of Asia's contested rise.

This series comprises two strands:

Asia's Transformations aims to address the needs of students and teachers, and the titles will be published in hardback and paperback. Titles include:

Debating Human Rights
Critical essays from the United States and Asia
Edited by Peter Van Ness

Hong Kong's History
State and society under colonial rule
Edited by Tak-Wing Ngo

Japan's Comfort Women
Sexual slavery and prostitution during World War II and the US occupation
Yuki Tanaka

Opium, Empire and the Global Political Economy
Carl A Trocki

Chinese Society
Change, conflict and resistance
Edited by Elizabeth J Perry and Mark Selden

Mao's Children in the New China
Voices from the Red Guard generation
Yarong Jiang and David Ashley

Remaking the Chinese State
Strategies, society and security
Edited by Chien-min Chao and Bruce J Dickson

Routledge Studies in Asia's Transformations is a forum for innovative new research intended for a high-level specialist readership, and the titles will be available in hardback only. Titles include:

1. The American Occupation of Japan and Okinawa*
Literature and memory
Michael Molasky

2. Koreans in Japan
Critical voices from the margin
Edited by Sonia Ryang

3. Internationalizing the Pacific
The United States, Japan and the Institute of Pacific Relations in war and peace, 1919–1945
Tomoko Akami

4. Imperialism in South East Asia
'A fleeting, passing phase'
Nicholas Tarling

* Now available in paperback

Japan's Comfort Women

Sexual slavery and prostitution during World War II and the US occupation

Yuki Tanaka

London and New York

What our fathers did not tell us

First published 2002 by Routledge
11 New Fetter Lane, London EC4P 4EE

Simultaneously published in the USA and Canada
by Routledge
29 West 35th Street, New York, NY 10001

Routledge is an imprint of the Taylor & Francis Group

Typeset in 10/12pt Baskerville by Graphicraft Limited, Hong Kong
Printed and bound in Great Britain by TJ International Ltd, Padstow, Cornwall

British Library Cataloguing in Publication Data
A catalogue record for this book is available from the British Library

Library of Congress Cataloging in Publication Data
Tanaka, Toshiyuki, 1949–
    Japan's comfort women: sexual slavery and prostitution during World War II and the
U.S. occupation / Yuki Tanaka.
       p. cm. — (Asia's transformations)
    Includes bibliographical references and index.
    1. Comfort women—Asia. 2. World War, 1939–1945—Women—Asia. 3.
Japan—History—Allied occupation, 1945–1952. 4. Soldiers—Japan—Sexual behavior. 5.
Soldiers—United States—Sexual behavior. I. Title. II. Series.

    D810.C698 T36 2001
    940.54′05′0922519—dc21   2001048307

ISBN 0–415–19400–8 (hbk)
ISBN 0–415–19401–6 (pbk)

For Mika and Alisa

Contents

Figure and tables

Figure

Tables

Plates

Foreword

By Susan Brownmiller

In December 1991, three Korean women who had been abducted into Japanese military brothels during World War II filed a dramatic class-action lawsuit in a Tokyo court. After a half-century of shame, anonymity, and hardship, the aged survivors were ready to tell their personal stories, and to demand an apology and reparations from the Japanese government on behalf of an estimated 100,000 victims.

The women's campaign had begun in Seoul with a call for a public memorial and had escalated into impromptu confrontations with Japanese diplomats. Their tactical leader, an active feminist, was Professor Yun Chung Ok of Ehwa Women's University. As a young schoolgirl, Professor Yun herself had narrowly escaped abduction and conscription into the brothels. Aided by church women and a sisterly coalition of Japanese feminists who were equally intent on righting an historic wrong, the Koreans' demand for belated justice was covered widely by the foreign media, putting the term "comfort woman" into the international lexicon.

Thus, the world learned of a highly organized trafficking system during the Pacific War run by the Japanese Imperial Army, secret police, and local "labor recruiters" using the ruse of legitimate jobs for good pay. Girls and women taken from country villages, or hijacked in broad daylight on city streets, became a human cargo that was transported to barracks on frontline posts, jungle airstrips, and base camps, where the captives remained in sexual servitude until the war's end.

Japan's military brothels were not exactly an undocumented story when the Korean comfort women launched their international campaign. Two books on the subject published in the 1970s had assumed a modest place in Japan's growing literature of conscience, but the research of Kim Il Myon, a Korean, and Senda Kako, a Japanese, had produced little interest and only scant indignation. It took the rise of an indigenous feminist movement in Asia to supply the moral outrage and place the dormant issue in a modern context.

Yuki Tanaka, the son of a Japanese military man, is the latest historian, and certainly the most meticulous, exhaustive scholar, to explore the dimensions of the comfort women story. In addition to ferreting out fresh documentation from buried and forgotten sources, he creates an original overview by moving backward and forward in time from the World War II era. He offers a capsule history of Japanese prostitution in foreign and domestic ports in the nineteenth century as Japan sought to expand its international trade (making the interesting point that the trade in women's flesh helped to jump-start capitalist enterprise). He compares Japan's wartime comfort stations with the brothels hastily set up by the defeated rulers for American soldiers during the postwar Occupation (the coercion was economic need rather than brute force). And he notes the similarities between the comfort women's slavery-like barracks and the "rape camps" holding Bosnian women in the ethnic wars that tore apart the former Yugoslavia.

Professor Tanaka offers no excuses for what his country did to women in the Second World War, but he sees it as part of a pervasive pattern of worldwide male aggression and domination. Trafficking in women has been on the increase, in China, Vietnam, Russia, and Eastern Europe, ever since the fall of communism exposed the destitute economies of these unfortunate countries. The moral law-lessness accompanying crude, rudimentary capitalism is not very different from the brutal sexual exploitation that accompanies warfare. The question for the future, of course, is can it be stopped?

Susan Brownmiller
author of *Against Our
Will: Men, Women and Rape*

Acknowledgments

This research project started as an extension of my last book, *Hidden Horrors: Japanese War Crimes in World War II*, in particular Chapter 3, "Rape and War: the Japanese Experience."

Initially I had no plan to cover the conduct of the Allied forces in relation to the comfort women issue. However, my two research trips to the US altered the original plan. In late 1995 and early 1996 I was asked to conduct research at the US National Archives in Maryland by Mr. Ōmori Junrō, a director of the TV documentary section of NHK (Japan Broadcasting Commission), for a documentary film project. My assignment was to find documents that would reveal why, at the end of World War II, the US military authorities were not interested in prosecuting the Japanese who had been responsible for the sexual exploitation of vast numbers of so-called "comfort women," despite their clear knowledge of this matter. On the first trip to the US in December 1995, I spent long hours at the US National Archives, searching any documents that might give some hint to the answer. I concentrated on the documents prepared during the Battle of Okinawa. As I knew that some of the US troops who landed on the Okinawan islands had come across many Korean comfort women abandoned by the Japanese forces, I hoped to find relevant official reports. The result was miserable. I could not find a single document that referred to comfort women, and I came back to Australia on Christmas Eve without any "Christmas present" for Mr. Ōmori. I was embarrassed to report this totally unsatisfactory result to him in Tokyo.

Therefore I was really surprised when he asked me to go back to the US to try again a few months later. This time I drastically changed my research strategy. I started investigating the US military documents in reference to their own soldiers' sexual conduct during World War II, hoping that I might find some clue using this indirect way of searching. My speculation was right. I was astounded by the amazing content and the large volume of vital documents that I found. I photocopied almost all of these documents and brought them back to Australia. As soon as I returned home, I visited the Australian National Archives and the War Memorial and started uncovering similar documents. The amount and content of relevant Australian documents that I subsequently found was a further surprise to me. Some of the results of these discoveries are included, mainly in

Chapter 4, but also in Chapters 5 and 6. If I had not been given the opportunity to visit the US National Archives twice, both times at the expense of NHK, the content of this book would have been very different. For this, my principal thanks go to NHK and Director Ōmori. The NHK documentary entitled *Asian Comfort Women* was broadcast in December, 1996.

I also thank the Australian Research Council for a grant in 1998 which partly funded my research trip to the National Diet (parliament) Library in Tokyo to collect further relevant information, which was used in Chapters 5 and 6.

As in my last book, Mark Selden offered the most detailed comments on my draft manuscript. I am grateful for his valuable comments and continuing help. Without his patience and generosity, I could not have finished this book. I extend sincere thanks to Gavan McCormack and his wife Fusako Yoshinaga. I particularly appreciate the hospitality they extended to me at their Canberra home every time I worked at the Australian War Memorial and the Australian National Archives. My discussion of a range of issues with them over the dinner table stimulated my thoughts and writing.

My special appreciation goes to Susan Brownmiller for her most articulate and concise foreword. It is a great honor for me to have an endorsement from one of the world's leading feminists whom I admire immensely.

I also offer my thanks to many colleagues and friends in Japan, Australia, the UK, and the US, who helped me in various different ways. In particular, Awaya Kentarō, Chita Takeshi, Fujinaga Takeshi, Hayashi Hirofumi, Igarashi Masahiro, Ikeda Eriko, Kawada Fumiko, Kim Booja, Matsui Yayori, Matsumoto Masumi, Nakagawa Sadamu, Nishino Rumiko, Ōwaki Michiyo, Takazato Suzuyo, Ueno Chizuko, Utsumi Aiko, Yoshimi Yoshiaki, Yun Myeongsuk, Martina Balazova, Cynthia Enloe, Stephen Frost, Michiko Hase, Laura Hein, Mary Katzenstein, Laurence Rees, Carol Rittner, Jean Ruff-O'Herne, Indai Sajor, Gary Sigley, Chris Smyth, Paul Tickle, Katharine Moon, and Nick MacLellan.

If there are any inaccuracies in this text, however, I alone bear responsibility for them.

For help in searching archival documents, photos, and pictures, I thank all the staff of the US National Archives, Australian National Archives, the Australian War Memorial, and the Japanese Diet Library, in particular, Rick Boyland, Esta Carey, and Ian Afflex.

Special thanks to my wife Jo, and my parents-in-law, Inge and Grahame. As in my last book, without their moral support, I could not have completed this project. This book is dedicated to our daughters, Mika and Alisa, hoping that some day they will find this book useful for cultivating their own thoughts and ideas on gender issues.

While completing this book project, my father, who was a young army officer during the Pacific War, passed away at the age of 84 years. While sorting out my father's old photos, I was made to re-appreciate the profound impact of the war upon his life. The latter half of his twenties was entirely given to the war. Usually, the experiences of one's twenties are the most important for shaping the foundation of one's own way of thinking. As the population of my father's generation, which had first-hand experience of unforgettable events in World War II, is now rapidly diminishing, I feel an urgent need to accurately record such important issues as the subject of this present book, and to re-examine that generation's wartime conduct from various angles. Ideally, such an exercise should be a co-operative work between the people of my father's generation and those of my own. That is an extremely difficult task, however, due to the enormous "generation gap" between us. Difficulties arise also as a result of the widespread silence on our fathers' side about certain relevant subjects. This book, I hope, will contribute to dissolving the estrangement between the two generations, and to bringing about something that we can learn from and, at the same time, that we can pass on to our children.

Author's note

I use the term "Asia-Pacific War" to include various battles in which the Japanese Imperial forces were involved, starting from the so-called Manchurian Incident in September 1931 and continuing on until the end of World War II in the Pacific in August 1945. The main reason for the use of this term is to clearly indicate that the Japanese military activities in China before the attack on Pearl Harbor in December 1941 and the war in the Pacific theater were closely interlinked and inseparable historical events. I believe that World War II in the Pacific theater can be adequately analyzed only when it is examined in this time span of 15 years.

All Japanese names, including authors of Japanese texts, have been cited in traditional Japanese order with the surname first.

Introduction

Sex becomes a source of brutality and oppression, instead of one of joy and life, when it is exploited in warfare. A lengthy and comprehensive argument is unnecessary to illuminate this point, which is well illustrated by the following extract from the autobiography of Maria Rosa Henson, a former Filipina comfort woman. The passage depicts clearly how military violence involves atrocious abuse of women's sexuality.

> Twelve soldiers raped me in quick succession, after which I was given half an hour rest. Then twelve more soldiers followed. They all lined up outside the room waiting for their turn. I bled so much and was in such pain, I could not even stand up. The next morning, I was too weak to get up . . . I could not eat. I felt much pain, and my vagina was swollen. I cried and cried, calling my mother. I could not resist the soldiers because they might kill me. So what else could I do? Every day, from two in the afternoon to ten in the evening, the soldiers lined up outside my room and the rooms of the six other women there. I did not even have time to wash after each assault. At the end of the day, I just closed my eyes and cried. My torn dress would be brittle from the crust that had formed from the soldiers' dried semen. I washed myself with hot water and a piece of cloth so I would be clean. I pressed the cloth to my vagina like a compress to relieve that pain and the swelling.[1]

Sex is a beautiful and extremely enjoyable human activity when it confirms and reconfirms the intimate relationship with a partner. When out of control, however, sex becomes ugly and monstrously abusive. Unfortunately these are the two diametrically opposing characteristics of sex.

This book is about how sex is used and abused to maintain military organization and discipline; ultimately it is about *control*. It investigates mass rape under the control of military forces in the years 1931–1945, and the half-century effort to suppress information about the system and its role in sustaining the Japanese military in World War II. It also examines the lives of the women whom the system abused. This study of the Japanese system of military sexual slavery is an attempt to understand the origins, uses, and abuses of the system, and to tell the stories of those who ordered and implemented it, as well as those of the many Asian women victims.

A heavy silence regarding this issue among the men of my father's generation who participated in World War II was one of many motives that inspired my research into this subject some years ago. However, this book is not only about Japan at war. I wanted to trace and understand the specific experiences that our fathers – not only Japanese, but also those from the Allied nations – did not tell us about and on which they still maintain silence. I introduce, therefore, discussion of American, Australian, and other nations' practices concerning wartime prostitution. I also discuss the experience of Japan under American occupation in order to point out certain continuities in Japanese government-directed prostitution during the US occupation, while distinguishing important and unique elements of sexual slavery in the wartime comfort women system.

During the war my father was a young officer – a lieutenant – of Japan's Kwantung Army and was stationed at a garrison near Harbin in Manchuria. Well before the end of the war, he was seriously injured in a battle with China's People's Liberation Army forces and was consequently sent back to a hospital in Japan. After recovering from injury, he was posted to a domestic military base and never returned to Manchuria. He married my mother shortly before the war ended while still serving as a military officer. He had three brothers, all army officers, who served in various places in Manchuria. All survived the war and eventually returned home. I grew up repeatedly hearing stories about the war in Manchuria told by my father and my uncles. The gist of these stories was how horrendous and absurd the war was, but also how honorably they personally had behaved. I heard stories again and again of how well they had protected and looked after the men under their command, and how well they disciplined their young soldiers. Yet very little reference was made to the lives of the local Chinese people and the relationship between the Japanese troops and the local population in Manchuria. There was certainly no mention of the various atrocities perpetrated by the Japanese troops against Chinese civilians.

My father and uncles were particularly silent about the issue of comfort women. Indeed, I knew very little about this subject until the early 1970s when, as a university student, I read a book by a Korean resident in Japan, describing the lives of Koreans who were forced laborers and comfort women during the war.[2] It was then that I first realized the scale and intensity of the sexual exploitation of Korean women by the Japanese forces. Although I had known little about the comfort women system previously, the book did not surprise me. I was vaguely aware of the issue from Japanese feature films I had seen in the 1960s, which were set in the war and occasionally depicted scenes showing the sexual exploitation of Chinese women by Japanese soldiers. It was many years later that I came to realize the necessity to question, not only why and how such crimes against women of various nationalities were committed, but also why it took so long for knowledge of the crimes to become public, despite the existence of many publications and films referring to this issue.

It is difficult to judge whether or not the fact that my father and uncles were silent about certain subjects, including the comfort women issue, means that they lied about their lives during the war. Was this a case of selective memory in which they suppressed entirely the issue of the comfort women and sexual slavery of the Japanese military? Or was it rather that even critics of the war long after Japan's defeat could not bring themselves to be frank about this and other sordid dimensions of Japanese colonialism and war? These are questions for which no answers are presently possible.

Yet, I think that both my father and my uncles firmly believed that they had adhered to high moral standards during the war – standards defined in the Japanese Imperial Code of Military Conduct. I am sure that they disciplined their soldiers quite well, considering their sincere personalities. I recall, for example, a story my father often told of how he succeeded in eradicating stealing by the men in his unit, through the implementation of various disciplinary measures. Yet, if he was so concerned about stealing, I wonder whether or not my father ever considered trying to eradicate the theft of Chinese civilians' possessions by his men, who were conducting warfare in a so-called "hostile district" in China. Was it not also true that Heinrich Himmler told his SS men not to steal because it would damage their soul and character? As Jonathan Glover clearly pointed out in his recent work,[3] no matter how high and clear the sense of moral identity, if it is not firmly rooted in basic "human responses" and "moral imagination," it is utterly useless or becomes weaker as a defense against inhumanities. In other words, no matter how strongly one embraces high moral standards, the lack of a sincere concern for dehumanizing others will paralyze true moral standards of humanity.

The extraordinary scale and brutality of the organized sexual violence committed by the Japanese Imperial forces against women is a powerful example of demeaning other people in the name of "high ideals" – in this case, Japan's claim to liberate Asian people from the toils of Western colonialism. Japan's military leaders organized the comfort women system based on the conviction that they were protecting the moral and physical character of their troops, and protecting Asian civilians, too. They regarded the system as a necessary and effective means of preventing Japanese soldiers from raping civilians and from contracting VD through contact with unauthorized prostitutes. They undoubtedly viewed their conduct as honorable. Yet, they were completely unaware that their moral standards showed a profound lack of humanitarian concern for others and that the system they had set up would victimize others irrevocably. Thus, they remained oblivious to the irreparable violation of the most fundamental human rights of the comfort women who were its victims. Focusing narrowly on the protection and control of their troops, Japan's military leaders were unable to consider the basic human rights of the victims of the system they created – the Asian comfort women drawn from Japan's colonies and other occupied territories.

Hannah Arendt, a German-born American-Jewish political thinker, once summed up the Holocaust with the phrase "the banality of evil," concluding that everyone is a potential perpetrator of atrocities against others. Describing Nazi "torturers," Primo Levi wrote that "they were made of our same cloth, they were average human beings, people of average intelligence, and average wickedness:

save for exceptions, they were not monsters, they had our faces."[4] The words "banality" and "average" are particularly apt when describing the crimes that Japanese committed against vast numbers of women, crimes committed not only by the architects of the comfort women system, but also directly by the officers and enlisted men who sexually exploited those women. For me, my father and my uncles were certainly not "monsters." Indeed they were "average" men and their faces were similar to mine. In other words, I need to face up to the fact that in other circumstances I could easily have become "a young Japanese officer" myself. This is my starting-point and it will also be the end point of this study.

An important question to consider is what causes the disjuncture between a sense of moral identity and human responses. Finding the answer is not simple, as this subject is not just a matter of individual psychology or ethics. It is closely intertwined with the structure of the military and state organizations and various ideologies such as masculinity, racism, and nationalism. We therefore need to approach this subject from two different directions – from the actions and responsibility of individuals and from the power structure of the military and state political machines. While the present study focuses on Japan, these are, of course, issues that pertain not only to Japan at war but to many other nations whose reach extends beyond their borders.

Japanese officers and enlisted men were *not ordered or forced* to abuse comfort women. They visited comfort stations by choice. Naturally, they were not punished for not using the "comfort service" organized by the military authorities. Clearly, this was a very different situation from cases in which soldiers were ordered to inflict violence on villagers or POWs, or to kill them. Crimes against POWs were in most cases carried out under orders, and soldiers could easily endanger their own lives by disobeying orders. The exploitation of comfort women, also a serious crime against humanity, was, however, a matter of personal choice, and in this sense, those Japanese men who chose to avail themselves of this facility undoubtedly bear personal responsibility for the crimes that they directly committed against the comfort women they used. Considered purely from a viewpoint of the "motive for the crime," personal responsibility in this situation is far more serious than in instances in which soldiers acted under orders to commit atrocities.

The question of the abuse of comfort women must be examined ultimately within the parameters of the intertwined ideologies of masculinity and militarism rather than exclusively within those of the Japanese military structure, even as we search for distinctive features of the Japanese system of sexual enslavement. In particular, it is imperative to closely analyze the symbolic parallel between the violation of a woman's body and the domination over others (enemies) on the battlefield or through colonial institutions. The question that needs to be asked here is why men find it necessary to demonstrate their power in this manner, particularly in a war situation. The structure of the Japanese military organization must be examined in relation to this fundamental question – how its specific structure and ideology created a strong propensity among soldiers to abuse women. The answer to the question – why so many Japanese soldiers abused comfort women – does not lie merely in a simple analysis of the organizational structure of the Japanese military.

In a broader sense, the ideology of masculinity is intrinsically interrelated with racism and nationalism. The conquest of another race and colonization of its people often produce the de-masculinization and feminization of the colonized. Sexual abuse of the bodies of women belonging to the conquered nation symbolizes the dominance of the conquerors. This helps us to understand why the majority of comfort women were from Korea – Japan's colony at the time. Therefore, in order to understand the nature of this system of forced prostitution – unprecedented perhaps both in its cruelty and in the magnitude of a state-organized system of forced military prostitution – it is necessary to study the broad historical context of the colonization of Korea and the military occupation of other areas in Asia. This also requires examination of Japanese overseas prostitution business, which began in the late nineteenth century and preceded the development of the prostitution industry in colonial Korea.

In the following chapters I will attempt to analyze these important issues and hope to reveal their complexity as well as to offer some useful guidance towards understanding them better.

Chapter 1 introduces the historical process that led to the establishment of the comfort women system, revealing the direct role of top-ranking officers of the Japanese Imperial forces in organizing and controlling the system. The close collaboration between government ministries – namely, the Ministries of the Army, Navy, and Foreign Affairs – and the military is examined in detail.

Chapter 2 analyzes the relationship between Japan's colonization of Korea and the sexual exploitation of Korean women, showing why and how Korea became the main source for procuring comfort women. The comfort women system expanded from the China theater to the entire Asia-Pacific zone after the attack on Pearl Harbor. The chapter examines the initiation of women into the comfort women system and the working and living conditions of women exploited by Japanese troops. In order to explain the ordeals that comfort women had to endure, I introduce the testimonies of several groups of Asian women who were the main victims of the Japanese – Koreans, Taiwanese, Chinese, and Filipinas.

Chapter 3 analyzes the sexual exploitation of the Dutch women who were taken from internment camps in Java to serve in comfort stations. This chapter also examines the enforced military prostitution of large numbers of Eurasian (Dutch-Indonesian) and Indonesian women that began in 1943. I explain, too, why the Dutch military authorities subsequently vigorously prosecuted those Japanese responsible for the exploitation of Dutch women, but not those who similarly victimized Eurasian and Indonesian women.

Chapter 4 considers why the US and other Allied forces failed to prosecute Japanese who had committed crimes against Asian women, despite the fact that they had accumulated ample evidence of the system of military sexual slavery. One answer to this question lies in US policies of military-controlled prostitution and the cover-up of the extent of this practice during World War II. The fact that British and Australian forces had similar policies to those of the US is revealed in this chapter, too, through the examination of a large number of relevant archival documents. The discussion raises the following questions which are dealt with in detail in the Epilogue. How distinctive were the Japanese military's comfort woman practices? To what extent were these practices common among contemporary military forces? In what other ways did military prostitution function in contemporary military forces? What larger issues are integral to the relationship of war and sexuality?

Chapter 5 uses both Japanese and American archival documents as well as personal memoirs to assess the extent and nature of sexual violence by US and Australian occupation troops immediately following their landing in Japan. I also discuss the responses of the Japanese government, police and women to these crimes. The aim of this chapter is to pinpoint the universal characteristics of military violence against women and to consider the fundamental causes of such sexual crimes. The point is not to mitigate or rationalize the crimes that Japanese men committed during the war by referring to similar or related crimes committed by the Allied soldiers immediately after the war. Rather, I aim to bring about an understanding of the broader dimensions of the problem, as well as to give some insight into the particularities of the Japanese crimes.

Chapter 6 examines how and why a military prostitution system with certain institutional similarities to the wartime comfort women system was established in Japan to serve the Allied occupation troops, and how the Japanese prostitution industry, the police, and the Japanese government collaborated with the General Headquarters of the Allied occupation forces to implement VD-preventive policies. It reveals not only how such polices failed but also how they contributed to the expansion of the prostitution business in postwar Japan.

In the final chapter, the Epilogue, the discussion focuses on two major issues. One is the question of how Japan's extraordinary military system of sexual enslavement came to be. The answer is sought in historical continuities linking the comfort women system and the *karayuki-san* system of overseas prostitution that involved large numbers of Japanese women. While noting continuities I delineate important differences between the two systems. The other is a theoretical analysis of the fundamental causes of military violence against women in general and of the specific characteristics of the comfort women system which differentiate it from other types of military violence against women.

Throughout this book, I use the words "comfort women." I am well aware that some historians and feminist scholars query the use of this term. Critics rightly note that these words evoke a false impression – suggesting that these women voluntary provided services, and indeed, the term masks the sexual and violent aspects of the system. Some of these critics suggest that the expression "sexual slaves" is more appropriate. As this study shows, the comfort women were indeed the "sexual slaves" of the Japanese military. At the same time, however, for reasons that I elaborate upon in the book, the "sexual slavery" of Japanese Imperial forces during the Asia-Pacific War assumed distinctive characteristics which cannot be found in other types of "sexual slavery." While the term "comfort women" was an official euphemism, it nevertheless is useful in underlining distinctive features of the system. Moreover, at this stage, I cannot find a more suitable alternative term to embody and connote this unique historical and socio-political phenomenon. Thus, I hope that my use of "comfort women" will not offend anyone who is concerned with the issue of violence against women.

Another important issue which concerns me deeply is that by putting "comfort women" in a special category, I do not intend to trivialize the victims of any other types of sexual violence. No matter how we historians and academics analyze various cases of sexual violence and classify them into different categories, the fact remains that, from the viewpoint of the victims, their individual experiences were invariably traumatic and unendurable. Each victim of sexual violence deserves to receive careful attention. I sincerely hope that the discussion in this book does not lose its foundation in the "human responses" to individual victims of sexual violence.

1 The origins of the comfort women system

The initial establishment of comfort stations

Exactly when the Japanese Imperial forces first set up *ianjo* (comfort stations) – military brothels – for the exclusive use of their soldiers and officers is still unknown. This is because a vast number of relevant official records were destroyed immediately after Japan announced its surrender in August 1945. However, a number of official Japanese documents related to this issue have been unearthed in the last several years. Information available in these newly discovered documents strongly suggests that the first Japanese military brothels for the exclusive use of troops and officers were those set up for the Japanese Navy in Shanghai, during the so-called "Shanghai Incident" in 1932.

On September 18, 1931, Japanese forces blew up the railway at Lake Liu (near Mukden in southern Manchuria), then claimed that Chinese forces had destroyed the railway. The Kwantung (Kantō) Army of the Japanese Imperial forces plotted this "sabotage" in order to provide a pretext for the invasion of northeast China. This marked the beginning of the so-called "Manchurian Incident." As Chinese forces avoided a major confrontation with the Japanese in this region, Japanese forces managed to occupy this part of China within a relatively short period. In January the following year, Japanese forces entered into an armed conflict with Chinese forces in Shanghai. The Japanese later named this military clash "the first Shanghai Incident." This "incident" was also plotted by the Kwantung Army, in order to divert the attention of Western nations from Japan's plan to establish the Manchuguo puppet state.

The Japanese Navy dispatched to Shanghai first set up military brothels in that city. According to a report prepared in late 1938 by the Japanese Consulate-General's office in Shanghai, "as soon as the Shanghai Incident occurred, some staff from our military forces stationed here established the navy *ianjo* (in reality, licensed houses) to serve as leisure facilities for its members, which continue to be operated since then."[1]

Before this time, the Chinese government had made efforts to abolish prostitution in Shanghai. In 1929, the operation of the Japanese brothels in this city was officially banned, as the Japanese Ministry of Foreign Affairs was placed in the difficult situation of co-operating with the Chinese authorities. However, Japanese

Plate 1.1 Japanese comfort women walking in the street where Japanese soldiers are
strolling. The exact location is unknown, although it is somewhere in north
China. The photo was taken in March 1939.
Source: Mainichi Shimbun

prostitutes were employed as "waitresses" at Japanese restaurants in the city, and
continued their business. Thus, although Japanese brothels existed in Shanghai
well before the Shanghai Incident, they were privately operated brothels for
Japanese residents and visitors, not exclusive military brothels.[2]

Probably only a few Japanese Navy brothels were set up at the time of the
Shanghai Incident. The report prepared by the Japanese Consulate-General's
office in Shanghai (mentioned above) recorded the existence of ten brothels in
late 1936, with 102 Japanese and 29 Korean women employed as "prostitutes."
Seven of these houses were navy brothels, and three others were so-called "Japanese restaurants." According to the same report, these seven brothels were for
the exclusive use of members of the Japanese Navy, and civilians were not allowed
to enter the premises. Twice a week, "prostitutes" at these houses received medical examinations conducted by a venereal disease (VD) specialist, accompanied
by a member of the naval force and a Japanese police officer attached to the
Consulate-General's office.[3] In other words, these navy brothels seemed to be
established primarily as a VD-prevention method, and operated under the close
supervision of navy authorities as well as the Consulate-General's office (i.e.
Japan's Ministry of Foreign Affairs).

Having had this experience in military-controlled prostitution in the early
1930s, the Japanese Navy started sending comfort women to China soon after

the Sino-Japanese War began in 1937. For example, on November 30, 1937, the Yawata police station in Fukuoka prefecture (Kyushu) granted permission to two Korean women to travel to Shanghai. The women, residents of the same prefecture, were to work at one of the navy brothels in Shanghai.[4] This evidence and other available information indicates that Korean comfort women sent to China early in the Asia-Pacific War were residents of Japan, mostly indentured workers, rather than coming directly from Korea.

The Japanese Army followed the navy's precedent and set up their own "brothels" in Shanghai in March 1932. This was initiated by General Okamura Yasuji, the Deputy Chief of Staff of the Shanghai Expeditionary Army. According to his memoirs, the General decided to set up similar facilities to the navy, in order to prevent further rape of Chinese civilians by Japanese soldiers – a serious problem during the Shanghai Incident. General Okamura requested the Governor of Nagasaki prefecture (Kyushu) to send a group of comfort women to Shanghai.[5] His choice of Nagasaki as a recruiting centre for comfort women was probably based on its historical background. Many so-called karayuki-san (Japanese prostitutes working at overseas brothels) of poor family background in Nagasaki had previously been sold by their parents to procurers and sent to various places in the Asia-Pacific region.[6] It is clear from Okamura's private record that the army intended to use Japanese professional women, rather than Koreans, as comfort women at this stage.

It is interesting to note that the army's explicit purpose in setting up such facilities in Shanghai was not only the prevention of VD but also the prevention of rape committed by their own soldiers. The diary of another senior staff officer in Shanghai, Lieutenant-General Okabe Naozaburō, further confirms this point. On March 14, 1932, he wrote:

> Recently I have heard a lot of scandalous stories, including that some our soldiers wander around seeking women. Such a phenomenon is hard to prevent as fighting becomes less frequent. Therefore the establishment of appropriate facilities must be accepted as a good cause and should be promoted. In consideration of our soldiers' sexual problems, we have decided to introduce various measures. Lieutenant-Colonel Nagami Toshinori is now responsible for this task.[7]

From these records, it is clear that the establishment of army comfort stations was initiated by top-ranking officers of the Japanese forces stationed in Shanghai. The actual plan was carried out by senior staff officers.

Why did the senior leaders of Japanese forces in Shanghai quickly introduce military-controlled prostitution? Undoubtedly, one important factor was the bitter experience of Japanese forces during the so-called "Siberian Expedition," between 1918 and 1922. Okamura, although only for a short period, served as the commander of the 14th Infantry Regiment which participated in this war against the Russians. Okabe was well known amongst Japanese military leaders as a Russian specialist, and he was an officer attached to the Special (i.e. secret) Service Agency in the Vladivostok headquarters during this expedition. For the majority of the

Japanese troops sent to Siberia, the mission of this military expedition was unclear, and the soldiers' morale was relatively low from the beginning. The discipline of these troops was also slack. Widespread looting and rape by Japanese troops on Russian soil gravely concerned Japanese military leaders.[8]

The Japanese commanders in Siberia were also troubled by the high VD rate amongst their troops. According to the official record, 1,109 soldiers were treated as VD patients between August 1918 and October 1920. The true figure was probably much higher. Even when the official figures are compared with 1,399 deaths and 1,528 casualties during the same period, one realizes how seriously VD affected the combat strength of the troops. In order to tackle this problem, the kempeitai (the Japanese military police force) was authorized to regulate private prostitution in Sakhalin and to force the prostitutes to have periodical medical examinations.[9] It can be said, therefore, that the establishment of military brothels in Shanghai in the 1930s, by both the Japanese Navy and Army, was a natural development from regulated prostitution in Siberia.

An official document confirms that a comfort station was set up in northeast China in April 1933, more than a year after the establishment of military brothels in Shanghai. On April 10, 1933, the Kwantung Army crossed the Changcheng Border, starting an invasion towards the east of China. The document, from the 14th Mixed Infantry Brigade of the Kwantung Army stationed in Pingquan, provides some evidence. According to some of the reports on sanitary affairs issued every ten days by the Brigade headquarters, local Chinese brothels were placed off-limits to Japanese soldiers, because of suspected high VD rates among the prostitutes working there. Instead, a station called the "Hygienic Facility for Prevention of Epidemics" was set up, housing 35 Korean women and three Japanese women. Medical examinations of these women were conducted by a Brigade medical officer. At the same time, two condoms were distributed to each soldier (a total of 15,528 condoms). The soldiers were instructed on how to use condoms and to apply prophylactic chemicals immediately after returning from this station. Although the word "*ianjo*" was not used in this report, there is no doubt this was indeed a comfort station.[10]

It is not hard to imagine that with the small number of newly arrived comfort women, this "Hygienic Facility" could not satisfy the demand of all 7,764 soldiers from the Brigade. Various units soon requested the Brigade headquarters to remove the off-limits placed on local brothels. As a result, after conducting medical examinations of prostitutes in these private brothels, the headquarters permitted soldiers to use these houses as well. However, it seems that senior headquarters staff were not in fact impressed by the results of these medical examinations, which showed a VD rate of 30 percent.[11]

Very few official documents have so far been found which refer to the establishment of comfort stations in northeast China at this time. However, this does not necessarily mean that there were only a few such stations attached to Japanese forces in this region. On the contrary, the following statement of Dr. Nakayama Tadanao (Director of the Nakayama Institute of Chinese Medicine) indicates that many comfort women were already being transported to this area of China at this early stage of the Asia-Pacific War. In June 1933, Dr. Nakayama

Plate 1.2 A Japanese officer standing by a large number of corpses, victims of the Nanjing
       Massacre.
Source: Ōtsuki Shoten

was on the way from Jinzhou to Chengde (the capital of Rehe Province), and
tried to secure a seat in an army plane:

> After I came to Manchuria, especially here in Chengde, I truly realized that
> *Joshi-gun* (Young Women's Corps) is not just a word of fantasy, and that they
> were a part of the military forces, indeed a military force itself. I was told
> by a commander in Jinzhou that the women will be put on a plane as a
> priority, as they are necessary goods. Wherever Japanese forces advance to,
> the first thing senior officers consider is the importation of *Joshi-gun*. Thanks
> to these women, the Japanese troops do not rape Chinese women. These
> women are therefore not just prostitutes![12]

As we will see later, there was no basis to Dr. Nakayama's belief that the provision
of comfort women would prevent rapes of Chinese civilians by Japanese soldiers.

A rapid increase in comfort stations after the "Rape of Nanjing"

Although it seems that a number of comfort stations were set up in Shanghai as
well as northeast China in early 1930s, Japanese forces adopted the military

comfort women system as a general policy from late 1937. As a result, a large number of women were mobilized as comfort women.

In July 1937, Japan started a full-scale invasion of China. By early 1938, the number of Japanese troops stationed in China (including Manchuguo) increased to more than a million. It was the first time that Japan stationed such massive numbers of troops overseas.

The sudden increase in the number of Japanese comfort stations in China was closely related to atrocities that Japanese soldiers committed during the "Nanjing Massacre." In 1937, Japanese troops fought a fierce battle in Shanghai (the so-called "Second Shanghai Incident") which continued for three months. Japan's Central China Area Army, led by General Matsui Iwane, then started advancing towards Nanjing in early November 1937. The members of this army committed crimes (eg. looting, massacre, arson, rape) at various places along the Yantzi River while proceeding towards Nanjing, as well as after entering the city.[13]

The leaders of the Central China Area Army soon recognized the problem of mass rape committed by their soldiers. On December 11, they instructed the commanders of each military contingent to set up comfort stations in order to prevent further rapes. On receiving this instruction, Iinuma Mamoru (the Chief of Staff of Shanghai Forces) ordered Lieutenant-Colonel Chō Isamu, his junior staff officer, to carry out this task.[14] The 10th Army, which was under the command of the Central China Area Army, also established comfort stations for their own soldiers. For example, on December 18, a staff officer of the 10th Army, Major Yamazaki Masao, wrote in his diary:

> Lieutenant-Colonel Terada, who came here to Huzhou before me, has set up a recreation facility by instructing the military police. I was told that initially there were four [women], but from today there are seven [women]. As women are still afraid [of the Japanese soldiers], not many want to work here, and the service is not good enough. However, if we assure them that their lives are safe, we pay an appropriate amount of money, and we do not make them work hard, I expect women will come to work one after another. The military police are unofficially saying that they will recruit 100 . . . Though we did not inform the soldiers [about this facility] and no signs were put up on the house, the soldiers got to know about it from hearsay, and the house is already full of the men. It is already warned that there is a tendency to driving [the women] hard. Needless to say, Lieutenant-Colonel Terada has already tested himself. When Major Ōsaka as well as Captain Sendō, who arrived here today, heard about this house, they could not wait any longer and went there together with the chief of kempeitai. About one and a half hours ago they returned . . . They seemed to be more or less satisfied.[15]

From this diary entry it is clear that local Chinese women were used as comfort women in this case. As the kempeitai (military police) were involved in setting up the comfort station, it was quite possible that these women were forcibly recruited. The fact that the kempeitai intended to secure 100 women also suggests that the Japanese forces were prepared to use coercion on Chinese civilians in the occupied area.

The Medical Unit of the 3rd Division set up a comfort station soon after they entered Yangzhou on December 18. A Chinese local security council was ordered to supply 60 women to this station. (These councils were organizations that occupying Japanese troops forced local civilians to establish.) Eventually 47 women were secured.[16] The 26th Brigade of the 13th Division, stationed in Bengbu, also set up a comfort station staffed with 10 Chinese women, which opened at the end of January 1938.[17] Therefore it seems that the Japanese forces which invaded Nanjing and neighboring areas used many Chinese women as comfort women. Some troops used devious methods to "recruit" these women.

However, the exploitation of local Chinese women in territories occupied by the invading Japanese troops did not become a general pattern. Before March 1938, some units such as the 104 Regiment stationed in Chuxian, were reluctant to use local women as comfort women. They did not set up a comfort station until mid-March when Japanese and Korean women were sent to this unit.[18] It seems that sooner or later troop commanders realized that it was not good policy to force local women into prostitution, out of consideration for the public. Another reason that the Japanese troops were generally reluctant to use local Chinese women was related to security. In particular, the kempeitai were concerned that local Chinese comfort women could be recruited as spies by the Chinese forces. In many places in China comfort station managers were instructed by the kempeitai not to "employ" Chinese comfort women. Thus, from March 1938, the number of Korean and Japanese women being sent to China began to increase.

Indeed, the full-scale mobilization of Korean women as comfort women from early 1938 is documented in Dr. Asō Tetsuo's personal memo as well as in photos he took. Dr. Asō was a gynecologist and a probationary medical officer at the Army Communication Hospital in Shanghai at the time. According to Dr. Asō, he examined 80 Korean and about 20 Japanese women on January 2, 1938. These women were to be comfort women at a comfort station in Shanghai which was soon to be opened. Dr. Asō claimed that these women were brought either from Korea or from various places in northern Kyushu. He also stated that, "interestingly, many women from Korea were relatively young and physically pure, but most of those [Japanese] from Kyushu were undoubtedly professionals in this business."[19] However, these Korean women were not from Korea but residents of Kyushu, according to Mr. Taguchi Eizō (a pseudonym), a former labor broker who was commissioned to recruit these women by the army in late 1937.[20] As has already been explained, in the early stage of the Asia-Pacific War, the Japanese recruited many Korean residents from poverty-stricken families as well as karayuki-san (Japanese prostitutes) from similar family backgrounds in Kyushu.

The Army's pool for recruitment of comfort women at this time was not, however, limited to lower-class Korean and Japanese families in Kyushu. For example, on November 20, 1937, the Ministry of Army called on brothel owners in several red-light districts in Tokyo, such as Tamanoi and Kameido. The military authorities asked them not only to recruit comfort women, but also to open comfort stations in mid-east China on behalf of the army. These brothel owners were assured that the Army would provide suitable buildings and they would be treated favorably in provision of food, payment, transportation and the like. In response to this request, in January 1938 one of these brothel owners, Mr. Kunii Shigeru, sailed to Shanghai with 53 Japanese prostitutes and opened comfort stations in Wusong, Nanxiang, and Nanshi.[21]

In May 1938, Japanese forces occupied Xuzhou. Wuhan and Guangdong also fell into Japanese hands in October that year. The number of Japanese troops stationed in China (excluding Manchuguo) was approximately 700,000 by this time. As the Sino-Japanese War became deadlocked, these soldiers were forced to stay in the occupied territories for a long period. Most of them were not given designated leave to return home. Military leaders believed that the provision of comfort women was a good means of providing their men with some kind of leisure to compensate for such unlimited tours of duty. Thus, by late 1938, the comfort women system became well interlocked with the Japanese military system.

As a result, the number of comfort stations, as well as the number of comfort women, rapidly increased in most occupied areas. For example, Table 1.1 was produced using information from various documents prepared between late 1938 and mid-1939 by the Ministry of Foreign Affairs.

The information in Table 1.1 was obtained from statistical data on occupations among the Japanese, Korean, and Taiwanese residents in these cities, compiled by the Japanese Consulate-General's offices.[22] The number of Chinese comfort women is not known. In addition, these comfort stations were all run by private proprietors under the auspices of the army. The number of comfort stations directly run by the army, therefore, is also unknown, and these statistics do not reflect the true situation. However, even from this limited information, it

Table 1.1 Number of comfort stations and comfort women, east-central China, 1938–1939

Place	Army comfort stations	Comfort women
Shanghai	unknown (seven navy brothels)	300
Hangzhou	4	36
Jiujiang	24	250 (143 Koreans & 107 Japanese)
Wuhu	6	70 (22 Koreans & 48 Japanese)
Wuhan	20	492 (not all of them were comfort women. Some were waitresses.)
Nanchang	11	111 (100 Koreans & 11 Japanese)
Zhenjiang	8	unknown
Yangzhou and Danyang	1	unknown

is clear that comfort stations were now established, not only in major cities but also in small and medium-sized cites as well.

The increase of comfort stations in mid-1938 was not a phenomenon limited to cities along the Yantzi River, but was also seen in northern China. Here too, Japanese soldiers raped many Chinese women, and comfort stations were established for the purpose of preventing mass rape. This fact is clear from an instruction issued to each unit commander in June 1938, by Lieutenant-General Okabe Naozaburō (then Chief of Staff of the North China Area Army). The instruction stated:

> According to various information, the reason for such strong anti-Japanese sentiment [among the local Chinese population] is widespread rape committed by Japanese military personnel in many places. It is said that such rape is fermenting unexpectedly serious anti-Japanese sentiment . . . Therefore, frequent occurrence of rape in various places is not just a matter of criminal law. It is nothing but high treason that breaches public peace and order, that harms the strategic activities of our entire forces, and that brings serious trouble to our nation . . . It is necessary to eradicate such acts. Any commander who tolerates rape must be condemned as a disloyal subject . . .
>
> Therefore it is of vital importance that individual acts by our military personnel be strictly controlled, and that, at the same time, facilities for sexual pleasure be established promptly, in order to prevent our men from inadvertently breaking the law due to the lack of such facilities.[23]

Thus, in order to prevent sexual crimes committed by members of his own Army, Lieutenant-General Okabe (who had played an important role in introducing comfort stations in Shanghai in 1932) again instructed commanders under his authority to set up comfort stations in northern China. The statistical data on occupations compiled by Japanese Consulate-General's offices in this region does not specify the number of sex workers at "*ianjo*." Thus, it is not known how many comfort stations and comfort women there were in northern China. One relevant document is the "Statistical Table on Occupations of Japanese Residents" prepared by the Department of Police Affairs in Northern China in July 1939.[24] In this table, 8,931 women were recorded as geisha, prostitutes, and barmaids. It is presumed that many of these women were comfort women. Yet, here again, Chinese comfort women were not included in this statistical survey, and therefore it is impossible to find exact numbers of comfort women exploited by Japanese forces in this part of China.

In reference to the situation in southern China, there is a relevant military document prepared by the 21st Army Headquarters stationed in Guangzhou (Guangdong Province). A ten-day report issued on April 20, 1939 contains a brief description of comfort stations under the control of this army, including Table 1.2.[25]

The nationalities of the 850 women listed in Table 1.2 are not specified in this document. However, according to this report, in addition to the 850 comfort women working under the direct control of this army, there were 150 Japanese

Table 1.2 The distribution of comfort stations and the sanitary conditions [southern China, 1939]

Unit	Place	Numbers of comfort women	VD rate (per 100)
Units directly under the Army	Guangzhou	159	28
Kuno Corps	East Guangzhou	223	1
Hamamoto Corps	North Guangzhou	129	10
Supply Unit	Henan	122	4
Foshan Sub-unit	Foshan	41	2
Iida Sub-unit	Haikou	180	not recorded
Total		850 [sic]	

Plate 1.3 A group of comfort women being transferred from a ship to a barge for landing in Shantou in South China. The date is unknown.
Source: *Mainichi Shimbun*

comfort women who were brought from the homeland of each unit. (Many units of the Japanese Imperial Army were made up of men from the same region.) However, as the kempeitai conducted this statistical survey with units stationed in the same places where it had offices, the numbers of comfort women working for the units outside its contact areas were not included. Therefore, the actual numbers were most certainly many more than 1,000.

Indeed, on April 15, 1939, Dr. Matsumura (the head of the 21st Army's medical section) reported at the section meeting that altogether between 1,400 and 1,600 comfort women were "imported" to serve the 21st Army. This was apparently based on the ratio of one woman to 100 soldiers. VD examinations of these women were conducted twice a week, and the cost of medical treatment of VD patients among these women was paid by brothel owners.[26] Dr. Matsumura's use of the word "imported" suggests that the majority of these women were Koreans and Japanese, not local Chinese women.

In July 1941, the Japanese Imperial Army started building up a large troop concentration (approximately 800,000 soldiers) near the border between the Soviet Union and northern China, planning to invade Soviet territory. In order to conceal their real intentions, the Imperial Headquarters claimed that the troops were concentrated here for a large-scale training exercise named "Kwantung Army Special Manoeuvres." It is reported that the Kwantung Army, under the command of Lieutenant-General Umezu Yoshijirō, planned to procure 20,000 Korean comfort women to serve these troops. For this purpose, a staff officer, Major Hara Zenshirō, requested co-operation from the Governor-General of Korea, General Minami Jirō, and eventually secured 8,000 Korean women.[27] However, no official documents have so far been discovered to prove this conduct, and it is necessary to rely on the testimonies contained in several individual accounts. One of those testimonies is that of a former medical officer who was involved in transporting 2,000 Korean women by cargo train from Korea to northern China.[28]

The military's policies can be summarized in the following manner, based on analysis of various documents and other relevant information. When the Japanese Imperial forces first set up comfort stations in the early stage of the Sino-Japanese War, the target for "recruitment" of comfort women was Japanese professional women rather than Koreans. Military leaders soon realized, however, that the recruitment of large numbers of Japanese professional women was far from easy. The exploitation of Korean women was then planned and implemented. Initially Koreans resident in Japan, and in particular from Kyushu Island, were used for this purpose, then massive numbers of young women from Korea were mobilized. As will be examined in more detail in the next chapter, the depressed economic conditions in the Korean Peninsula led to the migration of a large number of brothel proprietors and prostitutes from Korea to China in the late 1930s. This also contributed to the military plan to mobilize Korean women on a massive scale for the Japanese comfort women system. Local Chinese women were also rounded up by invading Japanese troops and pressed into hastily set up comfort stations. In particular, the exploitation of Chinese women occurred immediately after the Nanjing Massacre.

Comfort stations during the Sino-Japanese War can be categorized roughly into three different types. The first type were permanent stations attached to large supply bases located in major cities such as Shanghai, Nanjing, Tianjing, and Beijing. The second type were semi-permanent stations attached to large army units such as divisions, brigades, and regiments. Some of the stations in the first and second categories were managed by private proprietors under the strict control of the military authorities. Others were directly run by the military forces. The third type of station were those temporarily set up by small battalion-size units near the front lines in war zones. Most of these stations are believed to have been run by each unit.

For the first type of station, not only Koreans but also Japanese professional women were "employed" (although from 1939 very few Japanese women went to China to work as comfort women). On the other hand, in the second and third categories of stations, the majority of comfort women were either Korean or Chinese. The degree of coercion used for procuring women seems to have intensified according to the type of station and was most intense in the third type. It seems that the third category was often operated without obtaining permission of the central military authorities, as the troops were far away from headquarters. Thus, in these cases, many local civilian women were forcibly exploited, as it was difficult for these troops to access Korean or Japanese comfort women. It is clear that lack of authority from higher headquarters also contributed to wanton abuses by local troops in securing comfort women from the vicinity of their military bases.[29]

As we will examine later, when the Pacific War started, the operation of these three types of comfort stations was simply expanded geographically. Which type of comfort station became dominant in the area where Japanese forces were stationed depended on the local situation.

The organizational structure of the comfort women system

In order to clarify who was responsible for organizing the exploitation of women on such an unprecedented scale, it is necessary to analyze how the comfort women system became a general policy of the Japanese Imperial forces, and how this policy was implemented by military leaders.

At this time, however, it is quite difficult to conduct thorough research on this issue, mainly due to restrictions on access to relevant documentation:

- Firstly, many official military documents are still classified and not open for public inspection – for example, several thousand volumes of *Gyōmu Nisshi* (Records of Military Plans and Operations) and *Jūgun Nisshi* (Field Diaries) housed in the Research Library of the Japanese Defence Agency.
- Secondly, all documents prepared by the Japanese Police during the Asia-Pacific War are still closed.
- Thirdly, it is believed that many relevant documents were prepared by the Ministry of Home Affairs and the Ministry of Colonial Affairs, both of which had major responsibilities for colonial Korea and Taiwan. (From 1942, the Ministry of Home Affairs replaced the Ministry of Colonial Affairs

in charge of administration of Taiwanese affairs.) However, none of these official records has so far been released.

- Finally, it is also believed that Japanese government ministries – the Ministry of Labor, the Ministry of Public Welfare and the Ministry of Justice – still retain considerable numbers of relevant documents, but these are not accessible to researchers. The fact that there is no Freedom of Information Act in Japan makes it difficult to change the present research conditions.

In addition, many people who were directly involved in setting up and implementing the comfort women system are still alive, but they remain silent on this issue.

Therefore, the following analysis is based upon the limited number of official documents that have so far been discovered. A few documents as well as some testimonies are available, and these detail actual military instructions or orders to set up comfort stations (as detailed earlier). Let us look at these records more closely in order to clarify from whom such orders originated, and who was responsible for implementing the scheme.

- In March 1932, the Shanghai Expeditionary Army under the command of General Shirakawa Yoshinori set up comfort stations in Shanghai. General Okamura Yasuji (the Deputy Chief of Staff), and Lieutenant-General Okabe Naozaburō (another senior staff officer of this Army) instructed their junior officer, Lieutenant-Colonel Nagami Toshinori, to take charge of this task.[30] It seems very unlikely that the Army commander, General Shirakawa, was unaware of the fact that such instructions were issued by top-ranking officers of his own army. Shirakawa was the Minister of War between 1927 and 1929. In 1944, Okamura became the general commander of the China Expeditionary Army, the highest position within the entire Japanese forces stationed in China. Okabe was promoted to commander of the North China Area Army in the same year. Nagami later became the commander of the 55th Division.
- In December 1937, the Central China Area Army issued an instruction to each contingent force to set up comfort stations. The commander of this Army was General Matsui Iwane, and the Chief of Staff was Major-General Tsukada Osamu.

  On receiving this instruction, Iinuma Mamoru (Chief of Staff of the Shanghai forces) ordered members of the 2nd Section of the Staff Office to draw up a plan. His junior staff officer, Lieutenant-Colonel Chō Isamu, was responsible for implementing the plan. The commander of the 10th Army was Lieutenant-General Yanagawa Heisuke. This Army also set up comfort stations under the instruction of the Central China Area Army Headquarters. A staff officer of the 10th Army, Lieutenant-Colonel Terada Masao, set up a comfort station staffed with Chinese women. He used the kempeitai to procure these women.[31]

  After the war, General Matui was tried at the Tokyo War Crimes Tribunal. He was accused of responsibility for the Nanjing Massacre. It can be said that he was also responsible for the comfort women operations, as the commander of the Central China Area Army which issued an instruction to set up such facilities. Chō later became the Chief of Staff of the 32nd Army, and Terada was elevated to the position of head of the Armament Department in the Imperial Headquarters. The 10th Army commander, Yanagawa, later served as Minister of Home Affairs in Prince Konoe's cabinet in 1941.

• In June 1938, Lieutenant-General Okabe Naozaburō (then Chief of Staff of the North China Area Army) issued an instruction to each unit to set up comfort stations to serve several hundred thousand soldiers in this army.[32] The commander of these forces was General Terauchi Hisaichi. Terauchi was the Minister of War in the previous two years.

• The commander of the Kwantung Army was Lieutenant-General Umezu Yoshijirō, and the Chief of Staff was Lieutenant-General Yoshimoto Teiichi. It has been reported that in about July 1941, the Kwantung Army planned to mobilize 20,000 Korean women and requested assistance from the Government-General (i.e. the colonial government) of Korea. As a result, about 8,000 Korean women were reported to have been sent to northeast China (i.e. Manchuguo). Although no official documentation has been unearthed to prove such conduct, a number of testimonies refer to this operation, including one by a former staff officer of the Kwantung Army, Lieutenant-Colonel Hara Zenshirō.[33] It implicates many bureaucrats of the Government-General of Korea in procuring a large number of Korean women, and therefore the Governor-General, General Minami Jirō, was also responsible. Minami served as the Minister of War for a short period in 1931.

It is clear from these examples that senior staff officers of each army issued orders to establish comfort stations, and that staff officers of subordinate units made a plan and put it into operation. All were undoubtedly elite army officers. As commanders of each army, they had distinguished careers. Some of them were cabinet members of the Japanese government. In short, the comfort women system was created and developed as a well-planned policy by a group of top Japanese military leaders.

During the Asia-Pacific War, the Japanese Imperial forces stationed five armies overseas. These armies were under the supervision of the Minister of War and the Chief of the General Staff, who were subordinate to the Grand Marshal (i.e. the Emperor).[34] See Figure 1.1, which shows the locations of army headquarters in parentheses.

Each army engaged in warfare at the Emperor's orders. The Chief of the General Staff advised the Emperor in planning war strategies. The ultimate right of command over each army lay in the hands of the Emperor. However, in reality, the Chief of the General Staff was responsible for war strategies and military operations, and the Minister of War was responsible for military administration. As far as matters related to comfort women are concerned, the staff section of each army was responsible for dealing with them, and if necessary, the Ministry of War issued instructions to each army's headquarters.[35]

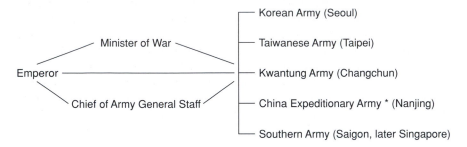

Figure 1.1 Japanese Imperial Army chain of command
*Note: The China Expeditionary Army was established in September 1939, with the Central China Area Army as the core force, to which the North China Area Army (headquarters in Beijing) and the 23rd Army (headquarters in Guangzhou) were subordinated.

In the Ministry of War, there was no particular section designated to administer the comfort women system. The relevant Bureau would give instructions to each army as the occasion demanded. For example, the Military Administration Bureau gave instructions on military discipline and troop morale in relation to comfort women and comfort stations, while the Medical Bureau was responsible for advice on matters related to VD prevention and sanitary affairs.

As already briefly mentioned, there were basically two different "recruiting" methods. The first method involved local civilians in the occupied territories. In these cases, staff officers attached to army divisions, brigades or regiments, together with members of the kempeitai, requested local leaders to supply certain numbers of young women. (The kempeitai in the occupied territories were under the control of the commander of each army.) As a result, a large number of women who were not prostitutes appear to have been forced to render sexual service to the Japanese troops. This point is proven by the following extract from the diary of a medical officer, Yamaguchi Tokio, who was assigned to conduct VD examinations of some selected local Chinese girls in a village near Dongshi (Hubei province):

> At the first VD check-up, one girl was too shy to take off her trousers for the examination of her sexual organ. My interpreter and the head of the local security council yelled at her, to force her to take them off. When I made her lie on the bed and started examining, she frantically scratched at my hands. When I saw her face, I realized that she was crying. Later I was told that she kept crying for a while, even after she left the examination room. The next girl also behaved the same way. I felt I would like to cry, too . . . I wonder whether these girls unwillingly came to see me because local leaders talked them into complying for the sake of the village's peace . . . This kind of work does not suit me, and I cannot get rid of the thought that this is a violation of humanity.
>
> (11 August 1940)[36]

Another method was that each army headquarters selected its own recruiting agents (i.e. brothel owners or labor brokers). They were then sent to Korea, Taiwan, and Japan to secure comfort women. These Japanese and Korean brothel owners/labor brokers, with support from the Kempeitai and the police forces in those countries, searched for and "recruited" suitable women. From various testimonies, including those of former Korean comfort women, there is no doubt that many of these labor brokers used dubious methods, including deception, intimidation, violence, and, in extreme cases, even kidnapping. It seems clear from diaries and individual testimonies that the Governments-General of Korea and of Taiwan made their kempeitai and police force available for this purpose. Although no official documentation has so far been discovered in relation to the activities of the kempeitai and police in this field in Korea and Taiwan, it seems that government officials well understood the nature of the work that these women would be engaged in. It seems likely that they also knew the methods used for such "recruitment."

We do, however, possess important official documentation concerning key aspects of the comfort women program. One document prepared by the Ministry of War is an instruction entitled "Matters related to the recruitment of female and other employees for military comfort stations," which was issued on March 4, 1938 to the Chiefs of Staff of the North China Area Army and Central China Area Army. It states:

> In recruiting female and other employees from Japan for the establishment of comfort stations in the place where the China Incident occurred, some deliberately make an illicit claim that they have permissions from the military authorities, thus damaging the Army's reputation and causing misunderstanding among the general population. Some others are causing social problems by trying to recruit [women] illegally through the mediation of war correspondents, visiting entertainers and the like. *Due to the selection of unsuitable recruiting agents, some have been arrested and investigated by the police because of their* [dubious] *methods of recruitment and kidnapping.* Thus, great care is necessary in selecting suitable agents. In future, when recruiting those [women], each Army must tighten control [of the selection procedure] by carefully selecting appropriate agents. In actual recruitment, each Army must work in closer cooperation with local Kempeitai or police authorities, thus maintaining the Army's dignity and avoiding social problems. The above is issued as a letter of proxy.[37]
>
> [Emphasis added]

This letter was drafted by the staff of the Military Administration Bureau and issued under the name of Colonel Fushibuchi Senichi. It was approved by the then Vice-Minister of War, Umezu Yoshijirō. It is important to note that this instruction was issued as "a letter of proxy," which means that it was also approved by the Minister of War, Sugiyama Hajime. In other words, top army leaders in the Ministry of War closely monitored the procurement of women in

Japan by the North China Area Army and the Central China Area Army. This was intended to control the use of "agents" of questionable character in order to prevent potentially explosive abuses, while sanctioning the basic comfort women system. While apprehensive about the methods of procurement, they made no attempt to stop their armies from operating comfort stations.

On the contrary, the following document endorses the fact that the Ministry of War promoted the comfort women scheme as an effective method to maintain military discipline and prevent VD. The document called "Measures for enhancing military discipline based upon experiences in the China Incident" was distributed as "educational material" to all army units from the Ministry of War on September 19, 1940. It states in part:

> [Since the Sino-Japanese War started], despite brilliant achievements in war, our soldiers have committed various crimes such as looting, rape, arson, murder of prisoners, and the like which are contrary to the essence of the principles of the Imperial Army. It is therefore regrettable that such conduct has created a sense of aversion both within and outside Japan, thus making it difficult to attain the object of our holy war . . . Having observed the circumstances in which crimes and misconduct were committed, it is recognized that many of them occurred immediately after combat activities . . . In the battle zone, it is necessary to make efforts to create a good environment, to pay considerable attention to the facilities for amenities, and to ease and control rough and low feelings from the troops . . . *In particular, the psychological effects that the soldiers receive at comfort stations are most immediate and profound, and therefore it is believed that the enhancement of troop morale, maintenance of discipline, and prevention of crimes and VD are dependent on successful supervision of these* [comfort stations].[38]
>
> [Emphasis added]

According to Mr. Shikauchi Nobutaka, who was trained to become a paymaster at the Military Paymasters' School in 1939, cadets were taught how to establish and manage military brothels. Incidentally, during the Pacific War Shikauchi was seconded from the Material Section in the Ordnance Bureau of the Ministry of War to the Kokusai Gomu Kōgyō (International Rubber Industry) Corporation, in order to supervise the production of condoms for military use.[39] The Army Accounts Department and the Supply Headquarters were responsible for sending condoms to forces stationed overseas, and officials ensured a ready supply. In 1942, for example, 32.1 million condoms were sent to units stationed outside Japan.[40]

There is no doubt that the Ministry of War was directly involved in transporting comfort women to war zones, since it was impossible to use any Japanese military ships without its permission. The operation of army ships was controlled by the Army Section of the Imperial Headquarters under the authority of the Commissary General. (This position was usually held concurrently by the Vice-Chief of the General Staff.) The Army Section of the Imperial Headquarters was

Plate 1.4 Comfort women together with Japanese soldiers being transported on a military
ship. This photo was taken in 1942.
Source: Mainichi Shimbun

staffed by the senior bureaucrats of the Ministry of War. From various available
documents and testimony it is clear that comfort women were transported by
army cargo ships from Japan and Korea to many places in the Asia-Pacific
region. In cases where Korean women were sent to China from Korea, the
Kyogi Railway in Korea and Southern Manchurian Railway in Manchuria were
used. Both railway lines were owned by Japanese companies. In China, local
railways controlled by the Japanese Army were used for this purpose. In places
where railway service was not available, army trucks were provided. In some
special cases, women were even flown by army planes to the front lines.[41]

However, the Ministry of War needed the co-operation of other governmental
organizations, such as the Ministry of Home Affairs and the Governments-
General of Korea and Taiwan, in order to facilitate the procurement and transportation of comfort women.

For example, on February 23, 1938, Tomita Kenji (Chief of the Police Bureau
of the Ministry of Home Affairs) issued an instruction to the governor of each
Prefecture in Japan, entitled "Regarding the treatment of female travellers to China."
In this document, he ordered that only prostitutes over the age of 21 should be
permitted to travel to northern and central China.[42] It could be interpreted that
such instructions, allowing only the travel of professional Japanese prostitutes to
China, was issued as a countermeasure to prevent illegal trafficking of women.

(Such illegal trafficking was against the International Convention for the Suppression of the Traffic in Women and Children of 1921, to which Japan became a signatory.) However, the fact that no such instructions were issued in Korea or Taiwan indicates that the Japanese government had no intention of suppressing illegal trafficking of Korean and Taiwanese women for military prostitution. It seems that officials believed this international law was not applicable to Japan's colonies.

Testimonies by former comfort women also indicate that police in Korea and Taiwan were involved in various ways in the procurement of comfort women. For example, Mun P'ilgi, a Korean woman from Chisu District, South Kyongsang, testified that a local policeman called Tanaka was with a Korean labor broker when she and other women were "recruited."[43] Another Korean woman, Mun Okuchu from Taegu city, said that when she was arrested by two members of the kempeitai for no particular reason, a Korean policeman accompanied them. She was then sent to northeast China to become a comfort woman.[44]

In both Korea and Taiwan, police forces were under the control of the Bureau of Police Affairs of the Government-General (i.e. the colonial government). No official documents regarding the involvement of the police of these colonies in procuring comfort women have been discovered so far. However, each police station under the control of the Bureau of Police Affairs was responsible for issuing passports. It was illegal for the police to issue a passport to a local woman knowing that she was being forcibly recruited as a comfort woman. If they did so unwittingly, then this should be condemned as "neglect of duty." It is most unlikely that the police in both colonies were unaware of forcible recruitment of comfort women, for it was standard practise for them to thoroughly investigate each traveler's age, occupation, family background, career, native language, and the purpose and intended period of travel before issuing a passport. Police should not have issued a passport unless the travel had a legitimate purpose.

One example of such misconduct by police in the colonies occurred in August 1940. Six Taiwanese minors (one 18-year-old, two 16-year-old, one 15-year-old and two 14-year-old girls) from Gaoxiung City were allowed to travel to Qinxian in Guangdong province with the wife of the owner of a comfort station that was attached to a Japanese Army unit stationed in Qinxian.[45] In this case, the Governor-General of Taiwan bore the final responsibility for this criminal conduct by police in Gaoxiung.

After the outbreak of the Pacific War in December 1941, the Ministry of War, on its own initiative, started implementing various policies to promote the establishment of comfort stations and to control the transportation of comfort women in the Asia-Pacific region. Until then, as we have seen, the Ministry of War played a somewhat secondary role in establishing the comfort women system, and the primary responsible body was each army headquarters.

Indeed, the Ministry of War's plan to set up comfort stations in future war zones was already under way several months before the attack on Pearl Harbor. For example in mid-1941, a Medical Officer, Major Fukada Masuo, was assigned to secretly conduct a field study in the Dutch East Indies (i.e. Indonesia).

After returning to Japan, he submitted his report to the Ministry of War on July 26, 1941, recommending the establishment of comfort stations in Indonesia immediately after the Japanese occupation commenced. He also recommended a "request" be sent to each village chief in occupied territory to provide local women to work at these stations. There is little doubt that "request" in this case meant "order." Major Fukada believed such arrangements would be necessary in order to avoid rape of local civilians by Japanese troops, as well as to prevent the spread of VD among the forces.[46]

In January 1942, the Minister of Foreign Affairs, Tōgō Shigenori, instructed his staff that comfort women should be issued with military travel documents and that they would no longer require a passport for overseas travel.[47] In other words, the movement of comfort women was now controlled by the Ministry of War, and thus the Ministry of Foreign Affairs lost its administrative power as far as controlling the travel of comfort women was concerned.

The following case reveals that permission from the Ministry of War was necessary for the travel of comfort women after January 1942. In March 1942 the Headquarters of the Southern Army made plans to set up comfort stations throughout Southeast Asia and the Pacific region, areas recently seized by Japanese forces following the attack on Pearl Harbor. One request was issued to Taiwanese Army Headquarters to procure 70 comfort women and send them to Borneo. The commander in Taiwan, Lieutenant General Andō Rikichi, and the Chief of Staff, Major General Higuchi Keishichirō, instructed the kempeitai to select three brothel owners to assist in gathering the women. The 70 women were in fact sent from Taiwan to Borneo, after military travel documents for them were obtained from the Ministry of War. These travel documents had the seal of the head of the Military Administration Bureau of the Ministry of War, Tanaka Ryūkichi, and his subordinate, Kawara Naoichi.[48] This indicates that involvement in decision-making about comfort women went all the way to the top levels of the Ministry of War.

Another document that shows a deep involvement of the Ministry of War in controlling comfort stations from 1942 is an instruction by the Vice-Minister of War, Kimura Heitarō, issued on June 18, 1942. The order went to all army units stationed overseas, calling for strict VD preventive measures in order to tighten hygiene control over comfort stations.[49]

The numbers of comfort stations are documented in a report prepared by the head of the Medical Affairs Section of the Medical Bureau in the Ministry of War, Kimbara Setsuzō, at a meeting of Ministry section heads on September 3, 1942. The report details the houses established overseas: 100 in north China, 140 in central China, 40 in south China, 100 in Southeast Asia, 10 in the Southwest Pacific, 10 in southern Sakhalin (i.e. 400 in total).[50] This report indicates that, by 1942, the Ministry of War had considerable detailed information on all comfort stations and exerted its controlling power over these military facilities to some extent.

Limited evidence has so far been found about the role of the navy in the exploitation of comfort women. One piece of evidence is a set of documents

written by Rear Admiral Nagaoka Takasumi, head of the Military Affairs Bureau
of the Ministry of Navy, on May 30, 1942. According to these documents, the
navy was to dispatch "*tokuyōin*" (which literally means "special staff," the term
used by the navy for comfort women) to various naval bases throughout Southeast Asia. For instance, 45 women were to be dispatched to the Celebes, 40 to
Balikpapan in Borneo, 50 to Penan, and 30 to Surabaya. This was a second
dispatch of comfort women to these bases. These documents were sent to Rear
Admiral Nakamura Toshihisa, Chief of Staff of the Southwest Area Fleet.[51]

According to a different document, at the end of the war there were 281
Indonesian comfort women in the southern part of the Celebes, of whom 250
were working at Japanese Navy comfort stations. These navy facilities were set
up by the Civil Administration Bureau of the Ministry of the Navy, and some of
them were directly run by the navy, while others were managed by civilian
employees.[52]

Available evidence on the navy comfort stations is quite limited. However, it
seems that the Ministry of the Navy played a more direct role in setting up and
running the stations than the Ministry of War. Further search of relevant documents is required to confirm this point.

Why comfort women?

There were several reasons why the Japanese military decided that comfort
stations were necessary.

As mentioned previously, Japanese military leaders were very concerned about
the rape of civilians by members of the Japanese armed forces – but not out of
concern for those civilians. For good strategic reasons, they believed that the
antagonism of civilians in occupied territories towards their conquerors was
exacerbated by such behaviour. They also believed that a ready supply of women
for the armed forces would help to reduce the incidence of rape of civilians.

Was the exploitation of women in military-controlled comfort stations effective
in preventing widespread random sexual violence by Japanese soldiers? The
initiator of the Japanese army comfort women system, General Okamura, reflect-
ing on the Japanese invasion of Wuhan in 1938, stated that random sexual
violence occurred in spite of the fact that the Japanese forces had groups of
comfort women attached to them. He admitted, therefore, that his scheme was a
failure.[53]

Until it was revised in February 1942, the Japanese Imperial Army Criminal
Law (Article 86, Clause 2) stated that army personnel who committed rape at
the same time as looting would be punished by between seven years and life
imprisonment. Here rape was regarded as a secondary crime, incidental to looting. It was also a general trend in the Japanese Imperial forces that looting and
rape, in particular during combat operations, were not only tolerated but even
encouraged by many troop commanders as a means of arousing the fighting
spirit in their men. Therefore, it is not surprising that only a small number of
soldiers were convicted of rape under this code of conduct each year. In 1939,

15 men were found guilty of looting, rape and manslaugter. Only four soldiers in 1940 and a mere two men in 1941 were convicted of the same crimes.[54] This Japanese official military data looks absurd when it is compared with actual evidence, such as various testimonies presented at the Tokyo War Crimes Tribunal regarding the Rape of Nanjing.

On February 20, 1942, the law was revised to acknowledge rape as a single major criminal offense. The amended article reads that "those who commit rape in the battlefield or in the territory of the Empire will be imprisoned for between one year and life," for the reason that "rape in the occupied territory is fundamentally different from rape in the national territory and will defame the Empire."[55] In other words, rape of women in occupied territories was regarded as a crime under the revised Army Criminal Law mainly because it brought disgrace on the name of the Japanese Empire, not because rape itself constituted a serious crime against humanity. Thus, in actual cases, it remained extremely rare that a soldier or officer rapist was court-martialed. The fundamental problem was that, regardless of what the law stipulated, rape of civilians in occupied territories was not considered a serious criminal act by Japanese military men. In fact, in his report about particular battlefield problems in China in 1939, Dr. Hayao Takeo, a medical officer and professor in psychiatry, stated that many officers deemed it necessary for their soldiers to rape women in order to stimulate aggression.[56]

The following testimony by General Okamura shows how reluctant even senior officers were to prosecute offenders. In August 1938, the Chief of Staff of the 11th Army reported to Okamura (then commander of this army) that some of their own soldiers had gang-raped the wife and daughter of the chief of one Chinese village in their occupied area. When Okamura was told that local civilians were refusing to co-operate in construction work of a Japanese military airfield because of this sexual violence, he ordered the kempeitai to arrest the offenders. However, the kempeitai chief told Okamura that the criminal act could not be established because the victims had not reported it. Hence, it would be inappropriate to prosecute the men. Okamura was shocked by the fact that the Army Judicial Chief also supported this kempeitai officer's opinion.[57]

What the military leaders, including General Okamura, apparently did not consider was the possibility that the highly oppressive and racist culture of their armed forces might be contributing to the problem. Thus, at least part of the solution would be to reform the military structure as well as to re-educate the men, to change their attitudes towards other Asian people in general, and towards women in particular.

As I also have mentioned, military leaders believed that the provision of comfort women was the most appropriate means of providing their men with some kind of leisure. Unlike US and other Allied soldiers, the rank and file of the Japanese military forces did not have designated leave periods or limited tours of duty. Military leaders had been advised by some senior medical staff that they should make greater provision for both the health and well-being of their men, including such measures as extended home leave. However, most of these suggested measures were never implemented. The notable exception was the provision of comfort women.

Another concern of military leaders was the incidence of VD among the armed forces. They believed that VD threatened to undermine the strength of their men (and hence their fighting ability). They also feared the spread of the disease could potentially create massive public health problems back in Japan, once the war was over. The leaders believed that a regulated system, such as the comfort stations, would enable them to take effective preventive health measures. The measures they employed were thorough if not completely effective. Those "recruited" were mostly young, unmarried women because it was believed they were the least likely to be infected with VD. Army doctors regularly checked the health of the comfort women to ensure that they had not contracted VD. Most of the women were examined for VD once a week or every ten days. The men were provided with condoms free of charge and were instructed to apply prophylactic chemicals immediately before and after associating with comfort women.[58]

However, such measures could not prevent VD, even if they went some way towards reducing its incidence. For instance, according to a report by medical officers of the 15th Division in north China in 1942 and 1943, 15 to 20 percent of comfort women were found to be suffering from VD each month.[59] Evidence from former comfort women suggests the figure could have been much higher. This was probably due to the fact that many soldiers refused to use condoms and did not bother applying prophylactic disinfectants. Numerous former comfort women testify that they had great difficulty in making the men use condoms. Official statistical data of new VD patients among the Japanese Army Forces in war zones between 1942 and 1944 also show a small increase in the number of cases (11,983 in 1942; 12,557 in 1943; and 12,587 in 1944).[60] It is presumed that the real figures were much higher.

Another reason for the difficulty of reducing high VD rates among Japanese troops was the disciplinary provision by which if a soldier was found to be infected with VD, he would be demoted two ranks. This punitive measure discouraged soldiers who were suffering from VD from reporting to their medical officers. Instead many secretly purchased medicines at a civilian pharmacy or on the black market. Needing money to obtain such expensive medicines, the soldiers were driven to looting.[61] Thus, the stringent VD control methods imposed upon soldiers as well as comfort women did not really alleviate the problem. Furthermore, they led to an increase in crimes committed by the Japanese men.

A further concern was security. Military leaders believed that private brothels could easily be infiltrated by spies and that prostitutes working in them could easily be recruited as spies. Kempeitai members were frequent visitors to comfort stations and kept close tabs on the women to ensure there were no spies among them. In order to limit the women's contact with people outside comfort stations as much as possible, they were not allowed to go outside the premises by themselves. So severely were they restricted that permission was required for them even to go for a walk to get fresh air.

The comfort women were treated as "military supplies," but relevant documents were either hidden or destroyed at the end of the war. It is impossible to know, therefore, how many women were exploited. The best estimates range from 80,000 to 100,000. According to the Japanese military plan devised in July 1941, 20,000 comfort women were required for every 800,000 Japanese soldiers, or one woman for every 40 soldiers.[62] There were 3.5 million Japanese soldiers sent to China and Southeast Asia during the war, and therefore, by this calculation, an estimated 90,000 women were mobilized. Of these women, 80 percent are believed to have been Koreans, but many also came from Taiwan, China, the Philippines, Indonesia, and Malaysia.

Why were comfort women almost invariably from Taiwan, China, or various places in Southeast Asia, and above all Korea? This might seem odd at first, given that the Japanese were notorious for their racism towards the people of other Asian countries. However, racial prejudice provides part of the answer to the question – that very racism helped make these women suitable for the role of comfort women.

Japanese prostitutes did serve the military abroad during the war, but most were in a different position from the comfort women. The Japanese prostitutes mainly worked in comfort stations that served high-ranking officers, and they

Plate 1.5 While comfort women were sexually exploited, Japanese women were expected to be chaste and encouraged to have as many healthy children as possible. This scene shows one of the healthy baby contests often held in Japan during the Asia-Pacific War. The photo was taken in April 1941.
Source: Mainichi Shimbun

experienced better conditions than the Asian comfort women. Apart from the difficulty in recruiting Japanese women into comfort stations, Japanese military leaders did not believe Japanese women should be in that role. Their mission was to bear and bring up good Japanese children, who would grow up to be loyal subjects of the Emperor rather than being the means for men to satisfy their sexual urges. The Japanese wartime government took its lead from Nazi eugenic ideology and policy in these matters. In 1940 the National Eugenic Law was proclaimed. The purposes of the law were to prevent miscegenation and the reproduction of the "unfit," such as those with mental illness that was believed to be inherited.[63]

According to widely held Japanese views at the time, a supreme virtue for a woman was to serve her husband from the time of her marriage until the end of her life. During the war, the Ministry of Health actually recommended that war widows remain loyal to their deceased husbands by not remarrying, unless they were less than 36 years old. In 1943, when Professor Kaneko Takanosuke from the Tokyo College of Commerce argued in a popular woman's magazine, *Fujin Kōron*, that all war widows should be encouraged to remarry, the military authorities demanded that the publisher issue a public apology. In addition, the government-regulated distribution of paper to this publisher was considerably reduced for the rest of the war period.[64] So hypocritical was the Japanese military leaders' attitude that on the one hand they strongly demanded that Japanese women be chaste, while on the other they did not hesitate to preside over the extreme sexual exploitation of other Asian women.

Korean and Taiwanese women were particularly targeted as sources of comfort women, not only because of the political and economic environment of these countries as Japan's colonies in which young women were easily procured, but also in light of their cultural proximity to Japan. Japanese language was compulsory in Korea and Taiwan, and people in these countries were heavily indoctrinated in loyalty to the Emperor and respect for Japan as their suzerain state. Physical similarity between Japanese and Koreans or Taiwanese also may have been a factor favoring procurement of women there.

In this way, Japanese forces exploited large numbers of Asian women under the excuse of preventing rape and VD. It must be concluded, however, that provision of comfort women did not function as an effective measure for either problem, and in particular for the problem of random sexual violence against civilians in occupied territories. Despite such official justifications for the program, it should not be forgotten that the estimated 80,000–100,000 women involved in the comfort women system were themselves victims of systematic, institutional rape and sexual slavery.

The following chapter examines in greater detail how these Asian women were "recruited" and what sort of life they led at comfort stations.

2 Procurement of comfort women and their lives as sexual slaves

The colonization of Korea and the growth of the prostitution industry

One cannot sufficiently explain the establishment and operation of the comfort women system, in particular the sexual exploitation of Korean women in that system, by viewing it from the perspective of military history alone. It becomes comprehensible only when we examine how the trafficking of young women came to be widely practiced in Korea well before the military brothel system was established. This trafficking was a by-product of Japan's various policies of colonizing the Korean peninsula.

Shortly after the Meiji Restoration in 1868, Japan began entertaining an ambition to extend its economic and political interests to Korea. Having succeeded in concluding the treaty of amity with Korea in February 1876, Japan started interfering in Korea's domestic affairs. China's Qing dynasty, which had long acted as Korea's suzerain state, was angered by Japan's intrusion. The antagonism between the Meiji government and the Qing over Korea eventually erupted into the Sino-Japanese War in August 1894. After eliminating Chinese influence over Korea by defeating China in this war, Japan then faced a threat from Russia, which had increased its activities in Korea and Manchuria. These moves threatened Japan's military and economic interests in northeast Asia, leading to the Russo-Japanese War between September 1904 and February 1905.[1]

On the eve of this war, Japan had taken steps towards colonizing Korea. In August 1904, the Japanese government imposed the "First Japan–Korea Convention" upon Korea. This convention allowed Japan to exert considerable influence in two fundamental state functions – administration of finance and foreign affairs. The convention forced Korea to accept Japanese "consultation" in these two areas. In early 1905, with Japan's victory in the Russo-Japanese War, the British and Americans accepted Japan's control of Korea. Japan was then able openly to colonize Korea. In November 1905, Japan's special envoy, Itō Hirobumi, forced the Korean Foreign Minister to affix the seal to the Protectorate Treaty (the so-called "Second Japan–Korea Convention"), surrounding the palace of the Korean King, Kojong, with Japanese troops. By this treaty Korea was completely deprived of its diplomatic power and autonomy in internal affairs.

Itō became the first Resident-General of Korea, now a protectorate of Japan. In July 1907, yet another convention was imposed on Korea. This "Third Convention" placed the administrative functions of the Korean government under the direct control of the Resident-General. Even the small remaining Korean Army – with about 9,000 troops – was dissolved by this convention. Finally, in August 1910, after the conclusion of the Japan–Korea Annexation Treaty, Korea officially became Japan's colony.[2]

After the annexation, the Government-General of Korea was established as a colonial administrative organ, and the Governor-General was posted to control the entire affairs of Korea. It was stipulated by Imperial Ordinance that the Governor-General was to be selected from among the generals of the Japanese Imperial Army or Navy, and that he was to be directly responsible to the Emperor for administering Korean affairs as well as defending Korea.[3] In other words, with the establishment of the Government-General, Korean society was virtually placed under martial law.

Aided by the military rule of the Government-General, Japan proceeded to transform the Korean economy. The most catastrophic change affecting social conditions in Korea was a new land ownership system, the result of a cadastral survey conducted between March 1910 and November 1918. Due to the loose nature of the traditional landholding system – which required no official registration – the newly introduced and complicated application system resulted in many illiterate peasants and petit-farmers losing their customary tenancy or land ownership rights. In contrast, the Korean upper-class landlords, called *yangban*, who knew how to get their land registered properly, benefited from the new system, thereby strengthening their contractual property rights. As a result, the commercial value of arable land increased. Large Japanese corporations, such as the Oriental Development Company, were given priority in purchasing the "public land." It is said that the Oriental Development Company alone came to own more than 20 percent of the arable land in Korea. This drastic change to the landholding system, together with a high tenancy rate (55 percent of arable land), rapidly decreased the number of small, independent farmers and turned them into poverty-stricken peasants. It is estimated that about 80 percent of the Korean population was engaged in agriculture in this period. Therefore, the impact of this change to the landholding system on Korean society was considerable.[4]

From the late 1910s a large proportion of rice produced in Korea was exported to Japan, cutting sharply into the supply of rice available for local consumption. In addition, in the coming years, Korean agriculture was severely hit by bad weather. Almost every year between the late 1920s and the late 1930s Korea experienced weather problems which further impoverished the peasants. Many peasants lost their jobs. For example, in the mid-1930s, the unemployment rate in rural areas during the slack season was as high as 85 percent. In 1932, it was reported that there were more than 20,000 beggars in South Kyonsang Province alone.[5] Excess labor in rural areas created a large influx of young men and women to cities. This trend of people seeking employment in the city brought chronic unemployment to urban areas as well.

Many Koreans went to Japan to work as indentured laborers. They worked under extremely harsh conditions. These Korean workers also suffered racial discrimination by the Japanese. One of the most extreme and tragic cases was the massacre of Koreans by Japanese civilians immediately after the Great Kantō Earthquake, which hit the Tokyo and Yokohama regions on September 1, 1923. Many parts of Tokyo and Yokohama were consumed by fire caused by the earthquake (450,000 houses were destroyed) and more than 100,000 people died. In the midst of the chaos caused by this natural calamity, an utterly ground-less rumor about Koreans was spread among Japanese civilians. Koreans were said to have poisoned the drinking water and to be preparing a large-scale political uprising. Many Japanese men, who believed this rumor, armed them-selves with swords, bamboo spears and the like, and randomly attacked and killed Koreans. In Kanagawa prefecture, where Yokohama is located, 4,106 Koreans were killed. In Tokyo, the death toll of Koreans was 1,347.[6]

Despite such deep-rooted, intense, and widespread Japanese prejudice against Koreans, the number of Koreans crossing the Korea Strait to Japan in search of work continued to increase. They were driven by the severe depression in their homeland. By 1931, 300,000 Koreans had come to Japan. Seven years later 700,000 Koreans were working throughout Japan. The Government-General of Korea also encouraged Koreans to migrate to Manchuria. By 1930, 1.3 million Koreans had moved to Manchuria. Most of them were engaged in rice production for export to Japan.[7]

In this way, a vast number of peasant-class men worked away from home, com-monly for long periods. Young women, too, picked up odd jobs to support their peasant families. Thus, large-scale urban migration took place throughout Korea in the 1920s and 1930s. For example, according to a survey conducted by the tax department of Seoul Municipal Office, the city population increased by 9,488 in one year from the end of 1932. Of this number, 6,690 were Korean women.[8] However, there were very few jobs in urban areas for uneducated, unskilled rural women. Most worked as low-paid factory workers, waitresses, barmaids, housemaids, nursemaids, and the like. Housemaids and nursemaids were mostly employed by Japanese families living in Korea.[9] (By the early 1930s about half a million Japanese were living in Korea, and most of them were government bureaucrats, policemen, school teachers, factory managers and their families.)

It is apparent that many young Korean women turned to prostitution to provide the essential income for their poverty-stricken families to survive. A series of articles entitled "Poverty makes prostitutes," that appeared in Septem-ber 1927 in the Korean newspaper *Dongah Ilbo*, clearly indicates this situation.[10] It seems that many young women were sold to brothels in return for an advance payment to their families. Many married women also became prostitutes due to financial difficulties that arose while their husbands were working away from home.[11] However, the amount of an advance paid for a Korean woman was far less than that paid for a Japanese woman. For example, in 1933, brothel owners in Inchon made an advance payment of between 200 and 700 yen for a Korean woman for a five-year contract, while between 700 and 2,500 yen was a usual amount paid for a Japanese woman.[12] In other words, destitute Korean families had to sell their daughters to brothels even though the return was small. In short, brothel owners could "employ" several Korean women for the same cost as one Japanese woman. It was quite common also for owners of "restaurants," "cafes," and "bars," who operated clandestine prostitution businesses, to pay far less – between 50 and 100 yen in advance – in order to employ Korean women under the pretence of being "waitresses" and "barmaids."[13] This "pricing mechanism," which was closely interlinked with chronic poverty caused by colonization, seemed to be one of the main reasons for a rapid increase in the number of Korean prostitutes under Japanese rule.

It was in March 1916 that the Government-General introduced in Korea a licensed prostitution system similar to that in Japan. In June 1922, the law regulating "prostitute employment agencies" was also enacted in Korea.[14] In other words, both brothel owners and "employment agents" had to obtain a license from the police to operate their business. Both Japanese and Korean proprietors were involved in the Korean prostitution industry. However, it was necessary for the Koreans to be seen as pro-Japanese by the authorities in order to secure a license and run a business smoothly. Thus, the licensing system created a tendency for the prostitution industry to be exploited by the Japanese administrators as a tool to foster Koreans who would collaborate with the Japanese. In the mid-1920s there were between 5,000 and 6,000 such "employment agents" in Seoul alone, "selling 30,000 women yearly for prices from 50 to 1,200

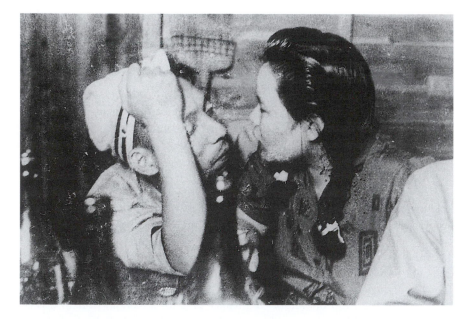

Plate 2.1 A comfort woman entertaining a drunken member of the Japanese Imperial Navy. The date and location are unknown.
Source: *Mainichi Shimbun*

yen."[15] In addition, many women were deceived by labor brokers who gave false promises of employment, such as factory work, and ended up as prostitutes.[16]

The prostitution industry in Korea was affected by the world depression in the late 1920s and 1930s. The economic depression contributed to an increase in the relatively cheap clandestine prostitution business, while the high-class brothel business declined. Partly because of the economic conditions in Korea and partly because of the rise of business opportunities provided by the Japanese occupation of Manchuria, brothel proprietors in Korea started moving into Manchuria. This began in late 1931. As the war in China dragged on, draining the Japanese treasury, the Government-General of Korea imposed austerity measures on the general population. For example, in April 1938, the tax rate on leisure services, food and drink was raised. This naturally included the services provided by brothels. As a consequence of the tax increase, the prices of alcohol and restaurant meals went up. In July that year, restaurants, cafes, bars and the like were ordered to shorten business hours. The police also changed their policy of tolerance. They started cracking down on clandestine brothels. It is strongly believed that such wartime stringency encouraged the brothel proprietors and clandestine operators to move out of Korea to seek business opportunities in China.[17]

Incidentally, the Korean situation turned out to be advantageous for the Japanese military forces stationed in China. As we have seen in the previous chapter, they had operated the comfort women system as an official policy since the early 1930s. The large number of Korean and Japanese proprietors, who moved to various places in China where Japanese troops were stationed, brought Korean women with them. Many of the women were bound by large debt through their "advanced payment." An example of this influx is seen near military camps in Jiujiang in Jiangxi Province, where 16 comfort stations and 46 restaurants were opened in 1940. Half of these newly opened comfort stations, and two of the restaurants, were run by Korean proprietors. As stated in the previous chapter, 24 comfort stations had operated in Jiujiang since mid-1939.[18] In Hankou, where there were only a few Koreans before Japan's invasion of China in 1937, the number of Korean residents increased to 1,614 by the end of March 1940. Most of these were owners of restaurants, comfort stations, small general stores and the like. Already by the end of 1939, Hankou had 20 comfort stations and more than 250 restaurants, cafes and bars at which prostitution operated mainly for civilian employees of the military.[19] It is therefore believed that by the early stages of the Asia-Pacific War many Japanese and Korean proprietors who had been operating prostitution businesses in Korea had moved to China due to economic problems in the colony and had started operating there for the Japanese troops and the military's civilian employees.

Procurement of Korean and Taiwanese women

As the war in China became deadlocked, the comfort women system, which had been firmly established as a matter of military policy, required more comfort women to be allocated to each unit of the Japanese Army stationed in China. It seems that "voluntary migration of proprietors and prostitutes" from Korea to China could no longer provide the army with a sufficient pool of comfort women. Thus, from 1938 the army itself became involved more closely in the procurement of women.

In March 1938, the army began carefully selecting and controlling "recruiting agents." By and large, there seemed to be two tiers of "recruiting agents." One group was those people who were directly selected by the Army and ordered to secure a specified number of women. These were mainly owners or managers of comfort stations already operating in China. In addition there were some private brothel owners from Korea and China. The other group was those who were commissioned by these brothel owners/managers to actually procure women – sub-contractors. The majority of these sub-contractors were local Korean "employment agents," labor-brokers, small proprietors in the prostitution business and the like. It is believed that most of these sub-contractors had already been operating businesses in the procurement of Korean women for prostitution, and many of them had been closely engaged in illegal trafficking of women.[20]

Some of the agents directly selected by the army, in particular the Koreans, returned to Korea to procure by themselves without using sub-contractors. In some cases Japanese and Korean proprietors collaborated to procure women in Korea. However, most "recruiting" seems to have been done by local Korean sub-contractors. Usually a Japanese or Korean owner/manager of a comfort station in China would go to Korea and stay in a port city, such as Pusan or Inchon. He would stay at an inn for some weeks or even a few months – long enough for his sub-contractors to secure enough women for him, and take them in at his lodging. In some cases, he would move from one city to another city, taking all the "recruits" with him. They would stay in an inn, again for a certain period until more women were procured. Once he had secured enough women they would travel to China. This "recruiting" procedure is verified by testimonies of many former Korean comfort women.[21] According to their testimonies, it was quite common for between 40 and 50 young women and girls to be "recruited" at once.

The most common expedient used in Korea was deceit – false promises of employment in Japan or in other Japanese occupied territories. Typically, a daughter of a poor peasant family would be approached by a labor broker and promised employment as a factory worker, assistant nurse, laundry worker, kitchen helper, or the like. While staying at an inn and waiting to be transported out of Korea, she would be relatively well treated. She would get good food and not need to work, but her physical freedom would be restricted. She would not find out the real nature of the work until she was taken into a comfort station and raped by members of the Japanese armed forces. This system provided many women from rural Korea. Jong Jingsong conducted research on 175 Korean women who came forward in 1993 as former comfort women. Of these, 105 out of 170 women whose birth places were identified had been "recruited" from rural areas in Kyongsang and Cholla Provinces.[22] In other words, sub-contractors had targeted young daughters of poor peasant families, knowing that it was relatively easy to trick them.

Kim Tokchin was a victim of this kind of deceit. She was one of five children of a poor peasant family living in South Kyonsang province. Her father had been arrested and beaten to death by the Japanese police over the illegal possession of tobacco leaves for his private consumption. After his death, her family's life became harder. She testifies:

> Making a living was not easy by any means. We were desperate for food. We dug up the roots of trees to eat, and my mother would work on a treadmill all day to bring back a few husks of grains as payment which we would boil with dried vegetables for our supper. . . .
>
> . . .
>
> It was the middle of January or perhaps a little later, say the beginning of February 1937. I was 17 years old. I heard girls were recruited with promises of work in Japan. It was said that a few had been recruited not long before from P'yongch'on, where we had lived with my uncle. I wished that at that time I had been able to go with them, but then I suddenly heard a Korean man was in the area again recruiting more girls to work in the Japanese factories. I went to P'yongch'on to meet him and promised him I would go to Japan to work.[23]

Yi Sunok, a 17-year-old girl in North Kyongsang, also became a victim of a false promise. According to her testimony, in 1938 she met a Korean man called Oh, who said that he had come to recruit young girls to work at a silk factory in Japan. She claims:

> He added that the factory would pay travel expenses and that many girls would be going. He also said that I could leave at any time if I didn't like the work there. Oh came and asked me if I wanted to go, and I answered that I would like to, given such good terms.[24]

Kim Tokchin was taken to a comfort station in Shanghai, and spent the next three years in China as a comfort woman. Yi Sunok was first taken to a comfort station in Guangdong, where she spent three years. Then she was taken to Singapore and forced to continue to serve Japanese soldiers there before being allowed to travel to Japan as a nurse on a Japanese hospital ship in 1944.

Some testimonies of former comfort women indicate that Japanese police in Korea collaborated with sub-contracted labor brokers. It is believed that the military authorities asked the police in Korea to assist local sub-contractors, to whom the work of procurement was commissioned by comfort station owners/ managers. The following testimony by a former comfort woman, Mun P'ilgi, for example, endorses such an interpretation.

> In our village there was a man in his fifties who worked as an agent for the Japanese. One day he approached me and told me he would give me an introduction to a place where I could both learn and earn money. I had

been so resentful that I hadn't been able to study, and his proposition was so attractive, that I told him I would like to take him up on the offer. . . . It was autumn 1943 and I was 18. . . .

. . .

After a few days, the man came to see me at dusk and told me to follow him. He said he wanted to take me somewhere for a few minutes. So I crept out of the house without saying anything to my parents. We walked for a little while, to a place not far from home. It was quiet; there were few houses around. There I saw there was a truck parked, *with a Japanese policeman, Tanaka, who worked at the village police station.*[25]

[Emphasis added]

In the case of the "recruitment" of Yun Turi, a young girl in Pusan, it seems that local policemen themselves were acting directly for a comfort station. According to Yun's testimony:

I was on my way home at about 5.00 or 6.00 p.m., and was passing the Nambu police station in front of Pusan railway station, when a policeman on guard duty called me over. He asked me to go inside, and I dutifully followed him in, thinking nothing could happen because I hadn't done anything wrong. It was sometime in early September 1943. There were three or four girls of my age already inside, and the policeman asked me to sit down. When I asked why, he said he would find me work in a nice place and told me to wait quietly. . . . At 11.00 p.m., a military truck arrived, and two soldiers loaded us on board.[26]

Yun was taken to No. 1 Comfort Station in Yongdo, an island just off Pusan, which was managed by a Japanese man called Takayama. Her mother and sister later found that Turi had been detained at this station, but they could not rescue her as the station was guarded by Japanese soldiers.

The fact that the police were involved in the "recruitment" in the cases of Mun P'ilgi and Yun Turi (both in late 1943) implies that, towards the end of the war, the military authorities used the police force to procure women. This probably was due to the scarcity of young women at the time.

Mobilization of the Korean labor force into war-related industries was greatly strengthened from 1943. In 1943 alone, nearly 140,000 people were mobilized by the Government-General.[27] In September 1943, the "Women's Voluntary Labor Service Corps" was organized throughout Korea. Through the corps many young, unmarried women were forced to "volunteer" for various types of work in wartime industries. In August 1944, a new law – the "Women's Voluntary Labor Service Law" – was enacted. This allowed the Governor-General of Korea to force any unmarried woman between 12 and 40 years old to engage in war-related labor for 12 months.[28] Under this law a vast number of young girls were mobilized and many were sent to Japan to work at large industrial factories. This policy probably created the situation in which procurement of young

Korean women for military comfort stations became difficult. As a result, it seems that the power of the police force was abused by the military authorities for the purpose of securing comfort women. According to testimonies of former comfort women, it appears that some representatives of the local Neighbour-hood Association, an organization that the Government-General required local civilians to establish, were also forced to act on behalf of owners/managers of comfort stations or their sub-contractors.

Some girls accepted offers of "employment" by labor brokers, or through the mediation of leaders of the local Neighborhood Association, in order to avoid being drafted into the Women's Voluntary Labor Service Corps. Ch'oe Myong-sun was one of them. In January 1945, when she was 19 years old, she accepted an introduction by a representative of the Neighborhood Association to a "good job" in Japan. She was sent to Hiroshima to become a mistress of a Japanese military officer for a couple of months. Then she was taken into a comfort station in Osaka, where she was forced to serve the Japanese soldiers until shortly before the end of the war.[29]

It was shortly after August 1944, when the Women's Voluntary Labor Service Law was enacted, that a rumor spread in Korea that all unmarried girls over

Plate 2.2 A group of Korean comfort women captured in Burma, who were interrogated by some bilingual Japanese-American soldiers in August 1944.
Source: US National Archives

14 years old would be forced to become comfort women. Many middle- and upper-class Korean families withdrew their daughters from women's colleges and hurriedly arranged marriages for them to avoid their being drafted.[30] However, some families in lower social strata felt trapped. For example, in September 1944, a girl called Kim T'aeson, who was then 19 years old and living with her uncle, was hiding in an attic of his house. One day when she came out of the attic and was having a meal downstairs, a Japanese man with a Korean partner visited the house, and offered her a "job" in Japan. Thinking that work in Japan would be a far better option than becoming a comfort woman, she accepted their offer. She ended up in a comfort station in Burma.[31] In this way, in the late stage of war, the method of deceit was closely intertwined with the political coercion imposed upon the colonial subjects.

It seems that in some cases an advance payment was made to a girl's family in a similar manner in which women had been sold to civilian brothels in the 1920s and early 1930s. Yet in these cases, too, labor brokers rarely told the girls and their parents the truth. They would give a false impression that the girls would be working as nurses, housemaids or factory workers. A survey of 20 Korean women captured in Burma, conducted by the Psychological Warfare Team attached to the US Army forces in the India-Burma theater, reveals that they were deceived and made to believe that their service would pay off family debts. The following is an extract from this official US survey:

RECRUITING
Early in May of 1942 Japanese agents arrived in Korea for the purpose of enlisting Korean girls for "comfort service" in newly conquered Japanese territories in Southeast Asia. The nature of this "service" was not specified but it was assumed to be work connected with visiting the wounded in hospitals, rolling bandages, and generally making the soldiers happy. The inducement used by these agents was plenty of money, an opportunity to pay off the family debts, easy work, and the prospect of a new life in a new land – Singapore. On the basis of these false representations many girls enlisted for overseas duty and were rewarded with an advance of a few hundred yen.
. . . The contract they signed bound them to Army regulations and to work for the "house master" for a period of from six months to a year depending on the family debts for which they were advanced.
Approximately 800 of these girls were recruited in this manner and they landed with their Japanese "house master" at Rangoon around August 20th, 1942.[32]

The "house master," i.e. the manager of this comfort station, was a Japanese man called Kitamura Eibun. Kitamura, his wife and sister-in-law had been running a "restaurant" in Kyonsong (now Seoul) before obtaining a commission to run a comfort station in Burma. Kitamura purchased 22 Korean women, who were aged 19 to 31, paying each family from 300 to 1,000 yen. In July 1942, Kitamura and his wife took these 22 women to Burma on a passenger ship which had more than 700 Korean women on board. The total amount of money

Kitamura used for advance payments must have been more than 10,000 yen, a large sum of money – surely beyond the means of a small "restaurant" owner at that time.[33] It is therefore speculated that the money may have been made available by the Japanese military authorities.

It seems also that in Taiwan (another colony of Japan) the most common tactic used for the recruitment of young Taiwanese women was false promises of employment in Japan or other Japanese occupied territories. Unfortunately, detailed information regarding the experiences of Taiwanese comfort women is not available. So far 50 former comfort women have been identified, of whom 30 are still alive. However we do know that, according to a report in June 1993 prepared by an organization called the Taipei Women's Rescue Foundation, 18 of the women had been working as either waitresses at restaurants or cafes, as bar hostesses or as maids at inns. It seems that most of these women had been sold to these places due to their families' desperate financial straits. About half of these women had been, in reality, working as prostitutes. They were approached by a labor broker and offered a job as a kitchen helper or a waitress at a military canteen, or a hostess at an officers' club. Another group of 12 women had been working as laundry workers, cleaning ladies, factory workers and the like. These 12,

Plate 2.3 A group of Taiwanese nurses leaving Taipei for Southeast Asia. Some of them were exploited as comfort women. Date unknown.
Source: Ōtsuki Shoten

also approached by a labor broker, had been promised jobs as a nurse helper, kitchen helper, or laundry worker for the Japanese troops. The "high salary" promised by the labor broker was also an attraction for these poorly paid women. Labor brokers came from both Japan and Taiwan, and, as was the case in Korea, it was common for a Japanese and a local to work as a pair.[34]

Unlike in Korea, there are cases of fully qualified nurses being recruited under the false pretence that they would be sent overseas as military nurses. Among the 50 identified Taiwanese comfort women, three were former nurses. One was ordered to go overseas by a matron of the hospital at which she was working and ended up in a comfort station. Another 17-year-old nurse was sent to Timor, together with more than 10 other nurses, believing that she would be working as a nurse. Yet as soon as she arrived, a VD check was conducted, she was raped by an officer and sent to a comfort station.[35]

Only three of the former Taiwanese comfort women so far identified genuinely volunteered to be comfort women, clearly knowing the real nature of the work. In fact, 31 claimed that they had been deceived and eventually forced to become comfort women, and seven testified that they were simply forced to serve as comfort women. Nine received an advanced payment, and it is believed that in most cases the payment was made to the girls' parents.[36]

The 1993 report compiled by Taipei Women's Rescue Foundation does not cover the cases of 14 Taiwanese aboriginal women who came forward between January and September 1996. (Two of the latter withdrew their cases due to fear that their own families would oppose the revelation of their past as comfort women.) All these women belong to three of 10 Taiwanese aboriginal tribes – the Tarokos, the Taiyas, and the Bunus. Most Korean and Taiwanese comfort women were sent overseas, but in these aboriginal women's cases, all (except one, who was sent to Hong Kong) were forced to serve Japanese troops stationed in their own home regions in Taiwan. Most were initially asked to work at a Japanese Army camp nearby to do domestic jobs, such as cleaning, sewing and cooking, where they were properly paid. However, after a few months they were gang-raped by soldiers and then forced to serve as comfort women in the evening, while continuing to do their domestic work during the day. In many of the cases this happened in 1944, a year before the war ended.[37]

It is believed that, towards the end of the war, small army units stationed deep in the mountains in Taiwan could no longer reach the service of comfort women, and thus used force to secure local young women as comfort women. Such actions by Japanese troops in remote Taiwan regions reflect the collapse of military morale due to their isolation in a prolonged war. According to the testimonies of some of these aboriginal women, local Japanese police also took part in the procurement of the women.[38]

Procurement of women in China and the Philippines

From the available testimonies of former comfort women, it is strongly believed that kidnapping and abduction were not widely used methods of procurement of comfort women in Korea and Taiwan.[39] In Japan's colonial territories, it was rare that military personnel were directly involved in actually "recruiting" women. As we have already examined, it was usually carried out by Japanese or local labor brokers. In the Dutch East Indies (now Indonesia), where the local population generally welcomed the entrance of the Japanese Imperial forces into the territories as "liberators" from Dutch colonialism, deceit was also a common tactic employed by the Japanese to procure local women. Forcible recruitment by intimidation or violence, such as the case of Dutch women and girls who were forcibly taken out of the detention camps in Java and pressed into comfort stations, was not a common method in this region, as we will see in more detail in the following chapter.

It is clear from the available evidence that Japanese troops used different methods in China and the Philippines.

As we have seen in the previous chapter, shortly after the Nanjing Massacre, Japanese army units set up their own comfort stations in areas in which they were stationed, like Nanjing and its nearby towns of Huzhou, Yangzhou, Changzhou, Chuxian and Bengbu. These comfort stations used Chinese comfort women, who it is strongly believed were local residents, not prostitutes. For example, in Nanjing, according to research conducted by Professor Su Zhiliang of Shanghai Normal University, the Japanese military authorities organized a group of Chinese collaborators who were ordered to "recruit" Chinese women. In one case, one of these collaborators visited the Nanjing University at the order of a senior Japanese officer. About 12,000 women had taken shelter at the university to escape Japanese atrocities. The collaborator tried to persuade the women to become comfort women, claiming that their safety would be guaranteed and that they would be rewarded for their service. This attempt failed. Then the Japanese troops and their collaborators raided civilian homes and abducted about 300 women, of whom about 100 were selected to work as comfort women.[40]

It was not long before comfort stations in China were staffed with Koreans rather than local Chinese women. This shift in the army's policy was probably made for three main reasons. Firstly, it seems that pressing local civilians into military prostitution was seen by the military authorities as an unwise strategy, as it would further arouse anti-Japanese sentiment among the local Chinese civilians. Secondly, Koreans were regarded by the Japanese as the people who were culturally and ideologically much closer to the Japanese than the Chinese were. The fact that many Koreans could understand the Japanese language – a result of Japan's colonization – was seen as another advantage of using Korean girls. It also seems that the Japanese were very concerned about the danger of local Chinese women, who they feared could be used as spies by the Chinese forces. Thus, at almost all of the officially approved comfort stations established in China from Manchuria in the north to Guangzhou in the south, Koreans were the most commonly exploited comfort women.[41]

This change of policy did not mean that Chinese women and girls escaped sexual violence committed by the Japanese soldiers. On the contrary, even after the full-scale mobilization of Korean women as comfort women, numerous sexual crimes were committed by Japanese men throughout the occupied territories in China. In particular, in the so-called "liberated districts" (or "hostile districts" in the Japanese military terminology, i.e. places where the Chinese Liberation Army's activities were strong) the treatment of local civilians by the Japanese was vicious and brutal, and many young girls and women were victimized. Many of these "hostile districts" were located in Shanxi and Hebei Provinces, where the Japanese Army adopted the tactics called "Shōdo Sakusen" – "scorched-earth strategy." This meant that, if a particular Chinese village or town community was identified as "hostile," Japanese troops had license to destroy the entire community, including the inhabitants. The Chinese called this atrocious practice "Sanguang zuozhan," which literally means "three lightening strategy," because the Japanese robbed the community of its possessions, killed all the inhabitants, and burnt down all the buildings. During such operations it was quite common for the Japanese men to take the attitude that they could do anything to the local civilians, including rape, because they were going to eliminate them all in the end, anyway.[42]

Among the army units stationed in areas in which "hostile districts" were located, it seems that some commanders set up comfort stations without higher official approval. In such cases, comfort women were civilian girls who were forcibly separated from their families, detained in military compounds for a certain period (up to six months), and continuously raped by Japanese soldiers, and, in some cases, by their Chinese collaborators as well.

A recent survey conducted by a local school teacher, Zhang Shuangbing, in Yu prefecture, Shanxi Province, disclosed that some 50 women have so far been identified as victims of this sexual crime in this prefecture. However, about 30 of them have died since they revealed their past as comfort women. The majority of these victims were young unmarried women between 15 and 18 years old at the time. One girl called Qiaolian was 13 years old.[43]

Li Xiumei was 15 years old when she was abducted by four Japanese soldiers from her home in a small village called Lizhuang, in Yu prefecture in September 1942. At the time, her mother was also at home but could not stop the Japanese men taking her daughter away. Li was taken to a village called Jingui, where a small detachment unit of the 14th Battalion had its garrison compound. Together with two other girls she was detained in a dwelling cave, which is quite a common feature in this region. Day after day they were raped by Japanese soldiers in the cave. Each day she was raped by at least two or three soldiers; sometimes by 10 soldiers. The cave was guarded by Chinese collaborators, making it impossible to escape. She was often taken to an officer's room in the fortress and raped there, too.[44]

One day, about five months after she had been abducted, she tried to refuse the commander who had been particularly wild in his treatment of the girls. He severely beat her with his waist belt. Her right eye was hit hard with the buckle, resulting in her losing the sight of that eye. When she continued to resist the officer, he clubbed her, knocking her to the ground. Later she was sent back home because her injuries made her physically unable to serve the Japanese men. However, on her return she found that her mother had committed suicide and her father gone mad. It appears that in order to get their daughter back, the family had paid the Japanese troops a ransom of 600 yuan, a large sum of money at the time. They had raised the money by borrowing from relatives. When they were told that it was not enough to secure her release, the mother hanged herself. The husband became insane with the shock of his wife's death.[45]

In her testimony, Liu Mianhuan – another victim of sexual violence committed by the same detachment unit stationed in Jingui – describes being taken from her parents in March 1941 by three Chinese collaborators. She too was detained in a dwelling cave and raped by the three Chinese before being taken to the Japanese commander. For the following 40 days she was raped by the commander at night and by Chinese collaborators and Japanese soldiers during daytime. It is not certain whether the Japanese commander who violated Liu Mianhuan was the same man who victimized Li Xiumei. Eventually Liu Mianhuan became too sick to be exploited by the Japanese. She was released in return for a 100 yuan ransom, which her father managed to raise, borrowing from relatives and friends.[46] "Sexual slavery hostages" rather than "comfort women" is a more appropriate term to describe the circumstances endured by Li and Liu. (Incidentally, the 14th Battalion which was responsible for the crimes committed against these Chinese girls was transferred to Okinawa in August 1944. Almost all perished in the Battle of Okinawa in 1945.)

When we closely examine the testimonies of the former Filipina comfort women, we note similarities between the procurement methods used in China and in the Philippines.

Several official documents which refer to comfort stations in the Philippines have been found in archives in Japan and the US. According to one of these documents, in Manila alone, in early 1943, there were 17 comfort stations for the rank-and-file soldiers, "staffed" by a total of 1,064 comfort women. In addition, there were four officers' clubs served by more than 120 women. No information is available as to the nationality of these comfort women. Other documents reveal the fact that comfort stations were also located at Iloilo on Panay Island, Butsuan and Cagayan de Oro on Mindanao Island, Masbate on Masbate Island, and Ormoc and Tacloban on Leyte Island.[47] It is almost certain that there were comfort stations at many other places in the Philippines. These documents do not disclose much information about the comfort women, but a few, such as those referring to comfort stations in Iloilo, mention a number of Filipina comfort women, including several girls between 16 and 20 years old.[48] It is almost impossible to know from the archival documents how these women were "recruited" and under what conditions they were forced to serve the Japanese troops.

It was in 1992, almost half a century after the end of the war, that the truly horrific picture of widespread sexual violence against Filipinas during the occupation first emerged. This was made possible when Maria Rosa Henson courageously came forward and revealed her painful past as a comfort woman.[49] Encouraged by her action, many women spoke out – one after another – and gave detailed testimonies about their wartime ordeals. Eventually, the testimonies of 51 women were collected by a group of Japanese lawyers and a local NGO called the Task Force on Filipino Comfort Women.[50]

In contrast to the military authorities' behind-the-scenes approach in Korea, Taiwan, and the Dutch East Indies, available testimonies, including that of Maria Rosa Henson, indicate that at many places in the Philippines the Japanese troops directly secured comfort women. Furthermore, their methods were wanton. They included abduction, rape, and continuous confinement for the purposes of sexual exploitation – similar to the Chinese case we have already examined. Both in China and the Philippines, it seems that the Japanese did not even try to conceal what they were doing to the civilians.

The main reason for such direct action by the Japanese troops in the Philippines may lie in the fact that the anti-Japanese guerilla movement was strong and widespread throughout the occupation period, as in "liberated districts" in China. It is said that there were more than 100 guerilla organizations at the peak, involving about 270,000 activists and associates.[51] Hukbalahap, which Maria Rosa Henson joined, was one of the largest of these guerilla organizations. It was comprised predominantly of peasants and workers under the influence of the Communist Party. As a result of this strong anti-Japanese movement, the Japanese were able

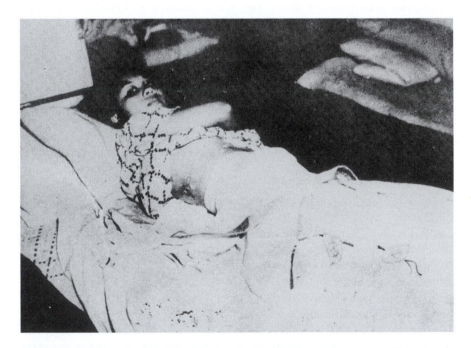

Plate 2.4 A Filipina girl, who was stabbed with a bayonet by a Japanese soldier because
       she tried to fight off being raped, lying on a hospital bed. The date and exact
       location are unknown.
Source: Ōtsuki Shoten

to control only 30 percent of the Philippines.[52] Guerilla activities were particularly strong on Luzon and Panay. The fact that the majority of the people who have so far been identified as former comfort women were residents of these two islands also suggests the close link between Japanese sexual violence against civilians and the strength of popular guerilla resistance. In areas of the Philippines where resistance was strong, Japanese troops tended to regard any civilian as a "possible guerilla collaborator," and therefore felt justified in doing anything to "women belonging to the enemy." Indeed seven out of the above-mentioned 51 victims testified that they were abducted by the Japanese during guerilla mopping-up operations.

In almost all of the 51 testimonies that have so far been collected in the Philippines, the victims were abducted by Japanese soldiers from home, work, or while walking in the street. In some cases, abductions were planned, but in many cases the women were simply picked up on the road by a small group of Japanese soldiers and taken to a Japanese garrison nearby, where they were raped day after day. The duration of captivity was usually between one and several months. In a few cases victims were confined for up to two years. In most cases the premises where they were confined were part of the garrison compound or right next to it. They were guarded by Japanese soldiers 24 hours a day, providing very little chance of escape. This was quite different from the typical comfort station in other parts of Asia, which in most cases was a facility completely separate from the barracks, and managed by a Japanese or Korean civilian proprietor under the supervision of the military authorities.

In the Philippines it seems that the usual practice was that about 10 young women or girls were held by each small, company-size army unit for the exclusive exploitation of the unit. Most commonly a victim would be raped by five to ten soldiers every day. None of the victims were ever paid and some were forced to cook and wash for the Japanese soldiers during the day and then provide sexual services at night. It is believed that, as in comfort stations in "hostile districts" in China, stations where these Filipina girls were confined were also set up without official approval by the regional headquarters.

Another distinctive feature of comfort women both in the Philippines and China is that they became victims of military sexual violence at very young ages. The average age of the Filippina comfort women for which we have information was 17.6 years. Many were younger than 15 years old and one was as young as 10 years old. Naturally, the younger girls had not yet begun to menstruate. The explanation why the Japanese victimized such young girls may require further investigation in the future.

Continuous rape in captivity was undoubtedly a tormenting experience for them, but tragically some of these Filipina girls had had to endure the additional horror of witnessing the murder of their own parents and siblings by the Japanese at the time of their abduction. For example, one night in 1942, two Japanese soldiers invaded the home of 13-year-old Tomasa Salinog and her father in Antique on Panay Island. As the two soldiers intruded, another two stayed outside on watch. Tomasa's father resisted the soldiers as they tried to take the child away. One of the Japanese, Captain Hirooka, suddenly drew his sword and severed the man's head in front of the girl's eyes. She screamed loudly at the sight of her father's head lying in the corner of the room, but the Japanese dragged her out of the house.[53] In another case Rufina Fernandez, a 17-year-old Manila girl witnessed the murder of both her parents and one of her sisters when Japanese soldiers broke into their home one night in 1944. The Japanese tried to take her and her father away with them. When he resisted he was beheaded. When her mother tried to do the same she was killed. Her youngest sister was also killed in front of her. Her two other younger sisters were crying as she was taken from the house. Their crying suddenly stopped, and she presumed that they, too, had been killed by the Japanese.[54]

The overall picture that can be drawn from these testimonies is strikingly similar to the situation experienced by many women in Bosnia-Herzegovina during the recent Bosnian War.[55] The only notable difference is that the Japanese had no intention of deliberately making the girls pregnant as one method of "ethnic cleansing." The words "comfort women" or "comfort station" are of course nothing but an official euphemism. As with the Bosnian case, "rape camps" is probably a more appropriate term to accurately describe the conditions of sexual enslavement into which many Filipinas and Chinese girls were pressed.

Life as a comfort woman

The experiences of comfort women at officially approved comfort stations were as inhumane as, if not worse than, those of the Filipina and Chinese girls that we have cited.

When the girls were informed about the real nature of the work, it was quite natural for them to refuse to work as comfort women. Some demanded that the comfort station manager send them back home as the job they had been promised was found to be false. Typically the manager would inform them that the large advance payment made to their parents had to be paid back before they would be sent back home. Even where no advance payment had been made, the manager would demand repayment of the cost of transporting them from their home to the locality of the comfort station, the cost of daily meals and clothes, plus interest on those costs. When they realized that they were trapped by this sort of "indentured system," it was too late to reverse the situation.

Yet some women still tried to refuse being made sexual slaves. Their resistance was met by force, often by torture, in order to get their consent, and some were maimed or killed. Yi Yongsu was one such woman who experienced extreme brutality as the result of initial refusal. The following is an excerpt from her testimony:

> The man who had accompanied us from Taegu turned out to be the proprietor of the comfort station we were taken to. We called him Oyaji [i.e. boss or master]. I was the youngest among us. Punsun was a year older than me

and the others were 18, 19 and 20. The proprietor told me to go into a certain room, but I refused. He dragged me by my hair to another room. There I was tortured with electric shocks. He was very cruel. He pulled out the telephone cord and tied my wrists and ankles with it. Then, shouting "konoyaro!" [i.e. "You rascal"] he twirled the telephone receiver. Light flashed before my eyes, and my body shook all over. I couldn't stand it and begged him to stop. I said I would do anything he asked. But he turned the receiver once more. I blacked out. When I came round my body was wet; I think that he had probably poured water on me.[56]

Comfort stations were allowed to be set up only at the premises designated by the military authorities – usually the regimental headquarters. Hotels, large restaurants, and large civilian houses were expropriated and used as military brothels. If such facilities were not available near the military camp, as in some regions, school buildings and temples were converted for such purposes. Usually comfort stations were set up a certain distance from the military compound. However, in some cases, such as a remote front line of a battle zone, military tents or a part of the army barracks were used.

Interior facilities and decorations differed from station to station. Those in large cities were lavishly decorated, with *tatami* mats on the floor, a chest of drawers, colourful bedding and so on in each room. However, most of them only had basic facilities; each room had a bed or *futon* on a mat or wooden floor and a small dressing table. As the building housing a comfort station was usually divided into a number of small rooms by thin plywood walls, each room was quite small and could not accommodate large furniture anyway. At some stations there were no doors on the rooms and no walls between the rooms. They used curtains to screen off the rooms. In bathrooms and toilets, disinfectant (potassium permanganate solution or cresol soap solution) was provided. Comfort women were instructed to wash their private parts each time after sexual intercourse. At some stations, vaseline was also provided in each room.

Each comfort station was tightly controlled by the regional military headquarters, even if it was owned and run by a private proprietor. Strict regulations were set out regarding the rates, business hours, available time for each soldier, sanitary conditions, regular VD examinations, and so on. The details of the regulations differed slightly from region to region, but by and large they had a similar format. Different hours were allocated for the service of different ranks of soldiers. Rank-and-file soldiers were allowed to visit the station between 9:00 am (or 10:00 am) and late afternoon. Visiting time for non-commissioned officers was between 4:00 pm and 8:00 pm, and the time between 8:00 pm and midnight or early morning was exclusively for the officers. Officers could visit the station as often as they wished, but non-commissioned officers and enlisted men were usually allowed to visit the station only once weekly – on an off-duty day. Different days of each week were designated as off-duty days for different units of the force. Therefore, there was hardly a respite for comfort women. Most comfort stations were closed only one day a month, giving one break a month for comfort women. Comfort stations for the exclusive use of officer-class men were often established in large cities. Most of the comfort women in these stations were Japanese. It seems that these Japanese women experienced much better conditions than other Asian comfort women.[57]

Each comfort woman served several men – up to 10 – on a normal day, but the number would sharply increase shortly before and after each combat operation. On such days, each woman was forced to serve 30 or 40 men a day. The available time for each man was regulated to 30 minutes. However, in the busy periods each soldier was allowed only a few minutes. The following extract from the testimony of Nishihira Junichi vividly describes the dreadful conditions that comfort women faced on just such a day during the Battle of Okinawa in 1945. Nishihira was a 13-year-old boy, who was drafted as a factotum at one of the comfort stations on the main island of Okinawa.

> Shouting "Come on, hurry up!" their eyes were bloodshot and their legs shook as they waited impatiently. Some even began to undo their belts and their bodies shook, even though there were many ahead of them in the queue.
>
> Most soldiers finished within twenty or thirty seconds and came out one after another in an infatuated state which greatly contrasted their behaviour while waiting. Some, however, took five minutes or more, although if they took too long a veteran soldier who acted as a supervisor would grab the offending soldier by the scruff of the neck and drag him out of the room.[58]

In such circumstances, there was no time for comfort women to follow the regulation that they should "wash their private parts each time." There is no doubt that such extreme sexual abuse caused considerable physical pain and health problems to many of the comfort women. One former comfort woman relates:

> Having to serve so many men made my sexual organs swell up, and I had to go to see a doctor. When I went the first time, my stomach hurt to the extent that I thought it was going to burst.[59]

According to a testimony of another former comfort woman:

> Yet, even though I had no venereal disease, I had to have treatment, because I kept bleeding and couldn't pass water. Perhaps it was a bladder infection. There were some women whose vaginas were so swollen and were bleeding so profusely that there was no space for a needle to be inserted inside.[60]

Managers of comfort stations were usually instructed to make sure that comfort women would not have intercourse during their menstrual periods. However, it seems that many women were forced to serve men during their periods. In her testimony, Kim Haksun describes how she managed to tackle this problem:

When our menstruation was due we used cotton wool obtained from the surgeon. We had to serve soldiers during our periods. We tried to avoid them at this time, but they just forced their way in and there was nothing we could do to stop them. We had to make small cotton wool balls and insert them deep inside our wombs so that no blood leaked out. When we didn't have enough cotton we had to cut cloth into small strips and roll this up to use instead.[61]

Soldiers were strictly instructed to use condoms provided by the supply department to each soldier through his unit or to the comfort station directly. The brand of condom supplied by the Japanese military was called "Assault No. 1." Despite the official regulation that anyone who refused to use condoms would be banned from associating with comfort women, many men forced comfort women to serve them without condoms. In some remote areas the supply of condoms was not sufficient. There the same condom would be used a number of times. After each time, it would be washed and disinfected by a comfort woman.[62]

It is not surprising therefore that many women suffered from VD. Most comfort women received periodic VD check-ups conducted by a medical officer or a medic. These checks were made once a week or once every 10 days. Penicillin was not available in those days. The most common treatment for VD was an injection of salvarsan, or "No. 606" in Japanese medical corps' terminology. Salvarsan is an extremely strong substance and some former comfort women who received the injections testified that they suffered from various severe side-effects. If a woman was found to be pregnant, a medical officer carried out an abortion. One former Korean comfort woman, Huwang Kumju, testifies:

The new girls were to serve the officers, as they were virgins. The officer didn't use condoms, so quite a few of us became pregnant quite early on, but we were naive and weren't aware of it. I was all right. But those who were injected with "No. 606" without knowing that they were pregnant, they began to feel chilly, their bodies swelled, and they started to discharge blood. Then they were taken to the hospital to undergo curettage. After curettage was operated three or four times, they became barren.[63]

A Korean woman, So Shindo, who spent seven years in various places in China, became pregnant several times. The first time, after a seven-month pregnancy, she had a stillbirth in her own room at the comfort station. She had been forced to serve men while pregnant. Later she gave birth to two babies – a few years apart. Both times she was forced to give the baby away, as comfort women were not allowed to keep children at the station. On other occasions she performed abortions on herself by using combined methods of fasting and drinking a herbal extract.[64] It is not clear from her testimony why the medical officer did not perform an abortion.

Although the fee charged for service at comfort stations varied according to regulations set by each military headquarters, prices generally differed little between the establishments. Charges were set according to the rank of the military

Table 2.1 Established rates of South Sector Billet Brothel [Manila, c. 1943 or 1944]

Classification	Summary	Time	Rate (yen)		
			Japanese	Korean	Chinese
Officers and warrant officers	1. Overnight stay will be from 2200 until 0600 the following morning.	1 hour	3.00	3.00	2.50
		Overnight stays:			
		from 2400	10.00	10.00	7.00
		from 2200	15.00	15.00	10.00
Non-commissioned officers	2. Persons staying longer than one hour will pay double for each hour.	1 hour	2.50	2.50	2.00
		30 minutes	1.50	1.50	1.00
Privates		1 hour	2.00	2.00	1.50
		30 minutes	1.50	1.50	1.00

"clients." Table 2.1, which was included in Japanese documents captured by the Allied forces during the war, is one example.[65] It is the chart of rates (probably in 1943 or 1944) at the comfort station set up within the South Sector Billet in Manila, the Philippines.

During the Pacific War, the monthly salary of an enlisted man was between 6 and 10 yen, depending on the rank. Therefore, 1.50 or 2 yen was a considerable amount of money for rank-and-file soldiers. Yet, it was almost certain that for these soldiers, seeking a temporary escape in sex from the horrors and threat of death they encountered daily, the high price weighed little on their minds. The fact that the system was similar to that of private brothels (where a client paid a prostitute for the service provided) also contributed to the soldiers' attitude that their deeds were legitimate; that they were indeed entitled to be served by a comfort woman in return for payment.

The managers of comfort stations were instructed by the military authorities about the "salary" arrangements for their "employees." For example, according to the regulations set out by the Army Headquarters of the Manila District in February 1943, half of the fee had to be paid to the comfort woman and the other half to the manager. Expenses for meals and bedding for the comfort women were supposed to be the manager's responsibility, while those for clothing, hairdressing and cosmetics had to be met by each comfort woman. In case of illness, it was stipulated that 70 percent of medical expenses be paid by the manager.[66] According to similar regulations set out in 1943 by the Japanese military government in Malaysia, the comfort woman was entitled to receive a set percentage of the fee. In the case of a woman for whom more than 1,500 yen had been paid in advance at the time of her recruitment, she would receive at least 40 percent of her takings. In the case of those who had received less than 1,500 yen in advance, the rate was at least 50 percent to her. If no advance payment had been made, the woman was entitled to at least 60 percent.[67]

A soldier who paid the fee at the front desk received a ticket in return. He would hand it to the comfort woman when entering her room. In some military districts, tickets were distributed to each unit and sold to the soldiers and officers who wanted to use the brothels. Every morning or evening, each comfort woman would give all the collected tickets to the manager. This method supposedly allowed the recording of the respective earnings of the comfort women. In reality, however, comfort women received hardly any payment. Managers did not give the women the details of their accounts. If they queried the matter, they were simply told that they still owed money to the manager. Most comfort women probably did not know that their managers had been instructed by the military authorities about the required sharing of the earnings. Obviously the managers took advantage of the lack of education and the naivety of their "employees," and gave them as little information as possible regarding their due payments and the expenses that the managers were expected to meet.

Available testimonies from Korean comfort women verify this point. For example, in her testimony, Yi Tungnam, a former comfort woman from Korea, described the "financial arrangement" she had with her manager, Kaneyama, whose real Korean name was Kim, while working at a comfort station in Hankou:

> Kaneyama said that he would keep 70 percent of our income and we would get 30 percent. He claimed to be keeping a record so that he could give us our money in one lump sum when we left the station. Sometimes, if we asked for money to buy clothes that we needed, he would give us about 20 yen each and say he had deducted it from our respective record. However, he barely gave enough money for new clothes, offering us a little perhaps once every few months. The money I had was given to me by soldiers once in a while. And even if I wanted to buy something, it was never easy to go out. Kaneyama disapproved of us leaving the station to buy anything from the merchants up the road. He argued that we might miss customers.[68]

Another Korean woman, Yi Sangok, who was taken to a comfort station on the Palau Islands, tells of a similar experience:

> We each had a room with a small wardrobe and bedding, the cost of which we were told was to be deducted from our income later on . . . My monthly income was said to be 30 yen. But the proprietor provided me with things like clothes, cosmetics and a mirror, and deducted the cost of these from my promised wages. So I never had any money in my hands. He said that we had to keep clean and have nice clothes in which to serve our clients, so he gave us Korean dresses, Japanese kimonos and Western dresses. He also offered us expensive food, but always deducted the expense from our wages.[69]

Most former comfort women testify that they received little payment from their managers, and the money they did get was mainly pocket money from occasional tips from their "clients." One Korean former comfort woman, Mun Okuchu, claims that she managed to save money given to her as tips by officers. She sent some of it to her home from Thailand. However, it seems that her case was exceptional. Even in her case, she lost all the savings she had deposited in a Japanese Post Office deposit account when she lost the deposit book at the end of the war.[70] Some women also managed to save small amounts of "cash," but in most cases they were saving the so-called Gumpyō – the Japanese military currency – which became totally worthless at the end of the war. As a result, most of the comfort women ended up penniless at the end of the war.

In addition to the financial strain, comfort women were constantly in danger of violence committed by their "client" soldiers and officers, in particular those who were drunk. Although drinking alcohol on the premises of comfort stations was prohibited, some men smuggled in liquor. Despite the military regulations banning intoxicated men from entering comfort stations, it was difficult for managers to refuse military personnel, especially officers. Intoxicated men often made various unbearable requests of the comfort women. They inflicted violence upon their "hostesses" when such requests were refused. The following extract from the testimony of Yi Sunok, a Korean woman who was taken into a comfort station in Guangdong, is an example of this.

> Among soldiers, some carried a flask of alcohol at their side. They would get drunk and become violent. Not long after I arrived [at a comfort station in Guangdong] I was stabbed on the thigh by one. This happened after I tried to refuse him when he went for me several times. I screamed when I was stabbed and the other women and soldiers in the station rushed to my room in surprise. I had to continue to serve the soldiers, even while I was receiving treatment from the military hospital. When this wound had nearly healed, another soldier pushed me backwards for not welcoming him. My hip was hurt, and my thigh began to swell because of the impact. It became so swollen and painful that I had to have an operation.[71]

Mun P'ilgi describes a similar experience:

> There were many times when I was almost killed. If I refused to do what one man asked, he would come back drunk and threaten me with his sword. Others simply arrived drunk, and had intercourse with their swords stuck in the *tatami*. This left the *tatami* scarred, but this sort of behaviour was more a threat to make me accede to their desires and give them satisfaction.[72]

Mun P'ilgi's testimony also refers to a man who tore all her clothes off, beat her, and eventually pressed a red-hot iron against her armpit, all as a result of her rejecting his unreasonable advances.[73] It seems that problems caused by drunken soldiers at comfort stations were particularly frequent towards the end of the war when morale declined as Japan faced imminent defeat. The following extracts from the Bulletin of the Ishi Corps, issued in the latter half of 1944, verify the low morale of the members of Ishi Corps stationed in the Naha and Urazoe areas of the main island of Okinawa. Almost all members of this army unit perished during the Battle of Okinawa the following year.

No. 62, September 28, 16:00
Item 7. Regarding Base facilities:
    1. Ensure there is an adequate supply of condoms.
      . . .
    4. Some soldiers have been seen drinking *sake* from water canteens while at the brothels. If found, all members of such a battalion will be banned from visiting the comfort stations.

No. 74, October 19, 12:00
Item 10. Regarding Base facilities:
    1. Although a warning was issued in Bulletin No. 62, some soldiers continue to enter the comfort stations without showing their tickets, peep into girls' rooms or forcibly demand service by grabbing a girl. Some soldiers came at night without tickets and when refused began pelting the reception area with stones. Ensure that this recalcitrant behaviour is not tolerated.

No. 79 October 26, 16:00
Item 8. Regarding Base facilities:
    1. Some soldiers are altering the time and date on their tickets, knowing full well that this is against the regulations. Others are turning up with four tickets all at one time, while still others turn up at the station at one o'clock in the morning. On September 24 one heavily drunk Warrant Officer (from 4283 Battalion, Ishi Corps) entered the station without a ticket, threw himself on the floor of the reception area and then went into a girl's room demanding service. Tickets on which the time and date have been altered are treated as invalid and those which are not used should be returned to the person in charge immediately.[74]

However, intoxicated men were not the only violent ones. Some men were equally violent when sober, as the following extract of Kim Hakusun's testimony indicates:

They [soldiers] varied in the way they treated us: while one soldier was so rough as to drive me to utter despair, another would be quite gentle. There was one who ordered me to suck him off, while he held my head between his legs. There was another who insisted that I wash him after intercourse. I was often disgusted by their requests, but if I resisted they would beat me until I gave in.[75]

Many comfort women were maltreated by their managers. Managers beat women as punishment if they failed to meet their daily quota of tickets, or contracted VD or became ill and were unable to serve the men for a long period.

Plate 2.5 Japanese soldiers waiting for their turn to be served outside a comfort station in China. The date and exact location are unknown.
Source: Ōtsuki Shoten

Many women contemplated escaping from the stations, but invariably they had little idea about exactly where they were and how they could find their way home. In addition, they could not speak the local language. Even those success-ful enough to escape the camp were soon arrested by the kempeitai. Ha Sunnyo was one woman who escaped but was forced to return to her station because she could not find her way home. The following is an extract from her testimony:

> After about a year in Shanghai, I ran away from the comfort station on a snowy winter's day. I ran as far as the rickshaw terminal. It was late at night. But there was nowhere for me to go. I couldn't communicate with anyone, because I didn't know Chinese. I crouched in the corner of the terminal and tried to sleep, waking frequently. I was frightened. In the morning, I still didn't have anywhere to go, so I returned to the comfort station. I crept back to the kitchen. I cooked breakfast, as usual, and sat down to have my own meal. But the proprietor knew. He came in and beat me all over, saying that he would teach me a lesson once and for all.[76]

It was natural that some women resorted to using narcotics to escape the phys-ical and psychological pain of their circumstances. They used opium and Philopon. Some managers apparently allowed their comfort women to buy narcotics, often as an incentive for the women to work harder. At some places where the purchase of such drugs was difficult, medics secretly provided some addicted women with morphine injections.[77]

Some women could not endure life as a "sex slave" and were driven to suicide. Some committed suicide by drinking cresol soap solution, which had been provided for them to wash their genitals. Others chose overdoses of drugs mixed with alcohol. There were also cases in which a depressed soldier forced a favourite comfort woman to commit double suicide with him.[78]

It is assumed that many women, especially those who were sent close to the battle zones, died as a result of being directly involved in warfare. Life was harrowing for the women on the battlefields. Pe Pongi was one such woman. She witnessed the deaths of her colleagues and experienced the hardship of surviving the Battle of Okinawa. She and six other Korean women were sent to the comfort station on Tokashiki Island, a small isolated island of Okinawa, in November 1944.[79]

On March 23, 1945, in anticipation of the US invasion, the Korean women were moved to a local school building where members of the Japanese naval unit were staying. That evening the school building was bombarded. A woman named Haruko was killed and two other women – Aiko and Mitsuko – were seriously injured. Aiko and Mitsuko were left in an air-raid shelter by themselves while the four remaining women, including Pe Pongi, followed the Japanese unit and hid in the forest. During the next five months, until mid-August when the Japanese surrendered, these young women lived in a cave with the Japanese soldiers. In the day time they prepared meals, washed the soldiers' clothes, gathered edible plants, carried ammunition and nursed injured soldiers. At night they worked as comfort women.[80]

Yi Tungnam, who spent the last few years of the war at a station in Sumatra, had a similar experience to that of Pe in Okinawa. Towards the end of the war, she and her colleagues would spend the day doing the laundry and treating wounded soldiers at a field hospital near their comfort station in the Sumatran countryside province of Aceh. In the evening they returned to the station to serve the Japanese men.[81] In other places women were forced to serve the men in underground shelters during bombing attacks by the Allied forces.[82] It is impossible to estimate how many comfort women died as direct victims of warfare.

When the war finished, most of the comfort women were simply abandoned by the Japanese.[83] Some were fortunately rescued by the Allied forces and eventually sent home, but many had to find their own means to travel the long distances back to their homes. There were unfortunate women, such as Mun P'ilgi and her colleagues, who were left behind in Manchuria and then had to face the danger of rape by the Russian troops who came southwards in early August 1945.[84] There were also women who decided not to return home because they felt stigmatized by the sexual abuse they had been subjected to. They could not face their families and friends again. They preferred to stay on in a foreign place and survive as second-class citizens. Today there are still such Korean former comfort women living in China and Kampuchea.[85]

Although we have so far dealt only with Korean, Chinese, Taiwanese, and Filipina comfort women, there is some evidence, supported by testimonies, to verify that other Asian women, such as Vietnamese and Malaysians, were also exploited for the same purpose by the Japanese.[86] Unfortunately, available historical documents on the comfort women from these countries are quite limited at this stage. Only a few former comfort women have been identified from these countries.

However, recently some information about comfort women in the Dutch East Indies (now Indonesia) under Japanese occupation has come to light. In the next chapter I will focus on the testimonies and documents from this region of Southeast Asia in order to examine the ordeal experienced by Dutch and local Indonesian women.

3 Comfort women in the Dutch East Indies

Japan's invasion of the Dutch East Indies and military violence against women

For the Japanese Imperial forces that entered the war against the Allied nations in early December 1941, the conquest of the Dutch East Indies (now Indonesia) was a high priority. This area had a number of major oil fields, particularly, in southwest Borneo, Java and Sumatra. In order to secure these oil fields as well as those in northwest Borneo, occupied by the British at the time, Japanese forces invaded northeast Borneo soon after the destruction of Pearl Harbor.

Seria and Miri oil fields and the refinery in Lutong were captured in mid-December, and by the end of January 1942 the whole of Borneo was in Japanese hands. By late February, Sumatra was also seized by the Japanese. On March 1, the Japanese forces landed at three different places in Java – Merak, Eretan Wetan, and Kragan.[1] On March 8, three days after the Japanese forces entered Batavia (present Jakarta), the Dutch forces, led by General Ter Poorten, officially surrendered. This was the beginning of a three-and-a-half year occupation of Indonesia by the Japanese Imperial forces. Java and Sumatra were put under the control of the Army, and the rest of the islands were administered by the navy.[2]

Japanese troops seem to have committed sexual violence against Dutch women at various places in the Dutch East Indies immediately after the invasion. For example, when they entered Tjepoc, the main oil centre of central Java, "women were repeatedly raped, with the approval of the [Japanese] commanding officer."[3] The following are some extracts from the testimony on this case given by a Dutch woman after the war, which was subsequently presented at the Tokyo War Crimes Tribunal as one of numerous pieces of evidence of war crimes that the Japanese troops committed against Allied civilians.

> On that Thursday, 5 March 1942, we remained in a large room all together. The Japanese then appeared mad and wild. That night the father-in-law and mother-in-law of Salzmann. . . . were taken away from us and fearfully maltreated. Their two daughters too, of about 15 and 16 had to go with them and were maltreated. The father and mother returned the same night,

fearfully upset, the girls only returned on Friday morning, and had been raped by the Japanese.

On Saturday afternoon, March 7, 1942, the Japanese soldiers (odd soldiers) had appeared in the emergency hospital where the women and children were seated together. The ladies were here raped by the Japanese, in which connection it should be mentioned that this happened where the children were not present. These ladies were myself, Mrs. Bernasco, Mrs. Mebus, Mrs. Dietzel, Mrs. de Graaf, Mrs. van Bakerghem, Mrs. Verbeek, Mrs. Warella.

This occurred from March 7 to 17, 1942; generally the Japs came at night, but by way of exception, also during the day. It was a mass, continuous merciless rape. The first afternoon that this happened, as mentioned, three enlisted men came, and everything took place under threat. After this happened, we managed to tell the Chinese doctor Liem. He went to the Commandant, whereupon that afternoon, Mrs. Dietzel, myself and one or two others had to appear before the Commandant. The Commandant said that we would be given an opportunity to point out the Japs who had misconducted themselves, and that they would be shot dead before our very eyes.

However, nothing happened and after an hour we were sent back to the emergency hospital.

That evening, at 8 o'clock, we were transferred to a classroom in a school near by. According to what we were told, this was done for our own safety, since the Japs would not come there.

Between 10 and 12 o'clock that night, when we were all asleep, a whole mass of Japanese soldiers entered with the above-mentioned commandant at the head. The Commandant sat on a table in our classroom and then watched how each of the women was dragged away, one by one, to be raped. He himself did not join in this.[4]

As only a part of this testimony was read at the Tokyo War Crimes Tribunal, it is not clear what happened to these women after this incident. However, Lieutenant Colonel Damste, a Dutch prosecutor who submitted this testimony to the Tribunal, claimed that this was "the same as happened when the Japanese entered the oil town of Balikpapan"[5] in southwest Borneo.

According to a Dutch government report, rape of Dutch women was also committed by the Japanese in Tarakan, Menado, Bandung, Padang, and Flores during the invasion and the early stage of the occupation.[6] It is also reported that at Blora, a place near Semarang on Java, about 20 European (presumably Dutch) women were imprisoned in two houses. Of these, 15, including mothers and their daughters, were raped several times a day for three weeks by the Japanese troops passing by. This was finally ended by a high-ranking Japanese officer who happened to visit.[7]

There is hardly any official record concerning sexual violence against Indonesian women committed by the Japanese at the time of invasion. Thus it is very

Plate 3.1 Japanese soldiers on bicycles moving along a road in Batavia, Java, in October 1942.
Source: Australian War Memorial, transparency number 127909

difficult to speculate how prevalent rape of Indonesian women was by the Japanese troops in various places of the Dutch East Indies, where many Dutch women became the victims of sexual violence.

There is no evidence of sexual molestation of Indonesians in the early period of the Japanese occupation. It seems that the initial Japanese behaviour towards Indonesians was relatively benign. This could mainly be attributed to the initial impression of Indonesians that the Japanese occupation would liberate Indonesia from Dutch colonial rule. In almost every town and city where the Japanese troops made their triumphant entry, crowds of local Indonesians lined the streets, greeting the victors with Japanese flags and *merah-putih* (Indonesian flags) and singing *Indonesia Raja*, the then national anthem.[8] Many Indonesians viewed the Japanese as their liberators from Dutch colonial rule. This was a totally different situation from that experienced in China or in the Philippines, where there was often deep-rooted local resistance against the Japanese military occupation from the beginning.

The peaceful honeymoon period between the Japanese invaders and the Indonesian population lasted only a short time, as the local people soon realized that the Japanese had no intention of giving them autonomous political power. Yet, it may not be wrong to speculate that Japanese sexual violence against the local Indonesian women was not a widespread problem *in the early stage* of the Japanese military occupation of the Dutch East Indies.

Exploitation of existing prostitutes by the Japanese troops

There is very little first-hand information available on the operation of comfort stations in the Dutch East Indies. There seem to be a number of relevant archival documents housed in the Dutch National Archives, but apart from a small number of war crimes tribunal documents which have so far been released, most are closed until 2025. In January 1994, the Dutch government published a short study report on this issue both in Dutch and in English.[9] This report has only a very short bibliography and no footnotes. None the less, when we combine this limited number of archival documents with other available information in Japanese and Indonesian, the following general picture of the comfort women issue in the Dutch East Indies emerges.

According to the above-mentioned Dutch official report, between 200 and 300 "European women" worked in the comfort stations in the Dutch East Indies during the war. Of these, 65 were "most certainly forced into prostitution."[10] The report uses the word "European" when referring to both Dutch and Eurasian (i.e. Indo-Dutch) women. But, given that there were well over 300 Indo-Dutch prostitutes anyway, the reference to "two to three hundred" women, most likely means Dutch women only. As we will see later, there were some Dutch professional prostitutes working, mainly in Java, before the war, and it can be presumed that some of these women were the professionals who continued business for the Japanese after the Japanese invasion. Some others might have been the so-called "volunteers" who reluctantly agreed to serve the Japanese in order to avoid the harsh living conditions they faced as captives of the Japanese.

The cases of forced prostitution using Dutch civilian women increased from mid-1943. Apart from the above-mentioned rape cases, there is little evidence that the Japanese between 1942 and early 1943 forcibly used Dutch girls and women in comfort stations.

This does not mean, however, that the Japanese military forces stationed in the Dutch East Indies did not set up comfort stations in the early stage of occupation. The following extract from the memoirs written by a former NCO, Nakamura Hachirō, testifies to the fact that the Japanese established comfort stations not long after their invasion into the territory:

> [One day in March 1942, at Meulaboh on the west coast of Sumatra] I was ordered by my commander to set up a comfort station. I consulted with a medical officer who was assisting in the settlement of our troops in this area and decided to establish the facility. An appropriate place was found quite easily. We decided to use a vacant hotel which had been used by Dutch travelers. It was a new Western-style building which had seven rooms, and I thought it was too good for a comfort station. My next task was the recruitment of women. This was not difficult either *as there were many*

unemployed women remaining in town after the departure of the Dutch forces. However, it would cause a serious problem if they had VD. Therefore, our medical officer conducted VD inspection on the women who turned up for the job. We selected only four who passed the medical check and put them in the hotel. The fee was set and thus I could start operating the comfort station.[11]

[Emphasis added]

The above memoirs indicate the presence of professional prostitutes in the Dutch East Indies before the war, and describe how the newly arrived Japanese troops used some of these women as comfort women. In this particular case, it seems that these women were Indonesians.

However, the memoirs of a Japanese journalist, Kuroda Hidetoshi, reveal the fact that white Dutch women were also used by the Japanese as comfort women, in particular at officers' comfort stations, from the early stage of Japanese occupation. Between November 1942 and May 1943, Kuroda traveled to various parts of Southeast Asia, with a group of Japanese journalists and writers, at the request of the Imperial Military Headquarters in Tokyo. He was to travel this region and report back to the Japanese populace about "the liberation of Asian nations from Western Imperialism."

When they visited Batavia in mid-November 1942, a public information officer took Kuroda and other members of the traveling group to one of these army officers' comfort stations in the city, where Dutch women were working as comfort women. According to Kuroda, the army also had officers' comfort stations staffed solely with Indonesian women. He states that the navy had Eurasian and Indonesian comfort women but did not have Dutch women at their officers' comfort stations. Kuroda believes that this was probably due to the fact that Java was controlled mainly by the army and that the army monopolized the Dutch women. Kuroda was also informed by an army medical officer in Batavia that many high-ranking army officers, such as staff officers of the Headquarters, had Dutch concubines.[12]

It was not only army officers who exploited both Dutch and Indonesian women. According to another journalist, Gotō Motoharu, the well-known Japanese writer Ōya Sōichi operated the "White Horse Riding Club" and "Black Horse Riding Club" at a large mansion in Batavia where he lived. Ōya was one of a few civilian writers who were sent to Batavia with the first Japanese Army contingent to the Dutch East Indies in order to engage in local propaganda activities. In fact, these clubs were "prostitution clubs," the one using Dutch and Eurasian women and the other staffed by Indonesian women. It is presumed that they were operated for Japanese civilians of high social status such as bureaucrats and businessmen living in Batavia. For a long period, the officers of the Army Headquarters believed that they were genuine "riding clubs," as there were several horses at this mansion. When army officers found out the real activities of these clubs, some also joined them.[13] In this case it is almost certain that the women who worked at these clubs were "volunteers" as the clubs were initially set up as "prostitution clubs" for civilians and not as military "comfort stations."

Indeed, prostitution had been widespread in the Dutch East Indies well before the Pacific War. The large number of Indonesian, Eurasian, and Dutch prostitutes in major cities like Surabaya, Batavia, and Semarang in Java served young unmarried Dutch men. Surabaya, where the Dutch naval base and garrison were located, was notorious for extensive prostitution. In fact, until well into the second decade of the twentieth century, many Dutch and Indonesian soldiers kept concubines in their own army barracks. For example, in 1911, 2,372 out of the 10,320 Europeans in the colonial army had concubines, the majority of the women being Indonesians. The existence of European prostitutes in Java was also recorded as early as the late nineteenth century. In Surabaya, Batavia, and Semarang, there were already well-known brothels owned by Europeans, employing white women to cater to European men.[14]

Under Dutch colonial rule it was quite a common phenomenon for divorced Indonesian women to leave their villages and work as prostitutes in nearby towns or cities for a few months each year over a long period.[15] Some of them worked as "house maids" for Dutch men. The work of "house maid" included offering sexual services as well.

As a Dutch medical doctor wrote in 1941, "a switch from the life of a prostitute to the normal life through marriage occurs very easily without deep conflict or radical change and is to be attributed to the great tolerance of the Javanese."[16] These "semi-professional prostitutes" often went back to their own villages, and if they remarried they were accepted back into the village community. Thus, prostitution, while widespread, appears not to have been regarded as an "immoral occupation" by many Indonesians in the colonial period. Perhaps such tolerance towards prostitution was partly due to the general poverty that Indonesians suffered under Dutch colonial rule. Prostitution was accepted as a means of survival for women.

Prior to the war, there were also small numbers of Japanese prostitutes (*karayuki-san*), who were brought in from Singapore or elsewhere by Japanese brothel owners operating in Java.[17]

So, when the Japanese troops entered the Dutch East Indies in March 1942, there were large numbers of prostitutes – Indonesian, Eurasian, European (mainly Dutch) women – who had lost Dutch clients due to the defeat of the Dutch forces and the subsequent internment of Dutch soldiers and civilians by the Japanese. It is therefore strongly believed that a significant number of these semi-professional and professional prostitutes were used by the newly arrived Japanese troops as comfort women and employed at both military comfort stations and civilian brothels/clubs catering to Japanese government bureaucrats and businessmen. It is also presumed that Japanese brothel owners, who had been operating businesses in Java before the Japanese occupation, were commissioned by the army to procure comfort women and run some of the newly established comfort stations. As has been mentioned, many of these prostitutes, in particular the Dutch women, seem to have become "concubines" of high-ranking officers of the Japanese Army.

Procurement of Dutch women

The Japanese began using coercion and deception to procure Dutch comfort women in mid-1943. This sudden increase of enforced prostitution on the young Dutch internees was undoubtedly related to the fact that, by this time, VD problems among the soldiers had become a grave concern for the Japanese military leaders in the Dutch East Indies. In order to reduce the high VD rates among their men, senior Japanese military officers sought to procure young, unmarried women free of sexual disease for military prostitution. The use of coercion seems to have coincided with the rapidly worsening living conditions of Dutch civilians under the Japanese military administration.[18] There is no doubt that the Japanese took advantage of the harsh living conditions in the internment camps to lure young women into prostitution.

According to Tokyo War Crimes Tribunal records, about 80,000 Dutch civilians in the Dutch East Indies were interned during the war. Of these, 10,500 died by the end of the war. The high death toll (approximately 13 percent) indicates the hardship these civilians experienced for the three and a half years under Japanese military rule.[19]

The internment of these civilians did not happen immediately upon the Japanese invasion of the Dutch East Indies. Until September 1942, apart from about 4,500 people who were regarded as "hostile civilians" detained in 19 different

Plate 3.2 A woman and six children inside a house at Kampon Makassar Internment Camp, Batavia, in 1945, showing the cramped, primitive conditions of the camp.
Source: Australian War Memorial, transparency number 305359

Plate 3.3 Exterior view of houses at Kampon Makassar Internment Camp, Batavia, in 1945, where one thousand women and children were interned in an area of less than half a square mile.
Source: Australian War Memorial, transparency number 305358

internment camps in Java, Allied civilians were free to move around as long as they carried the Alien Resident Registration Identification Card issued by the Japanese military government in Java.

After September 1942, all men between 16 and 60 years old were separated from their families and put into camps. The women, children, and old people were forced to live in designated places. Their freedom was further restricted in 1943 when the war situation turned against Japan and local resistance movements became stronger. By October 1943, 46,784 women, children and elderly people were interned in a number of camps in six different regions of Java. The private assets of these civilians were frozen. They were forced to rely on extremely meagre provisions of food, clothing, and medicine at the internment camps.[20] Around this time the Japanese apparently started to exploit the harsh conditions facing the Dutch civilians in order to lure young women into becoming comfort women.

For example, in March 1943, eight women in Chiapit Internment Camp on the outskirts of Bandung were taken out of the camp under the false pretence that they would be provided with meals at a Chinese restaurant and allowed to live outside the camp. However, they were taken to an officers' club instead, and ordered to work as comfort women. Despite persistent pressure by Japanese officers, six of these eight women refused the demand and two days later they were released. Two women, however, gave in and became comfort women at this officers' club. There were similar cases in Cirebon and Jember.[21]

In September 1943, a Japanese man, Aoji Washio, started operating a military brothel called the Sakura Club near Pasar Baru in Batavia, using Dutch women, as requested by a Japanese Army officer. Aoji was living with a Dutch prostitute who had been a brothel owner in Java prior to the Japanese invasion. This Dutch woman obtained permission to visit Cideng Internment Camp and re-cruited 11 young women by offering them jobs as "barmaids" to serve Japanese customers. However, once these women were brought into the Sakura Club, they were forced to act as prostitutes, being threatened that they would be handed over to the kempeitai (Japanese military police) if they refused to co-operate. Nine other Dutch women working at this club were brought from other camps in Java. Two of them were from Semarang; one of them was as young as 15 years old.[22]

In November 1943, the Japanese Ministry of the Army changed its policy of dealing with the civilian internees from the Allied nations. The Ministry shifted responsibility from the local military governments and placed all the internees in the Japanese-occupied territories under the direct control of each regional army commandant.[23]

The internees of the Dutch East Indies were placed under the control of the 16th Army, and until about April 1944 reorganization of the camps was carried out by transferring some of the internees from one camp to another.[24] It seems that, in this process, a number of women were forced to choose between moving to a different camp or working at a comfort station. There were at least two such cases in Bandung. The Japanese also tried to separate about 100 women during a transfer of internees from a camp in Surabaya to Gedagan Camp in Semarang. However, in the face of fierce opposition from the internees, this plan was abandoned.[25]

The enforced procurement of comfort women from the internment camps in the Dutch East Indies became more frequent between late 1943 and mid-1944. This was probably due to the fact that internment camps were now under the direct control of the army, making it easier for the army officers in charge of comfort stations to secure suitable women from the civilian internees.

There was a comfort station called the Magelang Club in Magelang. In December 1943, a group of Japanese, including the Resident (equivalent to "Governor" in the Dutch colonial administration) of Magelang and a kempeitai officer, visited Muntilan Internment Camp in the vicinity. They ordered the camp leaders to call up all female internees between 16 and 25 years old. About 100 young internees were gathered in front of the camp office and they were ordered to walk, one by one, before the Japanese. The Japanese selected about 50 of them and ordered the camp leaders to prepare a list of their names. In fact, the Japanese made sure that the camp leaders actually typed up the names of these internees on a piece of paper. The camp leaders were not given any reasons for such a request, but suspicions quickly grew among the camp leaders and mothers of young girls.

The camp leaders and an internee doctor, after conferring with their mothers, picked out most of the young girls from the list of about 50 people and put them in the camp hospital on the pretence that they were seriously ill.[26]

On January 25, 1944, the Japanese, together with about 50 Indonesian policemen, arrived at the camp in a bus and ordered the camp leaders to show them the name list. This time, there was a civilian among the Japanese who was believed to be a comfort station manager. The camp leaders told the Japanese that the name list had been destroyed, but the Japanese searched the camp office and found it. The Japanese scolded the camp leaders and ordered them to call up the 50 or so listed internees for immediate inspection at the church.

The camp leaders had no choice but to obey this order. The Japanese lined up the women in the church and inspected each person by lifting their skirts and checking their legs. The camp leaders and the doctor went inside the church building and complained to the Japanese. Eventually the Japanese selected seven women, who, according to testimonies of some internees, had had prior sexual relationships with some of the Japanese camp administrative staff, and eight other young girls. They were ordered to pack their belongings within half an hour. The Japanese did not explain where they would be taken, but told them that they would be looked after very well. Mothers of those eight young girls panicked and hid the girls in the camp buildings. As these girls did not turn up half an hour later, Indonesian policemen were instructed to go into the

Plate 3.4 A group of women at the Kampon Makassar Internment Camp, Batavia, in 1945. They were unable to leave the appalling conditions as they had no alternative accommodation.

Source: Australian War Memorial, transparency number 305360

compound and bring out the girls. The police brought out the girls, who were crying frantically, and dragged them to the gate. A crowd of a few hundred internees who were gathering near the gate tried to stop the girls from being taken away. When a scuffle broke out between the police and these internees, Japanese and Indonesian policemen drew swords and drove the internees away. The Japanese eventually took the seven women and eight girls out of the camp.[27]

Three days later, however, the Japanese came back to the camp and proposed to the camp leaders a plan to call for "volunteers" to replace some of the girls who had been taken away. It is said that this was an idea originally put forward to the Japanese by one of the internees, who was a former professional prostitute. Soon a few women "volunteered." As these women were reputed to have been former prostitutes, there was no protest from the internees this time. At the police station, in the presence of the camp leaders, the Japanese carried out a further selection of the girls and women including the "volunteers." As a result, four internees (one of whom was a 14-year-old girl) were sent back to the camp. The remaining thirteen women, including four unmarried girls, were taken on January 28, 1944, to Magelang, where they were examined by a Japanese doctor, raped, and forced to work as comfort women. A month later, mothers and relatives of these women and girls received parcels of tinned food and biscuits from the Japanese.[28]

Similar incidents happened at internment camps on other islands of the Dutch East Indies at about the same time. For example, at Padang Camp in Sumatra, the Japanese attempted to secure some women as "barmaids" on several occasions between the latter half of 1943 and early 1944. In fact, as early as February 1943, the Japanese tried to procure some women from this camp, but the attempt precipitated an uprising at the camp. Surprisingly, in this case, the kempeitai took the internees' side, and the Japanese abandoned the plan. However, in October 1943, the camp leaders were forced to agree to transfer a few hundred women from the camp to a building in the town of Padang. The camp leaders insisted that the detailed conditions of the work that these women were to be engaged in should be set out in writing, and that any form of forced prostitution should be excluded from these conditions. In addition, they set another condition that some of the camp leaders should be allowed to accompany the women when they were transferred.[29]

Once these women were taken out of the camp, however, the Japanese requested 30 "volunteers" for work as "barmaids" at a comfort station in Fort de Kock. Four women responded to this request and "volunteered." Another 17 women who subsequently "volunteered" were taken to a Japanese officers' "restaurant" on Nias Island, but for unknown reasons they were all returned to Sumatra a few weeks later. The Japanese selected a further 25 women who had not volunteered and tried to take them to Fort de Kock. The accompanying camp leaders managed to stop the bus which was to transport the women. However, the Japanese eventually succeeded in persuading 11 of these women to go to Fort de Kock. It seems that these women could not bear to return to the camp with its malnutrition and disease. In the end, the Japanese procured 15 women altogether for a comfort station in Fort de Kock. The rest of the women were returned to the camp. In December 1943, the Japanese attempted once again to "recruit" women, but this time no one came forward.[30]

It seems that, whether because of effective internees' organization or Japanese fears of using violence against white women, the situation differed from that faced by Asians.

Enforced prostitution at comfort stations in Semarang

The most detailed information concerning enforced military prostitution using Dutch internees is about the case in Semarang.

On May 17, 1943, the South Army Cadet School was established in Semarang. This school was set up to train young Japanese soldiers with relatively high academic background for eight months. On the completion of training, they were sent to the front lines as Second Lieutenant-class officers. Due to heavy casualties in the battlefields of Southeast Asia, it became necessary for the South Army to produce many such "lower-class" officers within a relatively short period.[31]

About October 1943, some teaching staff of the Cadet School contemplated setting up comfort stations in Semarang by procuring young women from the internment camps in the area. The main reason for the establishment of comfort stations in the area was the high VD rates among the cadets at the school. Two of the instructors at the Cadet School, Colonel Ōkubo Tomo and Colonel Ikeda Shōzō, submitted the plan to the head of the Cadet School, Lieutenant-General Nozaki Seiji. They thought that, by using young, unmarried Dutch women (who were the least likely to be carriers of VD) as comfort women, the VD problem could be limited and treated at the station. Nozaki endorsed this plan contingent on obtaining the permission of the 16th Army Headquarters in Batavia as well as from the authorities of the military government. In early February 1944, when Nozaki visited the headquarters in Batavia for discussions on other matters, he consulted the Chief of Staff, Kokubo (his given name is unknown), and another staff officer, Lieutenant-General Satō Yukinori about this plan to set up comfort stations in Semarang. Kokubo and Satō told Nozaki that permission would be granted if a formal request was submitted, but they insisted that the Dutch women had to be "volunteers" in order to avoid any possible legal problems. Upon returning to Semarang, Nozaki instructed his junior officers to discuss the matter with the administrative staff of the military government and to submit a request to headquarters.[32]

Major Okada Keiji, who was Ōkubo's Aide-de-camp, went to the 16th Army Headquarters in Batavia and submitted a formal request for permission to set up five comfort stations in Semarang. On the way back to Semarang, Okada visited Bandung and inspected some comfort stations there, in which Dutch women were working as comfort women, in order to study how such facilities operated. A few days later, permission to set up four comfort stations was sent from headquarters to the cadet school on condition that the comfort women were all "volunteers."[33]

In late February 1944, Major Okada instructed Captain Ishida to be responsible for "recruiting" young Dutch women from internment camps in the vicinity of Semarang. Seven women's camps were targeted for this purpose. Ishida met fierce opposition from the camp leaders of the first three camps he visited – Sumawono Camp in Ambarawa, and Bankong and Lampersari Camps in Sompok. Consequently he failed to "recruit" anyone. Ishida, who was a Christian, was reluctant to carry out the job that had been imposed upon him. In fact, he asked Okada if he could be released from this duty, but Okada insisted that Ishida continue the work. It seems that Ōkubo, Ikeda, and Okada soon realized that they could not leave this job to Ishida on his own. They decided to use more coercive methods by commanding other Japanese staff to accompany Ishida. When Ishida visited four other camps – Halmaheila, Ambarawa No. 6 and No. 9, and Gedangan – Japanese civil administrators of the Semarang region and other Japanese civilians, who were commissioned to be managers of these new comfort stations, accompanied him. Ishida was probably a person of weak character and he left the actual selection of the women to the other Japanese despite his apparently strong belief that the exercise violated human rights and the Geneva Convention. The selected women were never informed about the work they would be engaged in, and they were given no choice but to be forcibly taken away from the camps.[34]

At Halmaheila Camp all the women (about 40 in total), aged between 15 and 35, were summoned for roll-call. Each of them were ordered to walk in front of the Japanese, and eventually 11 were selected. Three of these were found to be too weak and sickly. So eight were taken away. These women were told that they would be employed as office clerks, nurses, or workers at a tobacco factory. A few days later, one of them, a 16-year-old girl, was returned to the camp. The reason given was that she was too young.[35]

At Ambarawa No. 6 and No. 9 Camps, 10 and 6 women respectively were selected from those who were unmarried and aged between 17 and 28. The leaders of these camps protested furiously against the Japanese actions, but their efforts were in vain. It seems that none of these 16 women were informed about their destination.[36]

At Gedangan Camp, several women were selected from the internees between 16 and 30 years of age. However, as they were about to be taken away, a large group of internees tried to stop them, and a riot similar to that at Muntilan Internment Camp broke out. Eventually the Japanese had to satisfy themselves with a few "volunteers" who showed willingness to co-operate with the Japanese. Here, too, some of the "volunteers" seem to have been former professional prostitutes. According to one testimony, one of the women took her two children (aged 2 and 4 years) with her to a comfort station.[37] It was unusual that a comfort woman was allowed to keep her children at the comfort station. It could be the case that she "volunteered" on the condition that her children would be fed at the station.

It is almost certain that at least 23 women from Halmaheila Camp and Ambarawa No. 6 and No. 9 Camps were forcibly taken out of the camps. According to the Dutch government report, a total of 36 Dutch women were put into four comfort stations – the Officers' Club, the Semalang Club, the Hinomaru Club, and the Seiun-sō. Some of these women were brought first to the Semalang Club (formerly the Hotel Splendid). Major Okada then distributed these women among a few different stations. Others were taken directly to particular stations. All of them were ordered to sign a contract which was written in both Japanese and Indonesian, stating that they were volunteering to become comfort women. When they refused to sign the paper that they could not read, they were severely beaten. Some of them eventually submitted and signed the paper, but others did not give in and kept refusing to do so – nevertheless they too were repeatedly raped as comfort women.[38]

On March 1, 1944, these four comfort stations were officially opened. When the women refused to serve the Japanese, they were threatened with torture and death for themselves and their families. They were eventually beaten, kicked, and raped on the opening night. Some of these women were raped by Okada himself as well as by some of the comfort station managers. One of the medical officers, who conducted periodic VD examinations of these women, also raped them.[39]

According to testimonies, one woman tried to commit suicide by taking massive doses of quinine, but failed. She was later sent to a mental hospital. Another woman also tried unsuccessfully to kill herself by slashing a vein. A few women tried to escape from the comfort stations, but they were soon captured and brought back. One girl was unconscious for two days due to the shock of being raped. Some became pregnant and had abortions.[40]

They experienced immense trauma at the time and the psychological legacy continues to plague these women even half a century later. Their experiences are clearly described in the following testimony of Jan Ruff-O'Herne, one of the women selected from Ambarawa No. 6 Camp, who was 19 years old at the time:

> The house was now filling up with Japanese military. We could sense their excitement, hear their laughter. We sat there waiting, huddled together till the time had come and the worst was to happen. Then they came.
>
> Lies was the first girl to be dragged out of the dining room and into her bedroom. Then, one by one, the girls were taken, crying, protesting, screaming, kicking and fighting with all their might . . .
>
> After four girls had been taken, I hid under the dining table. I could hear the crying coming from the bedrooms. I could feel my heart pounding with fear. I held tight to the wooden crucifix tucked into the belt round my waist . . .
>
> Sitting crouched up under the table, I saw the boots almost touching me. Then I was dragged out. A large, repulsive, fat, bald-headed Jap stood in front of me, looking down at me, grinning at me. I kicked him in the shins. He just stood there, laughing. He pulled me roughly by the arm. I tried to

free myself from his grip, but I could not. My fighting, kicking, crying, protesting, made no difference.

Don't! Don't! I screamed . . . He pulled me towards him and dragged me into the bedroom. I was fighting him all the time. Once in the bedroom he closed the door. I ran to a corner of the room, pleading with him in a mixture of English and Indonesian, trying to make him understand that I was here against my will and that he had no right to do this to me . . .

I stooped down and curled myself up in the corner like a hunted animal that could not escape from the hunter's net . . .

The Jap stood there, looking down at me. He was in total control of the situation. He had paid a lot of money for opening night and he was obviously annoyed and becoming angry . . . Taking his sword out of the scabbard, he pointed it at me, threatening me with it, yelling at me . . .

I told the Jap that he could kill me, that I was not afraid to die and that I would not give myself to him . . .

The Japanese officer was getting impatient now. He threw me on the bed and tore at my clothes, ripping them off. I lay there naked on the bed as he ran his sword slowly up and down, over my body. I could feel the cold steel touching my skin as he moved the sword across my throat and breasts, over my stomach and legs . . .

He threw himself on top of me, pinning me down under his heavy body. I tried to fight him off. I kicked him, I scratched him but he was too strong. The tears were streaming down my face as he raped me. It seemed as if he would never stop.

I can find no words to describe this most inhuman and brutal rape. To me, it was worse than dying. My whole body was shaking. I was in a state of shock. I felt cold and numb and I hid my face in the pillow until I heard him leave.

In the daytime, we were supposed to be safe, although the house was always full of Japanese coming and going, socializing, eyeing us up and down. There was little privacy and consequently we were often raped in the day as well. But my fear was worse for the evening to come. As it was getting dark, it would gradually build inside me until finally it was burning up my whole body.[41]

But worst of all I have felt this fear every time my husband was making love to me. I have never enjoyed intercourse as a consequence of what the Japanese did to me.

Fifty years of nightmares, of sleepless nights. Fifty years of pain that could never go away, horrific memories embedded in the mind, always there to be triggered off.[42]

While the sexual abuse of most of these women occurred at the four exclusive officers' comfort stations, some of the women were occasionally sent to comfort stations specializing in service for rank-and-file soldiers. For example, Ellen van der Ploeg, a 21-year-old internee from Halmaheila Camp, testified that every

Sunday she was sent out to a soldiers' comfort station and was forced to serve a large number of Japanese on that day.[43]

On April 1, 1944, all the women and girls forcibly taken out of the camps and put into comfort stations in Semarang were suddenly transferred to the Bogor Women's Camp. Shortly before this, Colonel Odajima Kaoru, a senior officer in the POW Management Bureau in the Ministry of Army, had visited Java from Tokyo to inspect the internment camps in the Dutch East Indies. During his inspection tour of Java, he had been informed about these Dutch women and girls by one of the camp leaders of the Ambarawa No. 9 Camp. Odajima promptly sent letters to the Headquarters of the 16th Army in Batavia, the Headquarters of the Southern Army in Singapore, as well as to the Ministry of the Army, urging that they close down the comfort stations in Semarang. Having received a letter from Odajima, the Headquarters of the 16th Army immediately issued an order to close down all four newly established comfort stations in Semarang.[44]

As soon as these women and girls arrived at the Bogor Camp, they were ordered never to tell anyone of what had happened to them. They were threatened that if they did, they and their families would be killed. Shortly after their arrival at Bogor, their mothers and siblings were also transferred to the same camp to be reunited.[45]

This case of enforced prostitution of Dutch women in Semarang was investigated by the Dutch military forces after the war. As a result, in February 1948, 12 Japanese were tried at the War Crimes Tribunal conducted by the Dutch Forces in Batavia. Colonel Ōkubo committed suicide in 1947, before the court hearing actually started. Colonel Ikeda was indicted on crimes carrying the death penalty. However, during the court hearing he feigned psychosis, and his trial was delayed. Eventually he was sentenced to 15 years' imprisonment instead of execution.

Major Okada was sentenced to death, and another officer received a sentence of 10 years' imprisonment. Two medical officers were sentenced to 16 and 7 years in prison respectively. Captain Ishida received a sentence of two years' imprisonment. Four comfort station managers were sentenced to between 5 and 20 years' imprisonment. One Japanese Army NCO and one civilian officer of the military government were found not guilty.[46]

For some unknown reason, the trial of Lieutenant-General Nozaki Seiji, head of the cadet school, who was most responsible for the entire matter, was conducted separately in February 1949, a year after the trial of his juniors. The prosecutors requested the death sentence, but the verdict was 12 years' imprisonment. It is interesting to find the following statement by Nozaki in the interrogation report prepared by the Dutch military prosecutors. He said:

> I must admit that such an undesirable situation arose as the result of neglecting my own duty to properly supervise junior officers. When I received an order to close down the comfort stations I was truly ashamed of myself. I went to see the commander of the Southern Army and sincerely apologized for bringing disgrace on the army cadet school.[47]

For Nozaki, the most serious crime was to disgrace the army's reputation. The violation of human rights of the Dutch internees did not concern him at all.

The Dutch military authorities' indifference towards Indonesian comfort women

During the investigation of the above-mentioned war crime committed by the Japanese in Semarang, the Dutch military authorities interrogated a number of Eurasian women who were also forced into prostitution by the Japanese.

According to these interrogations, on April 14, 1944, two weeks after the closure of the comfort stations in Semarang, about 100 local young women, including 20 or 30 Eurasians and a few Chinese women, were ordered to report to the Semarang Police Headquarters on April 16. According to one of the testimonies, some of these women were randomly picked up by the police while working at restaurants or walking in the street.[48]

At the police station, a Japanese officer told the women through an interpreter that, because many Japanese soldiers were now suffering from diseases, VD inspections would be conducted on the women. The women were told that, if they were found to be carriers of VD, medical treatment would be provided. If they were not carriers, the women would be allowed to return home.

They were then taken by car to the Hotel Splendid (the site of one of the comfort stations, the Semalang Club). There they were ordered to go into an inspection room one by one where, in front of a Japanese medical doctor and a few Japanese soldiers, each woman was told to take off her underwear and lie on the bed, with her legs apart. If she refused, the soldiers forced the woman to comply. When the doctor roughly inserted a metal instrument into the vagina, many women screamed and cried, scaring the other women waiting for their turn outside the inspection room. It seems that the purpose of this inspection was not a VD check but to find out whether these women were virgins.[49]

In the end, 20 women were told to remain, and the rest were allowed to leave. Eight of these selected women were Eurasians, one was Chinese, and the rest were Indonesians. That night they were forced to stay in four different rooms in the Hotel Splendid, and each was given 50 guilders. Some women realized what the Japanese were going to do with them and refused to accept the money. However, they were beaten and forced to take the money. Some tried to escape that night, but the building was guarded by Japanese soldiers.

It is interesting to note that the Japanese never produced any contracts for these women to sign, while they insisted that the Dutch internees enter a formal contract. It is obvious that the Japanese were not bothered about any legal problems as far as the "recruitment" of Asian women was concerned, whereas they clearly knew that enforced prostitution would be a violation of the Geneva Convention when they demanded signatures from the Dutch women.[50]

The following day these women were taken by three Japanese soldiers to Surabaya by train. They were detained in a house in Surabaya where the Japanese soldiers kept a continuous watch on them. A Japanese man, who was believed to be a brothel manager, lived in the house. They were waiting to be transferred to Flores Island. The boat sailed from Surabaya, but had to return twice, before successfully reaching Flores. The first time the boat was attacked by Allied airplanes and the second time it was followed by an Allied submarine. All in all they stayed in Surabaya for more than a month. During this time, two women managed to escape, and one became ill. Eventually, 17 women were taken to Flores.[51]

They were put into a comfort station in Flores, and forced to serve the Japanese from morning till midnight every day until the war ended in August 1945. In the morning, rank-and-file soldiers visited them; in the evening NCOs turned up; and at night officers came. On average, each woman was forced to serve 20 soldiers, two NCOs, and one officer every day. The comfort station manager received 1.5 guilders from each soldier, 2 guilders from an NCO, and the officers' rate was between 3 and 8 guilders, depending on the time he spent with the woman. On payment, each man was given a ticket which had to be handed to a comfort woman. Each comfort woman was expected to collect at least 100 tickets a week. Those who failed were physically punished by the manager. Each man was given a condom along with the ticket, and was instructed to use it without fail. But many would not use condoms and some beat into submission those women who refused service without a prophylactic. It seems the women rarely received payment, although sufficient food was provided every day. A medical officer visited the station once a week and conducted a VD inspection.[52] Undoubtedly their situation was very similar to that experienced by most Korean comfort women, as seen in the previous chapter.

According to the testimony of one of these women, a group of Eurasians at another comfort station was brought from Bandung. One of them, a 16-year-old girl, told her that they were soon to be taken to Timor.[53]

Despite the fact that sufficient evidence about enforced prostitution was collected through the interrogations of these women, there is no evidence that the Dutch military authorities charged the Japanese for the violation of the human rights of these Indo-Dutch, Indonesian, and Chinese women. It is believed that these interrogations were conducted in order to gather relevant information useful in the criminal cases of the Dutch victims. As much as the Japanese were unconcerned about the exploitation of non-Europeans, the Dutch were equally indifferent to victims who were not white and Dutch.

However, there were at least two exceptional cases brought by the Dutch military authorities to the War Crimes Tribunal, which addressed enforced prostitution involving non-Dutch comfort women. One of them is the case of a comfort station in Balikpapan. A Japanese man called Ishibashi Nakazaburō, the manager of the comfort station, was charged with kidnapping several Indonesian women and forcing them to render sexual services to the Japanese. However, three Indonesian "victims" who appeared in court as witnesses, actually testified against the Dutch prosecutors, claiming that, thanks to Ishibashi, they had a good life during the war. Thus, Ishibashi was found "not-guilty."[54] Incidentally, comfort stations in Balikpapan were set up by Nakasone Yasuhiro, later Japan's

Prime Minister, who was then a young paymaster of the Japanese Navy troops stationed in Balikpapan.[55]

The other case was the rape and enforced prostitution of five Indonesian women by the Japanese troops in Pontianak. Between October 1943 and June 1944, about 1,500 civilians – Indonesians, Chinese, and Indians – were arrested as suspects in an underground resistance movement, and the vast majority were eventually tortured and killed. During this period, some wives of the suspects were raped by members of the Japanese Naval Special Police Force, and then were forced to work at a navy comfort station for the following eight months. For this crime, Captain Okajima Toshiharu and 12 other members of the Naval Special Police Forces were found guilty. Okajima and two others received death sentences. The sentence was made in conjunction with verdicts on counts of torture and murder of 1,500 civilians, not just for rape and enforcement of prostitution.[56]

The Dutch military authorities made very little effort to seriously investigate the sexual crimes that the Japanese men committed against Indonesian women. However, testimonies by Indonesians themselves strongly support the speculation that, from 1943, at about the same time that Dutch women internees were taken out of the camps as comfort women, many young Indonesian women were also procured as comfort women.

According to a Javanese woman, Siti Fatimah, a daughter of Singadikarto, the Subdistrict head of Subang in west Java, she was told that she would be sent to Japan to study in Tokyo. In 1943, when she was 16 years old, she and four other girls from her home subdistrict were put on a ship at Tanjung Priok. They joined a few hundred Indonesian girls who had been deceived by the Japanese and believed that they were going to Tokyo. The ship went instead to Flores Island. As soon as they arrived, the Japanese attitude towards the girls suddenly changed. They were put into a camp and were forced to render sexual services to the Japanese soldiers. Each girl had to serve at least two soldiers every day. Three months later they were transported to the north of Buru Island, where they were put into a military compound. Here too, they were sexually abused every day until the end of the war.

In both Flores and Buru, many girls died as the result of maltreatment by the Japanese. Others suffered psychological trauma as the result of sexual abuse. Soon after August 15, 1945, Fatimah and some other girls asked the Japanese to return them to their homes. Their request was refused. Together with a few other girls, she ran away from the compound and sought help from the local Buton fishermen. She later married one of the fishermen and never returned to Java.[57]

Sukarno Martodiharjo, a seaman for a Japanese shipping company in Batavia during the war, recalled an incident in which about 200 Indonesian girls were loaded onto boats one night in March 1945. The girls, who looked to be schoolgirls aged between 15 and 19, were on five different cargo ships, part of a convoy at the port of Tanjung Priok. This convoy was to sail to Singapore and Bangkok. Sukarno was on board one of the vessels and, despite orders not to speak to the girls, managed to talk to a few of them during the voyage. He learned that they had been selected to go to Tokyo to study Japanese and to be trained as nurses or midwives. During the first few days of the voyage, they were very cheerful and full of hope about going to Japan. They sang Japanese school and military songs. One of the girls to whom Sukarno was able to talk was Sumiyati, a 17-year-old daughter of the head of one of the subdistricts in Kediri.[58]

A few days after they left Java, some girls started crying. One of them even tried to commit suicide for a reason that Sukarno did not know at that time. Sumiyati told him that they had been deceived by the Japanese. They had found out that what the Japanese had told them was a lie and just propaganda. At Singapore, the girls on two of the other ships disembarked. The convoy continued to sail on to Bangkok. When the ships arrived at Bangkok, all the other girls from Java were met by a group of Japanese and taken away. This was the only instance that Sukarno saw of the transportation of Indonesian girls from Java to other places in Southeast Asia, but he heard from a colleague seaman that similar transportation was carried out by a different convoy at another time.[59]

After the war, Sukarno continued to work as a seaman. In September 1947 he traveled from Singapore to Bangkok for sightseeing while his ship was harbored at Singapore. In Bangkok, he unexpectedly met Sumiyati on a city street. Sumiyati told him that she and her fellow Indonesian girls were taken to a comfort station somewhere near Bangkok and forced to serve the Japanese soldiers day after day until the end of the war. At the comfort station, 50 Javanese girls were strictly supervised by a Japanese woman. After the war, they wanted to go back to Java, but they had no money to do so. They were not paid by the Japanese except for a small amount of money that they were given on days when they were allowed to go into the city for leisure. They were all ashamed of being forced to work as "prostitutes" and could not face their parents even if they had been able to return home. When Sukarno met Sumiyati in Bangkok, she was married to a Thai who was a poor factory worker. At that time she told him that about 15 fellow Indonesians were living in Bangkok. She also told him that, when the war ended, some of the girls at the same comfort station were taken away by the Japanese.[60]

According to Pramoeda Ananta Tur, a well-known dissident Indonesian writer who collected many testimonies, including the two previously mentioned cases, many of the Javanese girls who became the victims of Japanese military prostitution were daughters of prominent local chiefs, such as subdistrict heads, village heads, policemen, and school headmasters. The military government made it known that the girls would be offered an opportunity to study in Japan, and this information was passed on to local public servants through provincial Japanese Residents (i.e. governors). Thus, many of the public servants who collaborated with the Japanese were placed in a difficult situation of having to show loyalty to Japan by sending their own daughters first.[61] It is not known how many Indonesian girls were "recruited" in this way, nor exactly where they were sent.

Dough Davey, a member of the Australian 9th Regiment, which acted as the British-Borneo Civil Affairs Unit, was in Borneo in August 1945. There he found some Javanese women who had been transported to Borneo by the Japanese.

They were living in the ruins of the Japanese comfort station at Beaufort (presently Weston) on the Padas River in the northwest. The Australian forces took them to a small island off the Borneo coast for medical treatment and rehabilitation with the intention of sending them back to Indonesia. But the women were afraid of going home because of the shame associated with their experience. One committed suicide.[62] It is possible that these women were also deceived by the Japanese in the same way. The Australian troops who landed at Kupan in the southwest of Timoa Island shortly after Japan surrendered also found 46 Javanese women who had been brought there as comfort women. The Japanese tried to camouflage this by making them wear Red Cross armbands.[63] The Australian forces apparently had no interest in finding out which Japanese were responsible for crimes against these Indonesian women. They took several photos of the women but never attempted to investigate the matter as a serious war crime.

These testimonies suggest that a large number of Indonesian women and girls were taken out of Java and put into comfort stations in various places in Southeast Asia, stretching from Thailand to New Guinea, from North Borneo to Timor.[64] Such extensive transportation of comfort women must have required a plan that was designed and implemented at a high level, by such Japanese military bodies as the Headquarters of Southern Army, and, most likely, in

Plate 3.5 Forty-six Javanese comfort women found by Australian troops in the southwest of Timoa Island shortly after Japan surrendered in August 1945. They were forced to wear Red Cross armbands by the Japanese in order to cover up the real nature of their work.

Source: Australian War Memorial, transparency number 120082

Plate 3.6 One of the Javanese comfort women found in the southwest of Timoa Island, delighted to be freed from sexual slavery enforced by the Japanese soldiers.
Source: Australian War Memorial, transparency number 120083

collaboration with the 16th Army which controlled all of Java. Yet, due to a lack of interest by the Dutch, Australian, and other Allied nations' military authorities, the unprecedented scale of sexual abuse committed by the Japanese on Indonesian women was consigned to oblivion.

Since 1993, in response to the Indonesian government's request, more than 20,000 Indonesian women have come forward, claiming that they were victims of sexual violence committed by the Japanese troops stationed in various places in the Dutch East Indies during the war.[65] Not all were comfort women; many seem to have been victims of rape. Some of these women may have been "semi-professionals," working at comfort stations or acting as concubines to Japanese officers.[66] At the peak time, 220,000 Japanese soldiers and military employees were stationed throughout the Dutch East Indies. Numerous comfort stations were operated to cater for these men. From the available information examined in this chapter, there is no doubt that a large number of Indonesians and Eurasians were forcibly pressed into prostitution at these comfort stations and ill-treated by the Japanese.

The Dutch Army sexually exploited large numbers of Indonesian women during its colonial period prior to the Pacific War. Its men stationed in the Dutch East Indies suffered high rates of VD as a result.[67] It followed that, when the Japanese invaded, the sexual abuse of the Indonesian and Indo-Dutch women by the Japanese was probably not viewed as a serious crime against humanity. It is in this climate, and because of previously accepted sexual "norms," that we see racial and gender factors closely intertwined. Due to racial discrimination against the Indonesian and Indo-Dutch women and sexual discrimination against women in general, the Dutch military authorities were unable to see the serious criminal nature of the comfort women issue except in so far as it affected Dutch women and girls. The same can be said about postwar attitudes of other Allied forces. They all failed to pursue legal prosecution against – or even to seriously investigate – the Japanese who committed crimes against numerous Asian women, despite the fact they had accumulated ample evidence. In the following chapter, this issue will be further examined by analyzing the relevant official military documents of the Allied forces, in particular those of the United States.

4   Why did the US forces ignore the comfort women issue?

US military indifference towards comfort women

Japan surrendered on August 15, 1945, and the occupation of Japan led by the US forces commenced less than two weeks later. The purpose of the occupation was "democratization" of Japan's entire political, economic, and social system. As one of the important exercises in this process, the International Military Tribunal for the Far East (usually known as the Tokyo War Crimes Tribunal) was convened to prosecute Japanese war leaders who had instigated the war against the Allied nations and bore final responsibility for the various war crimes committed by their own forces. The tribunal, which lasted two and a half years, was presented with massive evidence of such war crimes as rape, murder, and ill-treatment committed by the Japanese against Allied soldiers and non-combatants. Yet the issue of comfort women – a crime against humanity on an unprecedented scale – was never dealt with by this trial.

Does this mean that the US authorities were utterly unaware of this crime? On the contrary, well before the end of World War II, the US armed forces became aware of the comfort women system organized by the Japanese Imperial forces.

One piece of evidence is the existence of a report entitled *Amenities in the Japanese Armed Forces*, prepared in February 1945 by the Allied Translator and Interpreter Service (ATIS), which was revised and expanded for publication in November of the same year.[1] The report explains in detail how Japanese military "brothels" were managed and operated. It details the regulations which covered the "brothels" that were available for Japanese officers and soldiers in various places in Southeast Asia and the Southwest Pacific. The report is based on information obtained from captured materials, with information on "brothels" listed in Section II under the heading of "Amusements." Other ATIS documents, such as interrogation reports of Japanese POWs, also refer to the fact that Koreans, Chinese and Indonesians were used as comfort women at these military brothels.[2]

Only a few interrogation reports on comfort women have so far been found at the US National Archives. One of these is *Japanese Prisoner of War Interrogation Report, No. 49* prepared by the Psychological Warfare Team attached to US Army forces in India–Burma theater.[3] The POWs interrogated in this case were 20 Korean women "employed" by a Japanese couple, who had been serving the 114th Infantry Regiment of the Japanese Imperial forces stationed in Burma. The women were captured by the US forces in August 1944.

Another document is *Psychological Warfare: Interrogation Bulletin No. 2* published by the South East Asia Translation and Interrogation Centre.[4] This bulletin contains a section entitled "A Japanese Army Brothel in the Forward Area," which is also a summary of the interrogation conducted with the same Korean comfort women captured in Burma.

Why did a Psychological Warfare Team interrogate these comfort women? US Psychological Warfare Teams were formed for the purpose of gathering as much information as possible concerning the psychological conditions of Japanese soldiers in the battlefield. A particular function was to conduct thorough interrogations of Japanese POWs, to find out how they perceived the ongoing war and under what conditions they would decide to surrender. Such information was forwarded to the Foreign Morale Analysis Division in the Office of War Information, to be analyzed by such prominent psychologists and anthropologists as Ruth Benedict, Clyde Kluckhohn, and John Embree. These specialist opinions were taken into account in producing various propaganda leaflets designed to persuade Japanese soldiers and civilians to surrender rather than fight to the death. Tens of thousands of these leaflets were printed and scattered from the air throughout the Pacific region, in particular during the fiercest battle of World War II in the Okinawa Islands.

It is presumed, therefore, that the interrogation of comfort women was not regarded as an important task for the US Psychological Warfare Teams. Such interrogation could provide only secondary information on the psychology of members of Japanese military forces. A few years ago I interviewed Grant Hirabayashi, one of the former *nisei* interpreters attached to the Psychological Warfare Team mentioned above that interrogated the 20 Korean women captured in Burma. He explained that only a brief interrogation was conducted, simply because these women had unexpectedly fallen into the hands of US forces. According to Hirabayashi, only a summary memorandum was recorded in this case, in contrast to normal POW interrogation procedures in which every question and answer was precisely recorded.[5] In other words, information obtained from these women was not highly valued by the Americans.

Interrogation Report No. 49 prepared by the Psychological Warfare Team in the India–Burma theater clearly refers to the violation of these Korean women's human rights by the Japanese forces. It claims that most of these women were deceived into becoming prostitutes for the Japanese forces. However, it seems that the American interrogators did not regard it as a serious war crime against humanity, and had no intention of prosecuting the Japanese officers of the 114th Infantry Regiment for sexual exploitation of these women.

It is almost certain that the US forces captured many Korean comfort women in Okinawa. From the middle of 1944, a large number of Korean women were sent to comfort stations on the main island of Okinawa as well as many other small islands in Ryukyu Archipelago. The exact number of women sent to Okinawa is not known, but it is estimated to be at least 350.[6]

Two short US military government reports are available which give numbers for Korean women who were repatriated to Korea from Okinawa after the war.[7] According to these reports, a total of 150 Korean women (40 women captured on the main island and 110 women from other islands) were gathered in Naha, the capital of Okinawa, and then sent back to Korea in November 1945. The passenger boarding list on the repatriation ship to Korea made by SCAP contains 147 names of Korean women from Okinawa, many of whom had typical names of Japanese geisha in addition to their own Korean names.[8] Only a few Korean women stayed on in Okinawa after the war.[9] Thus, it is presumed that more than half of the Korean comfort women sent to Okinawa died during the fighting.

However, there is no documentation to prove that the US forces conducted interrogation of these 150 women. There is also no documentation to show whether crimes committed by the Japanese forces in Okinawa were investigated in order to prosecute Japanese officers who were responsible for violating the human rights of these Koreans.

Some photos of Korean, Chinese, and Indonesian comfort women captured by the Allied forces have been found at the Public Record Office in London, the US National Archives, and the Australian War Memorial.[10] However, the fact that no record of interrogation of these comfort women has yet been found implies that neither the US forces nor the British and Australian forces were interested in investigating crimes committed by the Japanese forces against Asian women. It can therefore be concluded that the military authorities of the Allied nations did not regard the comfort women issue as an unprecedented war crime and a case which seriously violated international law, despite their having substantial knowledge about this matter.

There were two cases in which some members of the Japanese Army were tried and prosecuted at B & C Class war crimes tribunals for the crime of enforced prostitution. One involved 35 Dutch girls in Indonesia, who were forced to work at military brothels for about two months – the case that we have examined in the previous chapter. The victims in the other case were islanders from Guam. However, these were exceptional cases in that the victims in the former case were Caucasians and the trial in the latter case was conducted in conjunction with an affront to the American national flag by the Japanese.[11]

The following incidents also indicate the disinterest of US forces in the comfort women issue. In early September 1945, a group of US military government officers flew from Okinawa to Kyonsong to take over the Japanese military government of Korea. The group included Brigadier-General Charles Harris, Colonel Swift and Colonel Argo of XXIV Corps. Shortly after their arrival, a dinner party was arranged at the Chosen Hotel by Japanese officers led by Deputy Chief of Staff, General Sugai. There were 28 officers, including five or six Japanese, at the dinner, and alcohol was served. About 12 or 15 Korean "geisha" were brought to the hotel by the Japanese after the dinner. The Japanese officers left early, but the Americans danced with the girls until 2 or 3 o'clock in the morning. All expenses for this dinner party were paid for by the Japanese. Some American officers who attended were later interrogated by staff of the Inspector General's Office of XXIV Corps. All denied allegations that they were provided with condoms and that they slept with the women.[12] These Korean women were probably comfort women who had been serving Japanese men during the war. Although the war officially ended on August 15, a few weeks before the dinner party was held, Korean comfort women continued to be exploited by the Japanese and the Americans. Some of these American officers were from G-2, one of whose duties was to collect information on war crimes, and Colonel Argo was the Chief of Police.

Why was awareness of the comfort women issue as a serious war crime clearly lacking in the mind of the leaders of the Allied forces? One reason probably lies in the fact that the majority of the women victims of this enforced military prostitution were Asians and were therefore neither white women nor civilians of the Allied nations. As we have seen in the previous chapter, the Dutch forces, who prosecuted Japanese officers for the crime of forcing Dutch girls and women into prostitution, did not even bother to investigate most cases in which Indonesian women were victimized. Some historians have pointed to the "absence of Asia" in the Tokyo War Crimes Tribunal.[13] Probably the comfort women issue was also ignored for the same reason. It took almost half a century for the enslavement of the comfort women to be considered one of the most serious and unprecedented war crimes in history.

Another reason can be sought in soldiers' common perception of women (i.e. their sexual ideas), which we find more or less universally in military ideology, regardless of its nationality. A common refrain is the idea that women are morally obliged to offer amenities to soldiers who are fighting at the risk of their lives, to defend their people and the nation. This kind of androcentric ideology has been, and still is, deeply rooted in most military forces and the societies that support them. For this reason, military men are generally quite insensitive towards the services rendered by women. American soldiers and officers during World War II were undoubtedly tainted with these attitudes, and this was probably one of the major factors that hindered them from correctly understanding the comfort women issue. Therefore it seems necessary to closely examine the sexual ideology of the US military forces and their relevant policies during World War II, in order to understand why the US failed to take up this issue as a serious war crime against humanity.

US military policies on the prevention of venereal disease in World War II

Very few first-hand documents have been unearthed containing information on official US policies regarding military prostitution and related matters during World War II. Yet secondary sources reveal that the US and other Allied forces had plans to establish military brothels to serve their own soldiers in various areas as they advanced. It has been argued that in some places such facilities were set up, but were forced to close down within a short period of time.[14] However, I have recently discovered a large number of relevant documents at the US National Archives which contradict this interpretation and require a new approach to this issue.

Most of the documents that I analyze below are from the records prepared by the US War Department over nearly three years between August 1942 and July 1945. Some relevant Australian archival documents are also examined. These documents can be roughly divided into two categories:

- the first group comprises those documents related to measures taken by the War Department to tackle persistent high rates of venereal diseases (VD) among US forces, especially those stationed overseas;
- the second set of documents is those detailing complaints over sexual misconduct by members of the US forces. These documents were submitted to the War Department from within as well as outside the military forces.

Among these documents, one of the earliest official records is a confidential memo dated August 6, 1942. Colonel W. A. Wood, Jr. (Director of the Requirements Division, General Staff Corps) sent a memo to the Surgeon General, informing him that:

> A special military requirement is established for provision of individual venereal prophylactic units to individual members of the military service located beyond the limits of the continental United States where no standard prophylactic measures are, or will be available for use, and where no individual protective measures are available for private purchase from the Army Exchange Service, commercial or other sources.[15]

Another confidential memo indicates that the army air force was responsible for the transportation of such "prophylactic units" to troops stationed outside the US, and that they were to be sold at cost.[16] The fact that prophylactic units were airlifted and not transported by ship clearly indicates that the distribution was a *matter of urgency*.

It was probably quite difficult for the Requirements Division to estimate how many "individual venereal prophylactic units" were actually required for distribution at this stage. Colonel Wood requested the Surgeon General to determine "the basis of the above requirement and procurement of such amount."[17] In response to this request, on October 15, 1942, an Executive Officer of Medical Corps, Colonel John Rogers, produced a report[18] which contains the following estimate:

> b. Requirements are established as follows:
> (1) Initial issue (tentative) per man overseas:
>   Mechanical prophylactic units – 12 (units of one)
>   Chemical prophylactic units – 12
>   This is considered to be a 3 months requirement.

(2) Maintenance issue 4 mechanical and 4 chemical per man per month or 4,000 of each per 1,000 men per month.

(3) Distribution factor – 3,000 per 1,000 troops strength or 25 percent of initial issue.

c. Cost for the calendar year 1943 is estimated as follows:

Unit cost of mechanical unit	$ .03
Unit cost of chemical unit	$ .15
Total cost of initial issue	$6,480,000. (*)
Total cost of maintenance	$25,920,000.
Total cost of distribution factor	$1,620,000.
Total cost for calendar year 1943	$34,020,000.

   (*) This figure is based on 3,000,000 men overseas in 1943.

On the assumption that each US soldier overseas had sexual intercourse once a week, the allocation of prophylactics would consume a staggering US $34 million of the military budget each year. This is equivalent to 17 percent of the entire money spent on the Manhattan Project, or 15.5 percent of the total cost of rifles distributed to the 8 million US soldiers during World War II. It is not surprising therefore that the War Department tried to distribute them at "cost price."

The War Department not only seriously deliberated over the distributions of condoms and venereal disinfectants but in fact implemented such plans in the latter half of 1942. Behind this massive enterprise lay the problem of a wide and rapid spread of venereal diseases amongst US forces stationed overseas. In particular, the diseases were prevalent among the forces stationed in Africa, the Middle East, and India. For example, in the case of one Afro-American ("coloured") unit stationed at Karachi, the VD rate was as high as 500 per 1,000 per year.[19]

The Inspector General who investigated this matter reported that the military authorities "could bring this problem out in the open as other countries have done, *establish supervised houses* and prevent a great number of our young men from being infected with the vilest forms of venereal diseases prevalent on this earth" [emphasis added]. Thus, he advocated that military-controlled brothels would be necessary to contain widespread VD amongst US forces stationed overseas. At the same time he criticized the War Department's official policy regarding prostitution, by claiming that "the provisions of War Department Circular 170, 1941 are scarcely applicable in foreign countries."[20] Circular 170, which was also called "the May Act," enabled the Secretary of War to issue orders to prohibit prostitution in a certain area, if prostitution in that area was found to be "harmful to the efficiency, health, and welfare of military personnel at the specified post, camp or station."[21] In other words, this Inspector General was implying that the prohibition of prostitution would not solve the spread of VD among the forces because it would encourage the business to go underground.

The War Department certainly did not adopt a policy of permitting or encouraging the establishment of "supervised houses." However, it arranged the mass distribution of condoms and disinfectants. The armed forces also instructed soldiers on how to apply chemical prophylaxis immediately after visiting brothels, by providing "prophylaxis stations" in red-light districts frequented by US soldiers in overseas theaters. It seems that such military prophylaxis stations were set up in various red-light districts in foreign countries from early in World War II.[22]

Despite such measures, VD apparently remained quite a serious problem among the US forces stationed in Africa, the Middle East, and India. On September 25, 1942, Colonel Stanhope Bayne-Jones (Acting Director of Preventive Medicine, Division of Medical Corps) advised Colonel Lawrence Hanley (Assistant Chief of Staff of G-1) to send Major William Brumfield, a VD control specialist, to these theaters for the purpose of investigating current conditions and recommending remedial action. As a result, Major Brumfield was assigned to this task on October 1, 1942.[23] His field investigation was conducted between the end of October 1942 and mid-January 1943, and on March 2, 1943 his report was submitted to the Assistant Chief of Staff.

In the meantime, it seems that the health situation for troops was worsening, and as a consequence, the distribution of "prophylactic units" to overseas areas was further increased. According to a report prepared by Colonel John Rogers on October 15, 1942, such overseas areas included Alaska, Canada, Newfoundland, and Panama. Furthermore, the bulk of those prophylactic units, initially for sale at cost, were now made available free of charge. Free condoms and chemical units were transported by air to 14 locations listed in the records, spread out over three different regions: South America (such as Brazil and Trinidad), Africa (including Lagos, Khartoum, and Cairo), and India (such as Karachi and Calcutta). The total distribution was 4,900 packets of condoms (each packet contains three) and 14,700 chemical units.[24] The fact they were airlifted and distributed for free to the troops in these three regions indicates the seriousness of VD problems in those places.

In addition, 100,000 packets of condoms and 150,000 chemical units were shipped out from the port of New York on September 29, 1942 to unspecified destinations, 55,000 packets of condoms, together with 165,000 chemical units, were dispatched from the same port again on October 2 of the same year. These were also intended for free distribution. According to the same report, by then condoms were made available at all foreign stations where post exchanges were located. The criteria for distribution were 2,160 packets per month per 1,000 men in temperate and cold climates, and 3,000 packets per 1,000 men in warm climates.[25]

It was not only troops stationed overseas but also those within the continental United States that were affected by VD. A memo dated October 8, 1942, prepared by the Personnel Division, G-1, indicates that VD among the domestic forces due to prostitution was becoming a serious problem.[26] By the end of 1942, the invocation of the May Act (mentioned above) began to be seriously discussed by the senior staff of G-1. It was concluded that its invocation could not be avoided "if the local authorities fail to take correct measures within a reasonable period of time."[27] In War Department Circular No. 77, issued on March 17, 1943, the 1941 regulations on "off limits" were amended and made more rigorous.[28] This indicates that prostitution near domestic military camps continued to be a problem.

Although the War Department's policy was that the May Act should be used "only as a last resort,"[29] conditions in some places, such as Fort Bragg in North Carolina and Camp Forrest in Tennessee, were so bad that the May Act was indeed invoked.[30] Furthermore it seems that commanders at certain camps connived at their soldiers' frequenting brothels. For example, in March 1945, civilians in Portland, Oregon complained to the War Department that the local US Army was associated with organized prostitution.[31] In his memo dated July 3, 1943, Brigadier-General Russell Reynolds (Director of the Military Personnel Division) also lamented that camp commanders were not wholeheartedly making efforts to eliminate red-light districts in their vicinity.[32] Such domestic conditions seemed to continue until the end of the war. In July and August, a Joint Army–Navy Vice Control Board had discussions on co-operative projects, such as gathering information on VD and prostitution, and designating "off limits" areas. Despite such efforts, there were ongoing problems: for example, in February 1945 it was reported that 47.7 percent of the members at Camp Polk in Louisiana was suffering from venereal diseases.[33]

However, it should be noted that the War Department's attitude towards VD and prostitution amongst forces based at home was quite different from its attitude towards the same problems overseas. There are no official documents to verify that the War Department distributed condoms and chemicals to soldiers within the US, free or otherwise. The fact that the May Act was actually invoked in some cases leads to the presumption, on the contrary, that the War Department adopted stringent measures towards these problems from the beginning. This was in stark contrast to its tacit approval of the use of "prophylactic units" and prostitutes by US forces overseas.

There seem to be a few reasons for this discrepancy. One key reason is probably that soldiers within the home territory could easily gain access to condoms and medical treatment for VD. Moreover, out of consideration for public opinion at home, it was vital to create and maintain the general image that US Army soldiers were healthy and morally sound. On the other hand, senior staff of the War Department were clearly aware that it would be quite difficult to suppress the sexual desire of soldiers stationed in overseas theaters of war, and that the spread of VD amongst those forces would have a serious effect on their day-to-day combat abilities. Thus, the War Department formally maintained an "official policy" not to allow its troops to use prostitutes regardless of their location, while in reality it took pragmatic measures to prevent VD among the forces stationed outside the US by providing individual "prophylactic kits" as well as setting up "prophylactic stations." However, this does not mean that all senior staff of G-1 in the War Department were happy with such arrangements. For example, Colonel F. A. Heilman (Deputy Assistant Chief of Staff for Operations) wrote a memo on October 29, 1942, stating that "the Secretary of War should give careful consideration to the implications of this program," because this "may be interpreted in the minds of certain military and non-military individuals as fostering immorality."[34]

The Brumfield Report and military-controlled prostitution

Let us examine the actual methods that the US forces adopted to tackle the problem of VD amongst its members stationed overseas.

We can start by analyzing the report submitted by Major William Brumfield, who investigated conditions in Central Africa, the Middle East, and India. It is clear from his field investigations in these regions that many units either directly or indirectly controlled local prostitution as an effective measure to suppress VD. This was done under the responsibility of local commanders who clearly knew that such actions were in contravention of the War Department's official policy. Usually in such cases, certain houses were selected from existing brothels in the vicinity of the military camp. Medical officers often conducted VD examinations with prostitutes working at those selected houses. Soldiers were instructed to use only those designated houses, and to make sure they visited a prophylactic station set up in that district immediately after visiting those houses. In some places, prophylactic facilities were provided to the designated brothels by the troops.

In some cases, however, new brothels were set up near US camps especially to serve Americans. For example, two "women's villages" were set up by the local government for US forces stationed in Robert's Field in Liberia, on the west coast of Africa. Women who wished to work in these villages had to pass VD examinations. If admitted, they were photographed and required to tag their own photos. They were also requested to purchase a thatched house with three rooms at a nominal price of $15. These women were examined weekly, and anyone showing infectious symptoms had her tags taken up and was treated. The tag was returned when all signs and symptoms disappeared. Soldiers were told not to have intercourse with the women without tags.[35] According to Brumfield, the troops at Robert's Field reduced their VD rates considerably in this way. However, he claimed that the rates were still higher than for those troops stationed in the US. He suggested in his report that the rates could be further reduced by putting fences around the villages to keep the local men outside, as well as by setting up prophylactic stations at the gate of the villages.[36] As a matter of fact, G-1 officers in the War Department were aware of the existence of such military-controlled brothels even before reading the Brumfield Report. For example, on December 18, 1942, R. Arnold (Chief of Chaplains of the US Army) reported to G-1 that he had received information that the 41st Engineers stationed in Africa had a brothel called "Paradise," staffed by "professional whores (natives)," which was being "operated by the United States Army."[37]

Brumfield also referred to five brothels in Eritrea (three in Asmara and two in Massawa), that were jointly controlled by US and British forces. These brothels were originally established by the Italian Army, but when the British occupied Eritrea in 1940 they were permitted to continue business under the British occupation forces. When Brumfield visited those places in late 1942 the brothels were "in-bound to both British and United States soldiers," and the soldiers were instructed not to associate with the Italian and native population outside these brothels. Military police were responsible for maintaining order in these houses as well as training attendants to administer prophylaxis. Alcoholic beverages were not permitted in the houses and soldiers under the influence of alcohol were not allowed to enter the premises. Brumfield described the "novel method of venereal disease control" practiced at these houses:

> Upon entering the house the customer is assigned a room by the madam. Upon leaving he is escorted to the prophylactic station where his name and serial number and the hour of prophylaxis are entered in a book. His name and serial number and the name or number of his sex partner are entered on a slip of paper and dropped into a locked box so that it is not available to unauthorized persons. Men are not allowed to leave the houses until they have had prophylaxis and have given the necessary contact information. The boxes from three houses [in Asmara] are delivered to the Surgeon's office each morning. There the slips are removed and the boxes returned to the houses. The slips are filed and should the man develop a venereal disease the consort is immediately taken from work and not allowed to return until it is determined that she is free from infection.[38]

Because of this rigid method of control, which was inherited from the Italian Army, Brumfield claimed that rates of venereal disease for both British and American troops were lower in Eritrea than in other places in the Middle East. According to Brumfield's report, there were similar type of brothels under the supervision of military police in Persia as well.[39]

There were some other places in the Middle East where the US and British armies were jointly stationed but which did not have designated brothels controlled by the military forces. In such places, the British and American troops set up prophylactic stations in red-light districts which were shared by both forces. Brumfield praised this arrangement and noted that "the cooperation between the British and US Forces was excellent."[40] Incidentally, Brumfield also noted that British forces in the Middle East captured over 5 million condoms from the Italians, and distributed them to its own soldiers free of charge, which was apparently "a departure from former policy."[41]

In Palestine, Brumfield also investigated the VD control methods of the Australian forces and was impressed by their thoroughness. He reported that:

> They established houses of prostitution under the rigid control of their medical and police officers, inspecting the girls and proffering prophylaxis to the men, and placing questionable areas out of bounds so that the troops would use the regulated places if they insisted upon sexual intercourse. It was

Plate 4.1 Australian and other Allied soldiers queuing up in front of a brothel in Cairo
  during World War II. Date unknown.
Source: Australian War Memorial, transparency number P419/02/01

indicated that venereal disease was less among Australian troops than among
English troops in Palestine. The lower rate was attributed to the method of
control.[42]

In fact, such rigid methods of control by the Australian forces were adopted
because of lessons learnt from bitter experience, when Australians were stationed
in the same region during World War I. During a five-month stay in Egypt
between January and May 1916, about 10,000 Australian soldiers suffered from
venereal diseases. The matter was so serious that the Australian forces set up the
"Cairo Purification Committee" and took various measures, including extensive medical examination of prostitutes and the supply of prophylactics to the
soldiers. As a result, the diseases were under control by the middle of 1917.
However, when the troops later moved into Palestine, another outbreak of
venereal disease occurred.[43] Thus, it seems that when the Australian forces
advanced in the Middle East in 1940, they arranged military-controlled brothels
from the beginning as a measure to tackle possible outbreaks of VD. The following excerpt from an Australian Army official report, *The Problem of VD in 7 Aust
Div. During Fifteen Months in the Middle East*, clearly endorses this point:

During the four months in Palestine, there were 138 cases of VD . . . With
modern methods of treatment the stay in hospital had been reduced, and

Plate 4.2 RAAF soldiers enjoying a drink in a night club in Cairo with some of the women "entertainers." Damien Parer, the photographer who took this photo, explained in the caption that "their exact profession is a matter for conjecture."
Source: Australian War Memorial, transparency number 004984

the combined effect of these various measures was that approximately 20 men – 0.14 percent div strength – were constantly under treatment . . .

At the termination of the Syrian Campaign, it was anticipated that the VD problem would be greatly enhanced with the div garrisoned in a Levantine area recently occupied by the French. Before the troops moved into the area, a conference was called of three gynaecologist specialists within the div to discuss the problem. The following recommendation was made: –

(I)   Certain brothels to be reserved for AIF [Australian Infantry Forces] soldiers only. This is to be strictly maintained by picquetting.

(II)   Any soldier who desires to patronise these brothels must produce to the guard his blue light [prophylactic] outfit.

(III)   Any soldier who has visited a brothel must attend immediately at the blue light centre and obtain a certificate of attention for his RMO [Regimental Medical Officer].

(IV)   The girls to be submitted to a satisfactory examination (clinical examination and smear, also culture and WR if practicable) before the opening night. Only those proved to be non-infectious to be employed. Such examination to be repeated at least once weekly.

(V)   The sale of alcoholic liquor to be strictly controlled.[44]

In the same report, it was recorded that during eight weeks of leave in Beirut, the 7th Australian Division's prophylactic stations served at least 27,000 men (i.e. over 480 men a day)! The result was relatively small numbers of incidents of VD – 61 in total.[45] This report also contains unusually detailed descriptions of how the 7th Division set up military controlled brothels. The following is a case in Tripoli:

At the port of EL MINA was a group of small houses on the water front, used for brothel purposes . . . Across the road from the Legoul Barracks was an empty building which, until closed, had functioned as a French regimental brothel. Surrounded by a high wall and barbed wire, it consisted of a large reception hall, opening by one door into a central bar or cafe, by another to a passage leading to twelve rooms, each with its bidet. A kitchen and a bathroom completed the accommodation . . . Unofficially, a series of Madames were paraded and the least objectionable – Madam OLGA – was selected . . .

It was explained to Madame that she had to produce 12 girls who were to submit to, and pass, a standard examination before the opening night and to a twice weekly snap examination thereafter.

Examinations would be carried out by a gynaecologist from the div and included inspections, smear, culture, Wasserman and Kahn. Each girl had to produce her identity book bearing her photo and result of MO's examination with date. Only these girls would be permitted to enter the premises . . . One Syrian pound was to be the price – nothing over half a crown . . .

The next few days saw a scene of hurry and bustle at the Emporium. In one room the gynaecologist with his pathologist were examining a series of girls temporarily in bathing gowns, down the passage were disappearing into the different rooms – large beds – easy chairs – wardrobes – suit cases and toilet articles. The Div Hyg Sec installed an excellent PAC in a room opening off the reception hall, which was decorated with warning posters. It was hoped that the horrible contrast between the real article and the poster would act as deterrent.

Within a week eight girls were passed as fit and the others had been admitted to the local hospital or had absconded. Madame produced a new and even uglier dress, and armed provost were posted at the gate. The girls were a mixed lot, Arabs, Lebanese and Greeks, all extremely unattractive, mostly grossly repulsive. . . . The youngest, LOLO, was 16 – a little dot from DAMASCUS. She alone seemed bright and happy until she developed an acute appendix . . .

Due to laxity of the provost, alcoholics were admitted and the place was partly wrecked – the usual accusations of brutality and thieving were made by Madame – but all was sorted out and business continued . . .

In the TRIPOLI area, with approximately 13,500 AIF troops, from September 14 to December 6, 12 weeks, there were totally 11,955 attendances in the controlled brothels, and unknown number outside – resulting in 134 cases of suspected VD. There was an average nightly attendance of 142.[46]

The above description of a brothel controlled by the Australian Army is strikingly similar to the situation of *ianjo*, i.e. Japanese comfort stations, although there is a fundamental difference. The women working for the Australians were professional prostitutes, while most comfort women were illegally forced to serve the Japanese men, and many of them were victims of rape. However, it was a breach of international law that the Australians used a 16-year-old girl as a prostitute knowing that she was a minor. Furthermore it is clear that the author of this report showed no guilt, and indeed strongly despised the women who became the objects of his and his fellow soldiers' sexual exploitation. Probably this was, and still is, a typical attitude of military men towards "prostitutes." This kind of raw information on the conditions of the military-controlled brothels is totally lacking in the Brumfield Report.

What were the rates of VD among the Australian troops stationed in the Middle East around this time? I have so far only found a few relevant statistical documents, including the following Table 4.1.[47]

If the figures of total cases in Table 4.1 are converted to ratios per thousand troops, in 1940 31.28 per thousand A.I.F. soldiers suffered from VD per annum, and in 1941, it was 40.33 per thousand per annum.[48] According to Brumfield's report, the rate for US troops stationed in Cairo in 1942 was 87.92 per thousand per annum, and 104.96 per thousand for the Persian Gulf Service Command. In the case of troops from the US Services of Supply in Karachi, the rate was as high as 218.4 per thousand per annum.[49] Therefore, the VD rates among the Australians were indeed much lower than those for the US forces. Incidentally, in Eritrea where the US and British forces shared the same brothels inherited from the Italian Army, the rate was as low as 22.16 per thousand per annum, even lower than the number of Australian cases.[50]

It should be noted, however, that as far as total cases are concerned, VD was the second most common disease after Sandfly Fever among the A.I.F. in the Middle East. Cases of VD ran at about 2.5 times the rate of Malaria or Dysentery cases, which were the third and fourth most common illness respectively.[51] Thus, it can be said that the problem of VD was the most serious health issue

Table 4.1 Incidence of VD, Australian Infantry forces in the Middle East, 1940–1942

	1940	*1941*	*1942(3/12)*	*Total*	*Average period*
Total cases	882	6121	1254	8257	25.6 days
Gonorrhea	284	1597	331	2212	33.46 days
Syphilis	71	247	45	363	28.2 days
Urethritis	288	1821	415	2534	26.2 days

that troubled US military leaders as well as those of other Allied nations. The Brumfield Report clearly proves that the US War Department not only distributed massive numbers of condoms and provided "prophylactic stations" to their own troops overseas, but also deliberately kept silent about the military-controlled brothels that their men frequented.

In the conclusion of his report, Brumfield proposed nine itemized measures to combat VD problems among US forces stationed in Africa, the Middle East and India. In Item 1, he suggested:

> That Army regulations be revised to permit the commanding generals in theaters of operations to institute such venereal disease control measures as may be deemed necessary in view of local conditions, regardless of whether such measures are considered applicable to venereal disease control in the United States.[52]

Although his wording is somewhat unclear, it is almost certain that he implied that commanders of ground forces in actual war zones should be given open permission to set up military-controlled brothels for their own men. The aim of using such facilities as an effective VD prevention method prevailed, despite the existence of the May Act, which was adopted within the US to some extent. Having actually seen many brothels controlled by the troops stationed in those regions, it seems probable that his true feeling was that in order to be relevant, the official military policy would have to change to come into line with the existing situation. However, senior officers in the War Department continued to maintain an official policy which was clearly in conflict with the actual methods they were using as "prophylactic measures."

In this sense, Brumfield's indirect criticism of his superior officers is understandable. However, he must be criticized for his interpretation of the causes of VD among US forces was fundamentally flawed. In the introduction of his report, Brumfield wrote:

> Among the factors influencing venereal diseases among the armed forces are: first, the characteristics of the people among whom soldiers are stationed. Their moral and customs, and especially the physical attractiveness of the native women have a direct bearing upon the desire of soldiers to associate with them and therefore the risk of sexual exposures. If the women lack physical attractiveness or if their customs prohibit intermingling with foreign men few sexual exposures will occur and low venereal disease rates will be the result.[53]

Here we find a perfect prototypical mixture of Orientalism and male chauvinism. To Brumfield's mind, American men are morally sound, healthy, and physically pure, but when they go to Asia and Africa they will be exposed to seductively exotic women inhabiting a morally corrupt society. In other words, US soldiers are viewed as naive "victims" of corrupt Oriental customs rather than as harsh "exploiters" of women in poverty.

Military prostitution in the Caribbean, Australia and elsewhere

Let us now examine the situation in other regions not covered by Brumfield's fieldwork.

It seems that VD was a serious problem among US forces stationed in the Caribbean from a relatively early stage of World War II. There are a number of relevant documents prepared by the War Department between August 1942 and December 1943. One of them is the memo sent to the Assistant Chief of Staff for Personnel from Brigadier-General F. H. Osborn (Director of the Special Service Division) on December 5, 1942:

Subject: Venereal Disease in Overseas Bases.

I. *Discussion*

1   Vigorous efforts by commanders and surgeons have not lowered the prevalence of venereal infection in many of the Caribbean bases.

2   *War Department procedure for prohibition of prostitution within reasonable distance of Military Establishments is not applicable to the problems of base commanders.*

3   In Surinam, 16 percent of the personnel have acquired a venereal disease. In St. Lucia, 10 percent of the forces are under treatment for syphilis. In British Guyana, the rate for the month of August was 331 per 1,000 per annum.

4   Civil authorities in British and Dutch colonies have no control over the widespread practice of prostitution by their impoverished, ignorant and diseased natives. Sanitary conditions in native village endanger in ways other than venereal the health of our troops.

5   Supervision of the sexual habits of soldiers is likewise difficult, particularly because of their long service in isolated areas, ready promiscuity, cheap rum and foreign service pay allotment.

6   Replacement of undesirable personnel and development of social and recreational diversions lowers the prevalence of venereal disease but is not feasible in all bases.

7   *Under such circumstances, commanders tend to tolerate quasi-control, such as sufferance of some illicit houses, to induce a degree of native cooperation and control.* Lacking the authority of higher headquarters, the thorough supervision of such ventures by the medical department is not possible.

8   Reconsideration of War Department policy and adaptation of prescribed procedures to the problems of overseas forces would seem desirable.

9   Prohibition of prostitution within reasonable limits of military establishments, as prescribed in Section II, Circular 170, War Department 1941, is dependent on cooperative action by civil authorities. *If such cooperative measures are not effective, as in the case of most overseas bases, it may be that commanders should be authorised to adopt control measures as warranted and as recommended by Venereal Disease Control Officers, within existing laws of the country in which troops are garrisoned.*[54]

[Emphasis added]

From this memo it is apparent that well before Major Brumfield submitted his report, one of the senior officers in the War Department had already suggested changes to the Department's policy, to permit commanders of overseas troops to adopt the method of military-controlled prostitution. Furthermore, in Item 7 of this memo, Brigadier-General F. H. Osborn admitted that some commanders in the Caribbean were actually condoning their soldiers' association with local prostitutes. It is also interesting to note that Osborn shared a similar view to Brumfield: the cause of VD problems was "impoverished, ignorant and diseased natives" rather than American men themselves.

Attached to this memo is a short report, *Prostitution and Venereal Disease in Caribbean Bases*, which was possibly prepared some time in the latter half of 1942. In this report, the situation in Panama, Aruba, Curacao, Trinidad, and British Guyana were briefly described. Another report entitled *Prostitution within the Caribbean area* was written by Inspector General, Major-General Virgil Peterson and submitted to the Assistant Chief of Staff, G-1 on April 6, 1943.[55] These reports give us a general picture of US military-controlled prostitution in this region.

In Panama, the Provost Marshal General's office organized a sort of educational tour for the soldiers to the red-light districts. They pointed out the designated brothels and instructed soldiers only to use those houses. The soldiers were not given a pass unless they attended this tour. The report admitted that there was some criticism that this expose served as an "introductory tour" rather than as a warning. As in Africa, the Middle East, and India, prophylactic stations were set up in red-light districts in the Caribbean. At one station near Quarry Heights, for example, as many as 200 to 300 condoms were given away every evening. In addition, all soldiers coming back drunk were required to be treated with prophylaxis at the camp hospitals. Yet, on the Pacific side some 400 VD cases were treated each month, and on the Atlantic side over 300 patients were admitted. At one stage, "no condoms had been on hand for almost a month until a few days previous, when an adequate supply had been sent down by plane."[56]

On the island of Aruba off Venezuela (then a Dutch colony), the town of San Nicholas immediately outside the US Army post had "active uncontrolled prostitution." Every two weeks 200 Venezuelan prostitutes from the mainland were flown by the Dutch airline to this island as well as to another island, Curacao. But for some unknown reason, these women were only allowed to stay on the islands for two weeks and then had to swap with another group. Prostitution at a hotel was prohibited, and so the business was carried out on the mountain nearby. The US command even set up a prophylactic station near the foot of the mountain and made sure to treat soldiers immediately after "each action." At one station which Major-General Peterson visited for inspection, 56 soldiers were treated by 9:30 pm.[57]

At Salinas in Ecuador, two brothels were designated in the red-light district and soldiers were allowed to visit these houses only between 4:00 pm and midnight. Here a quite similar method to that in Eritrea was adopted. A soldier had to surrender his pass to MPs at the entrance of the red-light district. The pass was delivered to a doctor at the prophylactic station set up in the district. The soldier could only regain his pass by appearing at the station for treatment, and without his pass no soldier could go back to his base. In this way, soldiers who visited the brothels were sure to be treated at the station. Moreover, at 4:00 pm every day, a US Army doctor with a local health officer visited these two brothels and checked whether every woman there possessed a health card verifying a recent VD examination. Any woman found without such a card was immediately removed by local police. In British Guyana, too, medical officers examined the prostitutes of designated brothels, and prophylactic chemicals were provided to one of those houses. Military police on patrol in the red-light district were authorized to request prophylactic treatment for any soldier picked up intoxicated.[58]

US forces stationed at Antigua in Guatemala took an extraordinary measure to reduce their soldiers' contact with local prostitutes, by bringing women from the US. One confidential document outlined seven different measures implemented by this unit which lowered its VD rate considerably in September 1942. One of these measures was "the importation of as many white women as possible, on any pretext possible, as hostesses, civilian aides, nurses, dates, etc." It is not known from this document whether these "white women" were professional prostitutes or not, or how many such women were "imported."[59]

Despite such VD prevention measures and the introduction of controlled prostitution, it still seemed difficult to reduce the VD rates among the troops stationed overseas. One reason for this was that many soldiers who came to the brothels were intoxicated and did not use condoms. It was also often too late to be properly disinfected when they visited a nearby prophylactic station a few hours after having had intercourse with prostitutes.[60] Intoxication among soldiers who frequented brothels was a common problem, not only in the Caribbean but also in Africa, the Middle East, and India, where Major Brumfield investigated. Moreover, doctors and medical orderlies were not always at prophylactic stations to attend visiting soldiers. The soldiers were expected to use prophylactic chemicals themselves, yet they were not properly trained to do so.

From these War Department documents, it can be verified that US military-controlled prostitution was widely practiced in the Caribbean as well as Africa, the Middle East, and India, in spite of the War Department's official disapproval of such activities. As already explained, it also reconfirms that senior officers in the War Department gave up applying the "May Act" to overseas troops from very early stages of the war. They condoned the implementation of prostitution controlled by their overseas commanders. Some senior officers of the War Department not only pretended to be uninformed about this matter but actively tried to cover up their knowledge. For example, on October 9, 1943, Eliot Ness (Director of the Division of Social Protection, Community War Service) wrote to Colonel H. A. Cooney of G-1:

Dear Colonel Cooney,
Following our telephone conversation on the Caribbean, I discussed the

matter of the statement "Venereal Disease Control Programs in the Caribbean Area," with Mr. Taft. We are in complete agreement with your point
of view that *while G-1 of the Army agreed in principle with the statement, the statement should not be published and made available for general distribution in its present form*;
and that statements relative to the movement of troops were detrimental
to the war effort if made available to persons outside the armed forces.

The statement will not be made available for general distribution in its
present form and any recommendations pertaining to the movement of
troops will be deleted from the statement, in as much as this recommendation has reached the proper official in the US Army.[61]

[Emphasis added]

There are a number of Australian archival documents which refer to the prostitution controlled by US forces stationed in Australia. None of the official US
documents I have found so far mention this activity.

As already explained, Australia's military forces made great efforts to suppress
VD amongst its soldiers stationed overseas from the very early stages of the war.
At the beginning of the war, the Australian government and its military leaders
were also concerned about growing VD rates amongst troops stationed within
Australia as well as in the general population.[62] Thus, unlike the US War Department, Australian authorities distributed condoms to their soldiers at domestic camps and bases and set up prophylactic stations in almost all red-light
districts in major cites and towns. According to relevant Australian documents,
US troops stationed in Australia had their own prophylactic stations, but at some
places they shared the same stations by agreement. US soldiers were also permitted entry for treatment in Australian military hospitals, though the Americans
preferred being treated by their own medical officers unless their diseases were
too serious to be attended to at ill-equipped camp hospitals.[63] It is not clear,
however, whether the US forces used the restricted brothels for their members in
Australia, apart from some specific cases that I will examine later.

During the war, the highly valued US currency induced many Australian
prostitutes to serve the GIs, and therefore some of these professional women
literally became "camp followers" of the US troops. There were some groups of
women who followed the US troops as the forces moved to different areas within
Australia: for example, not long after some US forces moved to Townsville in
the northern state of Queensland around February 1942, a large group of prostitutes moved into this town and boarded at civilian houses. Some of them
rented the houses and started "living with" Americans. The local and federal
government authorities were gravely concerned that the flood of these "immoral
women" would lead to a decline of morals in Townsville.[64]

The economic power, smart uniforms and flamboyant lifestyle of the American soldiers also attracted young civilian women in Australia. Many girls dated
GIs rather than "diggers" (i.e. Australian soldiers), which caused deep resent-
ments among Australian men. US troops were described as "over-sexed, over-
paid and over here." This situation created tensions between American and

Australian servicemen, and in fact led to a few incidents of street fighting between the two groups in major cities. On November 26, 1942, 3,000 soldiers from both sides and some civilians were involved in a two hour battle in Brisbane, which resulted in the deaths of two men and many injuries. Fighting continued the following day. Similar but smaller-scale battles also occurred in Adelaide and Perth. In February 1943, fighting took place in Melbourne between two forces involving 2,000 men.[65]

This kind of street fighting was also seen between two groups of US soldiers: white against Afro-American soldiers. It was tragic that the largest contingent of Afro-American soldiers on overseas service in 1942 was sent to Australia, a country with a strong "white supremacy policy." Many of these black soldiers were sent to Queensland, where the policy of racial segregation against Australian blacks (Aborigines) was rigorously implemented. Fighting between white and black GIs started in a red-light district in south Brisbane on March 11, 1942, and lasted for 10 days. Detailed information on this conflict is still not available, but it seems that the fighting broke out when black GIs were refused access to some brothels that white GIs were using.[66] This conflict was therefore a combination of racial and gender problems.

The series of violent racial incidents over 10 days triggered by this incident probably led the US forces to set up some special brothels for the black GIs in Queensland. The existence of such houses was referred to in the report *Civilian Morale in North Queensland*. The report was co-authored by Physiology Professor R. D. Wright of Melbourne University and Dr. Ian Hogbin, an anthropologist from Sydney University, and was submitted to the Prime Minister's Committee on National Morale in February 1943. It says:

> It is commonly believed in the southern states that there are licensed brothels in Queensland. This is not so, though the police insist that girls living in certain houses, who are known to be prostitutes, shall have regular examinations. In Brisbane, there are some twenty of these houses, and in Townsville, two or three. The American forces have set up several such places, with Australian girls, for the use of negro troops, much to the disgust of many civilians. The inducement to the girls to enter such places must be strong, for Sir Raphael Cilento stated that one increased her Savings Bank account by £3800 during twelve months.[67]

It is clear from this report that the US forces used pecuniary incentives in order to secure the service of Australian girls for their coloured troops. Such arrangements, which breached the "white Australia policy," angered one of the cabinet members of the Australian federal government, who read the report. On April 14, 1943, H. P. Lazzarini, the Minister for Home Security, wrote an indignant letter to the Prime Minister John Curtin, complaining that:

> This seems to me to be something so outrageous to Australian psychology that it is likely to become the gravest possible menace to Australia's war

effort, and I think myself deservedly so. Perhaps nothing embittered the German people more and provided such a fertile field of exploitation by Hitler in the early days of the rise of National Socialism, than the compelling of the German people to provide white German women to satisfy the lust of the African negroes, and the mere suggestion that the Americans are allowed to use Australian girls to satisfy the lust of American negroes seems to me incomprehensible.

I myself will not stand for it, and whenever it is raised I will attack it with all the vigour of which I am capable, and will dissociate myself at all times from such a vicious practice.[68]

There is an interesting contradiction in this letter: Lazzarini implies that it was vital to keep a racial segregation policy in order to avoid the rise of fascism, and thus virtually supported an unprecedented racist policy similar to that of the Nazis! It is not known how the prime minister responded to such vicious criticism from one of his own cabinet members. However, it is presumed that John Curtin remained silent and did not raise this matter with the US military authorities, knowing that American co-operation was so vital to defend his country against Japanese invasion.

Plate 4.3 US soldiers dating with Australian girls in the park in Melbourne, while an Australian soldier lies on the grass, watching enviously. Date unknown.
Source: Australian War Memorial, transparency number 011540

Plate 4.4 The Japanese knew the tension between American and Australian soldiers over Australian women, and tried to exploit this situation in order to further enhance the antagonism between two groups of the Allied forces. To this end, they produced various propaganda leaflets and left them in the battlefield in New Guinea, hoping to demoralize the Australian soldiers who would read them.
Source: Australian War Memorial, Japanese leaflets 7/42/3

Criticism, cover-up and a change in the War Department's attitude

Although they were probably in a minority, there were certainly some men within the US forces who also felt disgraced by their fellow soldiers' sexual conduct. In their letters home to priests, some soldiers in overseas forces mentioned the organized prostitution for their own troops. For example, in December 1943, a Catholic soldier at a US Army base somewhere in North Africa wrote to Reverend Edmond Kramer in New York:

> The Chaplain Dr. Kilbride, and the Catholic Boys of this Base are fighting our Army official for establishing a house of prostitution here as well as in the Base north of here. . . .
>   Father, you know the old saying: "when in Rome do as the Romans do". Well, that's just what's happening here. They say: "The French have them, so can we". They also say that it's necessary for a man to satisfy his desires, especially a married man.[69]

Some other Catholic soldiers at the same base wrote similar letters to their own priests at home. Those priests in turn passed this information to US Senator Robert Wagner and Congressman Hamilton Fish, asking them to investigate this matter. In response to the queries made by these two Congressmen as to War Department policy concerning prostitution, Colonel G. Ordway, Jr. (Assistant Executive of Operations Division) wrote a memo explaining that:

> It is recommended that the reply to Congressman Fish, as well as the other members of Congress who have inquired in a similar vein, should state in substance that houses of prostitution are not being operated by United States forces in Africa and that the War Department is definitely against the establishment or operation of houses of prostitution in North Africa and everywhere else.[70]

Another senior officer of Operations Division wrote a memo to General Hull, saying that:

> Since this brothel business could be very explosive indeed, . . . we should take every possible step to avoid a scandal. Particularly, we should avoid any semblance of equivocation. We should, therefore, query both Algeria and Cairo for the facts. If a denial from both theaters should be received, the War Dept. would be able to end the matter once and for all by making a categorical denial of Fish's accusation.[71]

The War Department communicated *pro forma* with the commanders of the troops in question, and of course those commanders denied and dismissed such allegations.[72] It is interesting to note, however, that the expression "*houses of prostitution are not being operated by United States forces in Africa*" could be interpreted as having a hidden meaning. It is possible to argue that this statement is correct: the brothels for American soldiers in Africa were not run by the US forces – rather they were operated by private businesses for the exclusive use of Americans. Indeed, that was the real situation, as described in the Brumfield Report. There is no doubt at all that senior staff of the War Department, when confronted with criticism from some church leaders and Congressmen, tried to cover up this fact by obtaining "suitable" answers from the commanders of the troops in North Africa.

In September 1944, one US Army soldier stationed in France wrote a letter home to his clergyman, condemning General Gerhart who "had taken it upon himself to open a house of prostitution for the soldiers of the 29th Division." This information was passed on to Right Reverend Mgr. Michael Ready (General Secretary of the National Catholic Welfare Conference), who subsequently questioned Secretary of War Henry Stimson about this matter. The War De-partment reported that an investigation found that "*through some error* a house of prostitution in the 29th Division area was allowed to open not off limits for the 29th Division but that the Division Commander, General Gerhart, discovered this fact four hours later and place was closed" [emphasis added]. The words "through some error" sound a poor excuse, and there is no evidence that the War Department conducted a thorough investigation on this matter. Yet, the War Department concluded that it "can safely consider this incident closed" and recommended that "no further action be taken."[73]

In January 1945, the Chief of Chaplains informed the War Department that a brothel called the "Pink House" had been operated outside of Noumea on the island of New Caledonia in the Southwest Pacific. Apparently this brothel had been "operating with the full consent of the local military and naval authorities to such an extent that army medical and military police personnel have been assigned to various duties in connection with its operation."[74] In fact, in June 1944, the Chief of Chaplains had previously complained about this matter and requested that the War Department take appropriate action to correct the situa-tion, but no action had been taken. At last, on February 17, 1945, Colonel C. E. Hixon (Director of Military Personnel Division) instructed the Commanding General of Pacific Ocean Area to investigate the matter. He stated that if the report was true, appropriate action should be taken.[75] It is not clear from the available documents what sort of action was eventually taken in this case. How-ever, the fact that the War Department did not do anything at all for almost eight months from the time the Chief of Chaplains first complained about this problem clearly indicates the reluctance of the War Department to investigate such allegations, not to mention taking any action to suppress such organized prostitution.

It is clear from these examples that the War Department maintained a dual policy in responding to various allegations, even as late in the war as February 1945. On the one hand, official policy promoted a ban of any form of organized prostitution controlled by US forces. On the other hand, such activities were not only massively condoned but institutionally supported, above all through the mass provision of prophylactics for overseas troops, but also through a practice of cover-up to shield against complaints. However, a change appeared in attitudes in late April 1945. This can be verified with a secret order from the Adjutant General, Major General J. A. Ulio, which was issued on April 25, 1945 to Commander-in-Chief of Southwest Pacific Area as well as to Commanding Generals of five different army organizations. Some excerpts from this document state:

1   Numerous unconfirmed reports have reached the War Department that in various overseas theaters the army has participated, and in certain areas is now participating, in the operation, supervision, sanction, designation, or condoning of brothels – so-called "G-I. Houses of Prostitution" – for the convenience of military personnel and for the purpose of venereal disease control. . . .

2   It is recognized that the social chaos among civilians existing in most overseas theaters presents unusually difficult problems in adjustment of relationship between soldiers and civilians, and that in many areas it is not practicable for the army to take action which will materially reduce contact between soldiers and prostitution. . . .

3   It has been repeatedly demonstrated that the toleration or fostering of organized prostitution is a completely ineffective method of controlling venereal disease, and that on the contrary prostitution contributes to a materially higher incidence of these diseases, especially among troops stationed in foreign countries. Furthermore, the operation of brothels under the partial or complete control or supervision of the army, or their designation for the use of military personnel is medically unsound, socially objectionable, potentially destructive of civilian and military morale, and in direct contravention of War Department policy.

4   It is therefore desired that necessary action be taken to assure compliance in your command with War Department policy concerning repression of prostitution by all means of available cooperation with civilian authorities in the countries concerned; and where civilian cooperation cannot be obtained, to employ all appropriate military measures to minimize the availability of prostitutes to military personnel.[76]

This order issued by the Adjutant General was the first of its kind in which War Department official policy was reaffirmed and emphasized, and instructions issued by one of the top staff of the Department for the suppression of military prostitution. Yet it is interesting to note that Major General Ulio still thought that "in many areas" it was "not practicable" to suppress the business of prostitution. It is also interesting to read his opinion that organized prostitution controlled by the Army was "a completely ineffective method of controlling venereal disease." As we have seen, military-controlled prostitution did in fact contribute to the reduction of VD rates among Allied troops *in certain area to some extent*.

Major General Ulio presumably knew this fact from various internal reports such as that written by Brumfield.

The question arises as to why Major General Ulio suddenly tried to abolish the dual policy and introduce stricter measures to suppress organized prostitution for American soldiers. One reason for this could be found in the state of the armed conflict, both in Europe and the Pacific. By this time, it was almost certain that the fall of Nazi power in the European theater was only a matter of time. US forces were advancing in various places in Europe and their contact with civilians suddenly increased. In the Pacific theater, too, large numbers of American soldiers were now in the Philippines and Okinawa, and control of large civilian populations became an important issue for the war administrators. It is quite possible that military leaders in the War Department gradually realized that it would be harmful for the US forces openly to operate military brothels in those areas and thus invite criticism from local civilians. However, it is not certain how much attention the Commanding Generals gave this order.

From this evidence, we see that the US forces widely used organized prostitution, controlled by themselves, as a VD prevention method during the war. They saw organized prostitution also as a means to improve troop morale with relative safety. It was evident also after the war – the topic we will examine in Chapter 6 of this book. It was therefore quite natural that they were completely unable to discern the criminal nature of the comfort women system implemented by the Japanese Imperial forces during the war – one of the most significant crimes against humanity in our history.

5 Sexual violence committed by the Allied occupation forces against Japanese women: 1945–1946

Sexual violence prior to the Allied occupation of Japan

There is no documentary evidence of mass rape by the Allied soldiers during the Pacific War. Although it is possible that some incidents have been censored or removed from the records, it is clear that such incidents were relatively limited, except in the final stage of the war. Although no relevant *official* documents exist, either on the US or on the Japanese side, there are numerous, credible testimonies of Okinawan women who were gang-raped by American soldiers during and after the Battle of Okinawa, the last battle in the Pacific War and the only one fought on Japanese soil.

The Battle of Okinawa, or "Operation Iceberg," as it was known in the US military, was the fiercest battle of the Pacific War. The US mobilized 548,000 men and 1,600 ships for this operation and fired 40,000 artillery shells from the sea during the seven days prior to April 1, the day that they landed on the main island of the Ryukyu (Okinawan) Islands.[1] At the time, the Japanese Imperial forces had only 86,400 men, with as little as 410 artillery pieces and 40 tanks on this island. Despite the vast difference in manpower and equipment between the two forces, the battle lasted two and a half months. The Japanese hunkered down doggedly in caves and huge lyre-shaped tombs, both of which are typical Okinawan features. They hid during the daytime, but came out and attacked the Americans at night.[2] In the end, American casualties totaled about 50,000, including 14,000 deaths. In addition, a few thousand US soldiers had to be withdrawn from the battlefield because of severe psychological problems. Japan lost 66,000 soldiers (76.4 percent death rate) in this battle, and a further 4,400 pilots perished along with 2,900 planes. Two-thirds of these planes were kamikaze on suicidal missions. Civilian casualties were also high, and although the exact number of casualties is unknown, it is estimated that more than 100,000 Okinawans died, i.e. one-fourth of the Okinawan population.[3]

It appears that US soldiers began viewing local women as "the women belonging to the enemy" as soon as the battle against the Japanese forces took place on the soil of Japan's national territory. It is almost certain that such a view, intensified by the bitter combat, contributed to the sharp increase in sexual

Plate 5.1 An American soldier fondling the hair of an Okinawan girl. Her face shows the
        intense dislike she has of this behavior. Date unknown.
Source: US National Archives

crimes committed by US troops on Okinawa. Such crimes were rare during the
previous battles in various Japanese-occupied territories in the Pacific region.
The above-mentioned horrific combat conditions in Okinawa must also have
contributed to the escalating brutality of the US troops against "enemy civilians."

Based on the research in oral history that he conducted over many years,
Ōshiro Masayasu, an Okinawan historian and former director of the Okinawa
Prefectural Historical Archives, writes:

> Soon after the US marines landed, all the women of a village on Motobu
> Peninsular fell into the hands of these American soldiers. At the time, there
> were only women, children and old people in the village, as all the young
> men had been mobilized for the war. Soon after landing, the marines
> "mopped up" the entire village, but found no signs of the Japanese forces.
> Taking advantage of this situation, they started "hunting for women" in
> broad daylight and those who were hiding in the village or nearby air raid
> shelters were dragged out one after another. It was no different from the
> "brutal acts of conquerors," committed by the Japanese forces in China
> earlier.

There was a communal taboo on this incident and no mention of it was made even after the men returned to the village after the war ended. Consequently it was a long time before it became public knowledge.

At the time, most of the women in the village had stopped menstruating [due to malnourishment], so only a few babies of mixed-race were born as a result of this war-time rape. This was undoubtedly the only consolation in this tragedy.

During the battle, violence against women occurred everywhere in Okinawa, although the true details will probably never be revealed.[4]

The above incident is reminiscent of the My Lai Massacre in which many Vietnamese women were gang-raped before being shot by members of Charlie Company.[5] The women of the above-mentioned village were at least lucky to emerge from their ordeal with their lives.

According to a survey conducted by a feminist group in Okinawa – Okinawan Women Act Against Military Violence – US troops landed on Zamami Island, a small island west of the main island, and began raping women there in March 1945, shortly after they had landed. They abducted the women, carried them one by one to deserted coastal areas and gang-raped them. After being raped, the women were allowed to go. There is also a testimony that some Okinawan nurses and local women patients who had been admitted to the US Field Hospital were raped by US soldiers. One of the victims, a young girl patient, was raped by a GI in front of her father who was in the tent attending to her.[6] These victims had nowhere to report the crime even if they had wished to do so, the Japanese police system of Okinawa having completely collapsed during the battle.

The rape of Okinawan women by American soldiers continued even after the war officially ended and there are many incidents in which American soldiers took young girls from civilian houses at gunpoint. These girls would later return with their clothes torn off. Some were even killed, although the perpetrators were never caught. As a result, villagers throughout Okinawa used a warning signal of banging on pots and pans to warn of approaching American troops. On hearing this, girls would hide until all was clear. Some women were also raped when they went to US camps to receive food hand-outs. During the first five years of the American occupation of Okinawa, 76 cases of murder or rape-murder were reported. This number was but the tip of the iceberg, as most cases went unreported.[7]

Fear and confusion before the landing of the Allied occupation forces

On August 16, 1945, the day after Japan officially surrendered to the Allied nations, major railway stations in Tokyo such as Shinjuku and Ueno were crowded with women and children who were desperate to catch trains bound for remote places far from the metropolitan area.[8] They feared that, if they remained in the city, they would be raped by US and other Allied troops who were expected to land soon in Japan. In adjacent Kanagawa prefecture, too, many railway stations were thrown into chaos as women tried to escape from cities like Yokohama, Yokosuka, Kawasaki, and Zushi. Yokohama and Yokosuka, two major port cities near Tokyo, were expected to be the landing places for the core of the Allied occupation forces. The authorities of the Kanagawa prefectural government were particularly concerned about the safety of women living in the coastal areas of its prefecture. Thus, they advised local councils in these areas to evacuate women and children to inland country areas as soon as possible. They also advised their own female staff and other public service workers to take refuge with relatives or friends in remote areas.[9]

Such fear was widespread, not only among the people in Tokyo and neighboring prefectures but in other cities, especially those cities with port facilities where the Allied troops were expected to land. For example, in Fukuoka on Kyushu Island, military officers of the Western District Army's headquarters held a meeting with Fukuoka prefectural officials in the afternoon of August 15 and discussed how to face the unprecedented situation. At the meeting, one army staff officer proposed the immediate evacuation of women and children from the city, as he thought that the ships carrying US reconnaissance forces would likely arrive there within the following few days, entering through Hakata Bay. As the first step in this plan, all female staff of the Fukuoka prefectural government were advised to evacuate to the country. A similar situation arose in Kure, a port of Hiroshima, and in Hachinohe, a remote coastal city in Aomori prefecture, where some residents believed a rumor that 30,000 Allied soldiers would be advancing on their city.[10]

The fact that this state of popular disorder continued until late August is clearly illustrated by some reports of actual cases which appeared in the series of secret reports entitled *Chian Jōsei* (Conditions of Public Peace and Order), prepared by the Headquarters of the kempeitai (the Japanese military police). For example, the report of August 23 includes the following cases:

- When the situation of women's evacuation from Kaname block and Chihaya block 6 in Toshima Ward [in Tokyo] was investigated, it was found that there were 31 households [from which women have fled.]
- The Neighborhood Association of Chihaya block 3 in the same ward is presently planning to form a vigilance corps consisting of all male residents over 18 years old in order to protect the virtue of women and girls in their block.
- Parents of young daughters are deeply concerned with their safety, being affected by speculative rumors such as "they will demand each neighborhood association to provide the service of young women" and "we must disguise young women as men, otherwise they will be in danger." (Tachikawa District)[11]

It seems that the Japanese government tried to restore order by using the influence of the media. From August 19 various articles related to this matter appeared in major newspapers. On August 19, *Asahi Shimbun*, one of the largest nationwide newspapers, published an article entitled "Looting and Brutality Are Not Possible."[12] This article claimed that the landing of the Allied occupation forces could not begin before the Japanese Imperial Government signed an instrument of surrender that General Douglas MacArthur was going to put forward, and that at this stage the landing places had not yet been designated. Thus, it implied that people would not need to worry about the Allied occupation forces immediately. The article also said that the collection of food and other materials needed for the occupation troops would be controlled by the Japanese government. Thus it concluded that "*in principle*, looting and brutality, which are quite common problems on the battlefield, should not occur" [emphasis added]. It is interesting to note that the words "in principle" indicate the psychological ambivalence of the journalist who wrote this article.

On the same page, directly above this article, *Asahi Shimbun* published a message from a Catholic priest, Father Patrick Barn, addressed to the US soldiers who were expected to land on Japanese soil as members of the occupation forces. Father Barn was an American citizen who was permitted to live near Mt. Hiei in Kyoto throughout the war without internment. In this message, entitled "To the American Soldiers Who Are Going to Land. Maintain Rigid Discipline!," he urged the US soldiers not to commit outrages against Japanese citizens, especially young women. He emphasized the similarity between traditional Japanese women's behaviour to choose to commit suicide rather than be sexually violated and the Catholic spirit of martyrdom. He asked the American soldiers to respect this sensitivity of Japanese women.[13]

This article was the Japanese translation of his message in English addressed to the US troops, which was broadcast by the NHK (Japan Broadcasting Commission) overseas service section. His message was aired many times between August 19 and the landing of the Allied troops at Yokosuka on August 30. In fact, Aragaki Hideo, then the chief of the Domestic News Section of the Tokyo head office of *Asahi Shimbun*, arranged the broadcast of Father Barn's speech with NHK, as he was seriously concerned about the possible violence against Japanese women by US occupation troops.[14] Thus, *Asahi Shimbun* published two contradictory articles on the same page of its newspaper. One reflected the "official stance" of the Japanese government and the other reflected the real concerns of journalists.

This kind of ambivalence of the press can be found in other major newspapers, as well. For example, on August 20, *Yomiuri Hōchi*, another national newspaper, published an article, "To be Driven by Demagogy is Foolish – We Would be Laughed at by the Rest of the World If We Show Too Much Confusion." This article cited a long commentary given by Mr. Horikiri Zenjirō, a member of the House of Peers, who had experience in serving as a Japanese representative to the Allied Committee on the Enforcement of the Peace Treaty in Germany after World War I. According to Horikiri, the discipline of the occupation forces stationed in Germany in those days had been maintained to a high degree and no unfortunate incidents had occurred. Yet Horikiri too ended up by expressing reservations about the strict discipline of the Allied troops in the following antinomic manner:

Of course it cannot be said so lightly that the Allied troops which are going to be stationed in Japan would behave in the same way. It can be expected that, in a war situation, looting and brutality are often committed when military discipline becomes slack to some extent and soldiers become truculent. But this time it is a peaceful station of the well-disciplined military forces, based upon mutual agreement. Yet some mishaps may possibly occur, depending on time and circumstances. Despite all these, we must not be driven and confused by unreliable rumors and make wrong decisions. Otherwise we would be laughed at by the rest of the world.[15]

Three days later, *Yomiuri Hōchi*, published two relevant articles. One called for calm: there would be no possibility of Allied troops looting or committing crimes of violence against them. Directly below this column, however, they printed an article entitled "Restrain Women from Walking Alone. Let's be Careful Not to Have a Licentious Appearance." This article listed as many as seven important issues that people should always keep in mind when dealing with the Allied soldiers. Item 2 urged people not to flee from homes, as peace and order would be maintained by police and the kempeitai as it always had been. However, items 4 to 7 were all designed to warn Japanese women to keep themselves away from the foreign troops as much as possible. Item 7 particularly warned the women who would have to live near the camps of the occupation troops not to walk alone in a quiet street, even in daytime, let alone in the evening.[16]

Almost every day until August 29, the day after 46 planes of the US advance party arrived at Atsugi airbase on the outskirts of Tokyo, almost all major Japanese newspapers ran such ambivalent and sometimes clearly contradictory articles on the same page. This fact is indicative of the situation at the time, in which the Japanese government somehow tried to persuade the populace to keep calm by influencing media publications, yet the press itself was extremely skeptical about the government view. It also showed that the government's wartime power to tightly control the press was rapidly diminishing.

Not surprisingly, these newspaper articles failed to reassure people that the Allied troops would not misbehave or commit serious crimes against Japanese citizens, in particular against young women. Some neighborhood associations in Tokyo circulated a notice warning female residents not to go out for a period after the landing of the Allied forces. It also instructed women, if they had to go out for some reason, to put on two or three pairs of underwear under *monpe* (women's work-pants).[17]

Indeed, political leaders and government bureaucrats themselves were far from confident that the Allied troops would behave decently. As we will see in more detail later, on August 21, less than a week after the announcement of Japan's surrender, Prime Minister Prince Higashikuni Naruhiko and his cabinet members held a meeting to discuss ways of dealing with the anticipated problems of "mass rape" by the Allied occupation forces. Along with the military leaders, they had been responsible for promoting wartime propaganda against the US in which Americans' proclivities to commit heinous crimes, such as rape and massacre, had been strongly emphasized. As a result of this mass indoctrination, it was a common belief of ordinary Japanese people during and immediately after the war that women would be raped and men would be massacred by the US soldiers if they surrendered or were captured alive. The most telling evidence for how deeply and widely this indoctrination had permeated into Japanese popular thought can be found in the historical fact that a large number of Okinawan civilians during the Battle of Okinawa committed group suicide in the caves in which they were hiding, having convinced themselves that they were going to be raped and massacred sooner or later.

In some sense it is therefore ironic that the Japanese Imperial Government, which had been guilty of creating this popular image of the enemy soldiers, suddenly instructed the Japanese people not to fear the US soldiers who were coming to Japan as an occupation force. A further irony is that they did so despite of their own fears of widespread misconduct by US troops. Beneath their anxiety undoubtedly lay one key factor – their acute awareness of the fact that their own soldiers had committed numerous crimes against civilians in many occupied territories during the war, most notably the case of the "Rape of Nanjing" in 1937, but numerous other instances throughout areas of Japanese occupation. They must have felt that this time their own women might become victims of military sexual violence.

Official reports on sexual violence committed by the occupation forces against Japanese women

The full-scale advance of US occupation forces began on August 30. From 6:00 am, every three minutes, a US troop transport plane landed at Atsugi airport, bringing a total of 4,200 airborne troops in that day alone. At 2:00 pm General MacArthur flew into Atsugi in his special C-54 plane, named "Bataan." The previous day about 380 ships (including 15 British ships) led by Admiral Chester Nimitz entered Tokyo Bay. From early morning of the following day, troops started landing at the port of Yokosuka. By 3:00 pm about 7,500 marines (including 450 British Navy staff) had landed.[18] The large influx of US troops continued for several months. By early December 1945 more than 430,000 US troops were stationed throughout Japan from Hokkaido to Kyushu. By then, 85,037 US troops had been stationed in Kanagawa prefecture, where Yokosuka, Yokohama, and Atsugi were located; in Tokyo, there were 33,890 US soldiers; in Aichi prefecture, of which Nagoya is the prefectural capital, there were 32,320; in Hokkaido, 20,241.[19]

The mass rape and murder of civilians, like that committed by Japanese army troops in Nanjing in December 1937 (and that the Japanese political leaders and civilians feared would occur when the Allied troops landed), did not take place. However, rape and other crimes committed by US soldiers were rampant from the first day of the occupation.

Japanese police intelligence reports compiled by the Police and Security Bureau of the Ministry of Home Affairs contain statistical data on crimes committed by Allied soldiers against Japanese civilians in Kanagawa prefecture.[20]

Plate 5.2 General MacArthur arrived at Atsugi airport in his special plane "Bataan" on August 30, 1945.
Source: Australian War Memorial, transparency number P0633/03/02

According to this data, on August 30, two rape cases were reported, together with one case of kidnapping, one case of bodily harm, one act of violence, and 197 cases of extortion. On August 31, one rape case and 212 cases of extortion were reported. The record for September 1 shows 12 rape cases, one case of bodily harm and 75 extortion cases. Almost every day from August 30 till mid-September, rape, bodily harm, extortion, burglary, and murder were reported. According to this data, the number of reported criminal cases committed by the occupation troops in Kanagawa sharply declined from September 19. It is not certain whether this is due to the fact that the Japanese victims gave up reporting to the police because they soon found that their police had no power to investigate the cases, let alone arrest the American perpetrators, or because the US soldiers' conduct improved. Probably both factors contributed to the decrease.

The source of information for the above-mentioned statistics is not clear, although it is presumed to be the Central Police Office of Kanagawa prefecture. According to the official published history of the Kanagawa prefectural police, 1,900 criminal cases were reported to the police by the end of January 1946. Among them were 58 rape cases.[21] However, these official figures hardly reflect the reality of the time. The real situation was far worse than this data indicates. Due to the chaotic circumstances of immediate postwar society, communications between different levels of the police force were extremely poor. And the methods used to collect accurate data were not well established.

Thus, internal information available from the Central Liaison Office (CLO), for example, offers quite a different picture. The CLO was established by the Japanese government on August 26, 1945, as a body attached to the Ministry of Foreign Affairs.[22] Its function was to liaise with the GHQ of the Allied occupation forces. According to a document that the Yokohama city police office submitted directly to the CLO, 957 crimes committed by GIs were reported in Yokohama city alone during one month between the beginning of September and the beginning of October, 1945. Among them were 119 rape cases.[23] As rape victims were usually extremely reluctant to report to the police, the real number of rape cases was probably several times greater than the official figures.

Many of the extortion cases involved attempts by GIs to steal sabres and pistols from Japanese policemen. In some cases a small group of GIs surrounded a few policemen on patrol in the street or on duty in a police box and forced them to hand over their weapons.[24] It seems that many GIs wanted to take these arms back home as "spoils of war." Some of these extorted pistols were also used later in burglaries of Japanese homes and shops.

Many privately owned and public cars and trucks were also extorted. For example, in Yokohama city alone, at least 32 vehicles were extorted within one month of the Allied landing.[25] One day, when a US soldier demanded that a Japanese civilian in Yokohama "lend" him a car, the Japanese man asked the soldier to write a letter guaranteeing that he would return the car. The following is what he wrote:

> One car (Buick)
> Model "1930". To be used by the U.S. Gov. for purpose of transporting high ranking officers on official business. After all who won the war, you or me? This certifies that *this car is to be used to pick up any girls who fuck*, and further more who cares what the hell is it to you.
> G. I. Johpha (signed)
> 17-fort [sic] soldiers of the winning army, U.S.A.
> on this date 19. Sept. 1945.[26]
>
> [Emphasis added]

Indeed, some of these vehicles were used for kidnapping and raping young women and for transporting goods (particularly, beer and *sake*) extorted from shops and storage.[27] Stolen vehicles made it difficult for the authorities to find the GIs involved in such crimes, and the Japanese police were helpless to intervene in such cases anyway.

Let us examine more closely the sexual violence against Japanese women that GIs committed in the first several weeks of the occupation. As far as the major official reports on crime committed by the Allied occupation troops are concerned, I have so far found four groups of documents. The first is a series of secret daily reports that the Governor of Kanagawa prefecture, Fujiwara Takao, submitted

Plate 5.3 A group of Japanese policemen in Yokohama in September 1945. Japanese policemen were often harassed by the members of the Allied occupation troops.
Source: Australian War Memorial, transparency number OG3439

to the Minister of Home Affairs, Yamazaki Iwao.[28] Although these reports do not specify the sources of information, it is almost certain that information was gathered by the Central Police Office of Kanagawa prefecture. Second is the above-mentioned series of secret reports entitled *Chian Jōsei* (Conditions of Public Peace and Order) prepared by the Headquarters of the kempeitai.[29] The information in this case was provided by various regional offices of the kempeitai throughout Japan. Third are the letters and radio messages from the CLO addressed to the GHQ, complaining about various crimes committed by the US occupation troops, which include the details of some crime cases.[30] In addition to these groups of documents, there are reports prepared by the Police and Security Bureau of the Ministry of Home Affairs.[31] These last reports include the documents collected and analyzed by Tokkō, the notorious Special Intelligence Police, which was the Japanese equivalent of the Gestapo during the war.

As mentioned above, two rape cases were reported in Yokosuka on August 30, the day that the US marines landed there. At about 11:00 am, only a few hours after the landing began and three hours before General MacArthur stepped out of his plane at Atsugi airport, two marines on an "inspection tour" entered a civilian house in Yokosuka, and raped a 36-year-old mother and her 17-year-old daughter at gunpoint.[32] About 6:00 pm that day, two other marines entered another home in Asahi-chō and found a housemaid at home alone. While one of the marines was on watch at the door, the other made lewd gestures and tried to grab her. In fear she fled upstairs. The marines followed and raped her in turn in a small room upstairs.[33]

On August 31, a US Marine advance party landed at Tateyama in Chiba prefecture. Three days later the US occupation forces to be stationed in Chiba arrived there under the command of General A. Cunningham. On September 1, many small groups of marines from this advance party visited villages nearby and entered some public buildings and private houses, claiming that they were conducting "inspections." The following are some of the incidents that occurred at that time and were eventually reported to the Adjutant General's Office of the GHQ through the CLO:

1   Around 12:30 am on September 1, three American soldiers intruded in to the house of Mr. B. I., [the details of the address], Awa district in Chiba prefecture. These intruders showed something like a ten yen bank note to the housewife N., 28 years old and claimed intimacy to her by making gestures while upon receiving her flat refusal they brought her to the inner room and raped her in succession.
2   At about 2:00 pm the same day another four American soldiers intruded into the house of Mr. A. T., [the details of the address], the same village. They threatened the wife, T. aged 30 as well as his mother and then chased the three to the next room and one of the Americans violated T. in the first place. But at that time another three American soldiers entered the same house. They withdrew from the house without attaining their intended purposes satisfactorily.
3   At the same hour on that day seven American soldiers while ransacking the village office in Nishiki village, resorted to indecent acts such as touching breasts of the girl clerks or rubbing their cheeks.
4   Another several Americans resorted to the same acts to the girl clerks in the post office located in the same village.[34]

In addition to these cases, six cases of attempted rape, one case of kidnapping, three cases of indecent acts, six cases of extortion and 16 cases of house-breaking were reported on the same day in this area.[35] In this instance GIs committed rape in a fishing village during the day when most elderly men of the community were at sea fishing. There were very few young men in the village, as they had been conscripted to the Japanese military forces.[36] However, as we will see later, the presence of men at home did not guarantee the safety of women.

One aspect of the above-mentioned first rape case is that the woman was offered "something like a ten yen bank note." It seems that this refers to the currency known as B-Yen notes, distributed by the US forces to their members before the landing. At the request of the Japanese government, the use of this military currency was banned by the GHQ on September 3.[37] It is interesting to note that there were many rape cases in which perpetrators first offered a woman a small gift, such as a handkerchief, candy, chewing gum, chocolate, or cigarettes, and, when the offer was refused, they resorted to violence. Sometimes they were holding a gun when offering such gifts, thus forcing the victim to "consent." For example, on September 9, a 14-year-old girl living near Tachikawa air base was suddenly confronted by a naked GI in the backyard of her own house. Holding a gun, he offered her candy and demanded she perform oral sex.[38]

As US troop "inspections" became more frequent, cases of kidnapping young women for purposes of gang rape occurred. The following is the first reported case of this kind:

> About 6 o'clock, in the afternoon of September 1st, two American soldiers in a truck forced two Japanese to guide them around the Yokohama city. When they came to Shojikiro, at Eirakucho, Naka-ku they forced Miss K. Y., aged 24, a maidservant, to board the truck against her will and absconded to the US Barracks in Nogeyama Park. There altogether 27 of the American soldiers violated her in turn and rendered her unconscious, though she later recovered her consciousness through the care of some other American soldiers and was sent home on September 2nd.[39]

In another abduction case, at about 3:30 pm on September 2, a policeman and some civilians walking down a street in Isogo ward, Yokohama city, saw a woman in her thirties who was madly crying for help in a car driven by a GI. Another GI was in the car, too. Neither the policeman nor the civilians could do anything to rescue her.[40]

At around 6:00 pm on September 4, a 28-year-old married woman was walking in a street in Yokosuka city on the way home from the funeral of an acquaintance. She was escorted by a male friend. Two GIs in a truck ordered her at gunpoint to get into the vehicle. The man escorting her insisted that he should go too and the GIs agreed. However, when the truck was several blocks away, the GIs forced the man to get out and drove away with the woman.[41]

On September 5, at about 4:30 pm, two GIs forced a 23-year-old woman, Hosono Mieko, to get into their car in the street near Ashina Bridge in Yokohama. As they drove away she desperately tried to escape but the car was going too fast. However, when the car slowed down at a crossroads, she jumped out of the car and escaped.[42]

There are many other similar cases in Yokosuka and Yokohama. Cases arose in Tokyo, too, as the US troops moved into the metropolitan areas from September 8. As already mentioned, many of the vehicles used by GIs for this purpose were stolen, making it difficult to find out to which unit the soldiers belonged.[43]

It was not just healthy young women who fell victim to GIs sexual violence. Some sick and retarded women were also violated. For example, on September 9, two American soldiers guided by a Japanese man came to the house of Mr. K. T. in a village near Atsugi airbase. They asked to exchange a packet of their cigarettes for 10 onions. K. T. accepted this barter. However, at around 4:00 pm on the same day, these soldiers, then heavily intoxicated, returned and gang-raped K. T.'s sister, a 47-year-old woman, who was in bed suffering from spinal caries.[44] It seems that the purpose of their first visit was not to obtain onions but to find out whether any women were at home. On September 26, a 26 year-old, mentally handicapped woman was gang-raped by five GIs in Yokohama. One of the GIs took a photo of this woman's vagina after they raped her. This was witnessed by an 11 year-old boy.[45]

From mid-September, reported cases of attempted rape at night increased in the area near the base camps of the Allied troops. In many of these cases, small groups of GIs would intrude into a Japanese civilian house while the family members were asleep to rape the women. Typically, while a few of the soldiers were inside the premises, others were on watch outside the house. If any family members dashed out of the house to call for help, the men on watch would grab and beat them.

For example, at around, 1:30 am on September 16, an American soldier entered the house of the Hayakawa family in Fujisawa city, Kanagawa prefecture. Only the mother and her 21-year-old daughter were at home at the time, sleeping in the same room. As the mother was struggling to prevent the soldier from attacking her daughter, the daughter managed to run outside, calling for help. She was grabbed by three other soldiers at the door and was severely punched in the face and jaw. Her clothes were ripped off and she was almost raped. Luckily, policemen were on patrol nearby and the GIs ran away after the mother struggled free and called for help.[46]

At around 2:00 am on September 25, three soldiers entered the house of Mr. Yamamoto Umekichi in Hiratsuka city, Kanagawa prefecture. Umekichi, his wife, Takiko, and his 18-year-old daughter, Yuriko, were all asleep. One other soldier was on watch outside the house, holding a gun. Both Umekichi and Takiko tried to protect their daughter, but were severely beaten by the men. However, all three kept screaming and calling for help. Neighbors awoke and came out of their houses, causing the four soldiers to run away without harming Yuriko.[47] In this case, too, it seems almost certain that the GIs had found out beforehand where young women were living, possibly while on a daytime "inspection tour."

A number of similar cases appeared in the official reports. All were cases of *attempted* rape. No actual rape cases are found in these documents. However, according to various unofficial information, it seems that many women were victims of rape, but their families decided not to report it to the police or to tell their neighbors about their "family tragedy."

For example, according to the testimony of Sugita Tomoe (pseudonym), one night two drunken GIs barged into her house on the outskirts of Tokyo at around 10:00 pm. They threatened her father with a knife and demanded money. Once they got the money, they bound her father to a pillar and raped her mother. While the mother was being attacked, Tomoe and her 15-year-old sister, Naoko, were too terrified to move or call for help. After the soldiers had raped the mother they bound her to the same pillar and proceeded to rape Tomoe and Naoko in front of their parents. Naoko died from blood loss. Her father later reported Naoko's death to the police station, but he falsely testified that Tomoe and her mother had run out of the house and that only Naoko had been raped. Two policemen and a doctor came to the house and took evidence, but that was the only time that police contacted them about the matter.[48]

The fact that rape and other crimes were committed by US troops from the very beginning of the occupation is also confirmed by the diary of General R. L. Eichelberger, the commander of the 8th Army. On September 2, immediately after the surrender ceremony on the *Missouri*, Eichelberger "received an order to report to the Chief [General MacArthur]"[49] at 5:00 pm that evening. He wondered what MacArthur wanted. The following sentences in his diary clarify the topic of the meeting:

> At 1700 I was called to General MacArthur's quarters for a conference concerning some reported rape cases on the part of Marines. There are also reports of some "acting up" on the part of 11th Airborne troops . . .[50]

It is interesting to note that the subject of the very first meeting between the top two military men of the US occupation forces immediately after the surrender ceremony was neither "the democratization of Japan" nor "the future status of Emperor Hirohito," but "rape by Marines."

The following record in his diary of September 3 also indicates that the crimes committed by the men under his command were already a serious issue:

> In the evening General Hall, General Swing and a representative from the 1st Cavalry Division met with me to discuss the actions of our soldiers in Japan. We have had assault cases reported and a stern directive was given

Plate 5.4 Commander US 8th Army, R. L. Eichelberger (centre), together with General MacArthur (right) and H. Robertson, Commander-in-Chief of BCOF (left), watching the parade past the reviewing stand to celebrate US Independence Day at the Japanese Imperial Plaza in Tokyo, on July 4, 1948.
Source: Australian War Memorial, transparency number 145602

to everyone concerned that rowdyism, looting and vandalism would not be tolerated.[51]

Almost every day from early September, the Japanese government officially complained to GHQ, through the CLO, about numerous crimes that the US occupation troops were committing against Japanese civilians and public servants, in particular policemen. The CLO reported the details of the serious crime cases to GHQ and kept requesting that it take strict measures to prevent the recurrence of such incidents.[52] In response to these continuing complaints, GHQ asked the Japanese authorities to provide more detailed information on offenders, claiming that the Japanese victims should be able to identify any offenders by the mark on the shoulder straps of their uniforms.[53] Thus, on September 4, some newspapers published the pictures of the US shoulder marks together with an article encouraging local people to strengthen the neighborhood associations' activities in order to protect themselves.[54]

At the same time, on September 4, the Japanese government instructed the Kanagawa prefectural government to allow schoolgirls and female college students, particularly those from schools near the Allied bases, to stay at home and study by themselves until conditions improved. The girls were also instructed not to go out of their homes alone. These instructions were also publicized in the major newspapers on September 5.[55] According to the *Asahi Shimbun*, on that day the 8th Army instructed all its troops that they had to obtain a leave slip if they were going outside the permitted areas and told them that military police would conduct random inspections of soldiers' leave slips on the street.[56] On September 15, the *Yomiuri Hōchi* newspaper reported that, as the result of a request from the Metropolitan Police Office, 5,000 MPs had been mobilized in Tokyo in order to suppress US soldiers' criminal activities.[57]

On September 27, GHQ further asked the Japanese government to ensure that any report of criminal offences committed by soldiers be accompanied by some clue to identify the criminal.[58] However, it was quite difficult for ordinary Japanese people to describe the particular features of the US soldiers (who wore the same uniforms), let alone to quickly identify and memorize a shoulder mark while being subjected to physical threat. It seems that this request by GHQ also contributed to discouraging victims from reporting to police.

One GHQ report on crimes committed by US troops in Tokyo between October 4 and November 17, says that "of approximately 100 reported cases of rape of Japanese women by US servicemen, only six have been substantiated." As evidence could be provided for only six cases, the author of this report proudly claimed that these figures reflected "the absence of serious crime waves" in Tokyo for this period.[59]

Yet there is no doubt that newspaper reports on the increasing number of crimes committed by the occupation forces upset GHQ staff considerably. On September 19, the Office of Supreme Commander of the Allied Power (SCAP) issued a memorandum on the "press code for Japan"[60] and started controlling press reports by introducing post-censorship. This "press code" had ten Articles, including the following one:

4   There shall be no destructive criticism of the Allied Forces of Occupation and nothing which might invite mistrust or resentment of the troops.

As a result, the *Asahi Shimbun* was not permitted to distribute its papers for a couple of days between September 19 and 20. From September 22, similar regulations were applied to radio broadcasts. From October 8 pre-censorship was applied to all articles published in five major newspapers. From January 1946, pre-censorship was extended to the publication of journals and magazines, and to the content of films and theatrical plays. This censorship was introduced not only to suppress any information on crimes committed by the occupation troops, but also for many other purposes, such as information about the effects of the A-bombs dropped on Hiroshima and Nagasaki.[61] The tight control on information about the increasing number of crimes committed by GIs against Japanese civilians was undoubtedly one of the important roles that this censorship was expected to play.

Therefore, news reports of crimes committed by the occupation forces vanished from newspapers after September 19. After that, we see only articles applauding Americans such as a long article entitled "the Essence of American Democracy"[62] published in *Yomiuri Hōchi* on September 23, and an article about a US medical officer who saved the life of a sick Japanese girl, which appeared in the *Asahi Shimbun* on September 26.[63]

Unfortunately, the most informative official reports, such as the kempeitai's secret reports, *Chian Jōsei*, and the reports prepared by the Police and Security Bureau of the Ministry of Home Affairs, including the documents that Tokkō prepared, cover only the first several weeks of the occupation.[64] Thus, we do not have comprehensive official documents which could reveal the full extent of sexual violence committed by the US occupation troops against Japanese women.

However, according to statistical data compiled by the Metropolitan Police Office, the following numbers of rape and attempted rape by GIs in the Tokyo and Kanagawa areas were reported to police between March and September 1946:[65]

Table 5.1 Reported cases of rape and attempted rape in the Tokyo and Kanagawa areas, March–September 1946

Month	Reported cases	
	Rape	*Attempted rape*
March	15	10
April	15	20
May	35	30
June	30	30
July	20	20
August	30	30
September	20	25

These figures, which record only a small fraction of cases of rape and attempted rape, indicate that, even a year after the beginning of the occupation, GI rape was still a serious problem for Japanese women.

In addition to the US forces, the BCOF (British Commonwealth Occupation Forces) also participated in the occupation of Japan from early February 1946. The advance party of the BCOF, sent from Hong Kong, arrived at Kure, the port of Hiroshima, on January 31, 1946. On February 13, 1,000 Australian troops landed at Kure. By June the numbers of the BCOF had increased to 39,000. They were composed of British, Australian, New Zealand, and Indian soldiers. The largest group was 12,000 Australians – 32 percent of the BCOF. The BCOF was stationed in the Chugoku area of Honshu Island and on Shikoku Island. They functioned as the supplementary troops for the US forces. The bulk of the troops, however, were concentrated in Kure and Fukuyama of Hiroshima prefecture.[66]

According to statistical data compiled by the Hiroshima prefectural police office, 263 crimes by occupation forces were reported to police in the prefecture between October and December 1945. Among them were 84 rape cases. As these crimes were committed before the BCOF's arrival, it is presumed that the offenders were mostly Americans. In 1946, 800 crimes were reported, of which 303 were rape cases – the single most common crime, consisting 38 percent of the total crime cases reported to the police. This figure is twice the rate of the second-most-common crime – extortion.[67] Most of these crimes are believed to have been committed by members of the BCOF because the majority of the US occupation troops had left Hiroshima prior to the BCOF's landing.

Unfortunately, unlike the cases in the Tokyo and Kanagawa areas, detailed official reports on individual cases of sexual crimes committed by the Allied soldiers in Hiroshima prefecture are not available. However, in his memoirs, Allen Clifton elaborates upon some cases that he investigated during the occupation. Clifton was a young Australian junior officer of the BCOF who acted as an interpreter and criminal investigator. The following passages are some extracts from his memoirs:

> I stood beside a bed in a hospital. On it lay a girl, unconscious, her long, black hair in a wild tumult on the pillow. A doctor and two nurses were working to revive her. An hour before she had been raped by twenty soldiers. We found her where they had left her, on a piece of waste land. The hospital was in Hiroshima. The girl was Japanese. The soldiers were Australians.
>
> The moaning and wailing had ceased and she was quiet now. The tortured tension on her face had slipped away, and the soft brown skin was smooth and unwrinkled, stained with tears like the face of a child that has cried itself to sleep.
>
> Staying indoors was not sufficient to give women protection. One evening a young married woman was reading a book in bed in a hotel. Her husband was absent for the night on business. In the next room, separated only by

the paper sliding partitions, a party of Japanese men were playing cards. It was a hot night and she fell asleep in the middle of her reading, with the light still burning. She awoke a little later to find a huge Australian soldier kneeling beside her, and another swaying in the doorway, his drunken leer telling more clearly than any speech or gesture what was to follow . . .

The men in the next room heard and watched; saw all and did not intervene. To call them cowards would be to presume the obvious and improbable. The reason lay elsewhere: in their blind unquestioning acceptance of instructions from the Government that placed the Shinchugun [occupation forces] beyond criticism and Japanese justice . . .

Instead the Japanese went and told the police. The police, having no power, could do no more than inform us, when it was too late . . .

At the Court Martial that followed, the accused was found guilty and sentenced to ten years' penal servitude. In accordance with army law the court's decision was forwarded to Australia for confirmation. Some time later the documents were returned marked "Conviction quashed because of insufficient evidence."[68]

Testimonies of victims of sexual violence committed by the occupation troops

The official documents conceal important dimensions of how sexual violence was committed by the occupation troops. Rape of Japanese women took various forms. It is necessary to closely examine first-hand testimonies of the victims of sexual crimes in order to understand the nature of the crimes committed.

A number of Japanese publications on this subject were published between the late 1940s and early 1950s – shortly after the Press Code by GHQ was removed. Among those publications, the most reliable are *Nippon no Teisō* (Japan's Virtue), published in 1947, and *Kuroi Haru* (Black Spring), published in 1953. Both include a number of first-hand testimonies of victims of sexual violence committed by GIs.

According to some testimonies, members of the military police, who were supposed to be responsible for investigating rape cases and arresting rapist soldiers, themselves sometimes raped Japanese women. One woman, Ono Toshiko (pseudonym), states in her testimony that she was a victim of rape by three military policemen in Kyoto. Shortly after Toshiko's parents were killed in the firebombing of Tokyo in March 1945, she moved to Kyoto to live with her aunt's family. She continued to live there after the war as she had nowhere else to go.[69]

She does not give an exact date when it happened, but one evening a Japanese police officer came to see Toshiko and informed her that the military police were investigating her on suspicion of illegal possession of US military goods.[70] Stealing of military goods by GIs was rampant in the early period of the occupation. Goods such as tinned food, blankets, and clothes were stolen from the base stores or from trucks and freight trains while in transit from one place to another. They were then sold to Japanese black-market brokers, who in turn sold them to black market dealers.[71] Many Japanese bought these items at high prices, given the acute shortage of essential goods at that time. The military police arrested GIs involved in stealing large quantities of military goods and also arrested black-market brokers, who operated the business widely, but they rarely arrested individuals who had purchased items at black-market stalls. Given that the Japanese police were aware of the US military police policy towards individuals accused of purchasing stolen goods, the Japanese officer must have suspected the military policemen's real intentions. However, he probably could have done nothing but obey their orders.

The police officer took Toshiko to the three military policemen, who were waiting for her in an army jeep outside her aunt's house. Leaving the Japanese policeman behind, they took her a long way out of the city and repeatedly gang-raped her until midnight. When they had finished, one of them offered her a cigarette, which she refused. Becoming angry, the military policemen stuck the cigarette butt on her stomach and left her alone in the bush.[72]

According to various other testimonies, it seems that rape by members of the military police was far from rare. There is even testimony that one military policemen, who interviewed a rape victim in order to collect evidence, later returned and raped her.[73] One Japanese policeman complained to a Japanese interpreter employed by the US occupation troops that if the police reported a rape case to the military police they usually showed very little interest. On the other hand, they would immediately investigate other crimes, such as arson.[74] In rape cases which implicated members of the military police, victims had no-where to go because the Japanese police had no power to interrogate American suspects.[75] It is very difficult to determine the prevalence of rape by military police as there are very few official documents about the problem – either on the Japanese side or on the US side.

Another type of rape which is missing in the official documents, but which is confirmed by testimonies of many victims, is the rape of young Japanese women employed at various offices of the occupation forces. Each military base employed numerous women as telephone operators, typists, and in other office work. Newly recruited Japanese women were often subjected to rape by occupation soldiers and officers. In other cases women were deceived into having sexual relationships on false promises of marriage.

A woman under the pseudonym of Kawabe Satoko was employed as a tele-phone operator at a US occupation base near her home. Within a few weeks of being employed she found out that many of her colleagues had been raped by GIs, especially during night-shift work. She was surprised to learn that some perpetrators offered tinned food to their victims as a token gesture of apology. Perhaps the GIs thought that this changed their actions from rape into commer-cial sex, i.e. the familiar transaction of prostitution except for the fact that it was paid for with goods, not money. Some victims reported such incidents to the local police office only to be told by the police that it was their own fault and to be careful to avoid being raped.[76]

Shortly after starting work, Satoko became friendly with a sergeant, her super-visor, who was particularly kind to her and who always tried to protect her. After

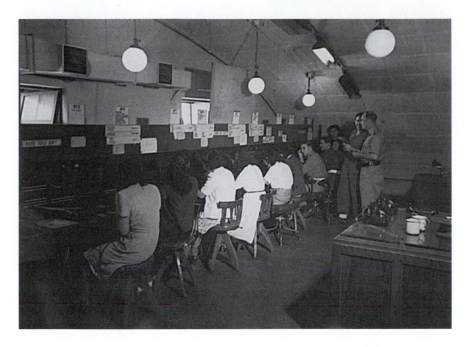

Plate 5.5 Japanese young women working as telephone operators at the headquarters
Signal Regiment, BCOF in Kure in September 1948. Many Japanese employees
of the occupation forces were victims of sexual harassment.
Source: Australian War Memorial, transparency number 145831

about a month the sergeant took her in his car on a picnic during a day off. He
stopped the car in a forest and raped her. He kept promising that he would
marry her in the near future, and continued the relationship. Eventually, however,
she was fired.[77]

Another woman, Hamada Mieko (pseudonym), worked as a typist in a ware-
house office at one of the US bases. One evening GIs at her office held a farewell
party for one of their colleagues who was going back to the US. The Japanese
staff were also invited. When Mieko went to the restaurant where the party was
held she was surprised to find a musical band and two striptease artists. Before
long the GIs became drunk and started frolicking with the strippers. While this
spree was going on, the GIs made her and other Japanese staff drink. When the
striptease show finished, the GIs started dancing with Japanese women, touching
their hips and thighs and kissing them. Feeling nauseous, after drinking more
alcohol than she was used to, Mieko decided to go home. An officer named
Major Wilson offered to take her home. She accepted this offer and got into his
car. Wilson took her to a barley field far from town and raped her in the car.
Eventually he left her at a nearby railway station.[78]

Mieko did not go to the office for the following four days. However, she
eventually decided to return to work, blaming herself over her carelessness that

invited Wilson's misbehaviour. Just a few days after returning to work, another GI raped her in the office. It took place when she was working overtime and everyone else had gone home. While she was being raped a member of the military police watched through an office window. Far from trying to stop the rape, he said, 'Hey, hey, nice' and disappeared. Indeed, all the other GIs at the same base knew that she had been raped by Wilson.[79] As a result they probably believed that Mieko would consent to having sex with anyone.

There are a number of similar testimonies of women employed by the occupation forces. In fact, according to some Japanese men who worked as interpreters for the occupation troops at various camps, lists of names of officers and junior officers were put up on the wall in the officers' club and in their canteen. Next to each officer's name appeared lip marks signifying how many Japanese women that officer had "conquered."[80]

At Camp Sendai, there were two different kinds of lists. One was similar to the above mentioned officers' lists with "MV" (abbreviation of Military Victory) marks instead of lip marks. The other was a series of pictures of all the female Japanese workers. These pictures were pinned on the wall and above some of the pictures a cross was marked to identify that that woman had lost her virginity. According to Itsushima Tsutomu, one of the former interpreters at this camp, of the 200 photos only about ten photos did not have cross marks; they were all newly employed women. These lists were organized by a group called "Charming Members to Musumesan." This group consisted of about 500 officers, including all the junior officers at the camp. They competed with each other over how many women they had "conquered." GIs called this competition "hunting for moose," punning on the similarity of "musumesan" ("young women" in Japanese) and "moose."[81] Holding parties was only one of their various strategies to create opportunities for them to rape Japanese female workers. According to another former interpreter, he often heard GIs discussing how to take the "virginity" of newly employed women. Indeed, some GIs proudly gave him detailed accounts of the rapes they had committed.[82]

Here we can see a striking similarity between the sexual conduct of these officers of the occupation forces in Japan and a more recent case of the rape ring at the Aberdeen Proving Ground in Maryland, USA. In 1997 it was revealed that some officers and drill sergeants at the Aberdeen Proving Ground played a secret game, competing to have sex with newly arrived female trainees.[83] The difference is that the victims of rape in the latter case were "fellow American soldiers" rather than foreign "employees," and that the rapists in the latter case were court-martialed and in some cases convicted rather than getting away with it, as was the case of the former.

There were also many blurred cases which are difficult to define either as rape or as consensual sex. This is particularly so in the cases of women employed as "maids." For example, in April 1946, Saitō Yūko (pseudonym) became a "maid" at the Officers' Club of Camp Toneyama. At this club, there were about 20 "maids" doing washing, cooking, and cleaning for about 20 junior officers. In other words, each junior officer had his own "maid" who looked after him. In the same building where these officers' individual private rooms were housed, much smaller maid-rooms were also located. Yūko was assigned to look after an officer, First Lieutenant Sallet. The first night she moved into this building, Sallet came into her room and slept with her. In the same camp, there were many individual houses built for married officers, but less than one-third of these houses were occupied by married couples. The remainder were occupied by single officers, each with his own "maid." About a month after Yūko had started work at the club, Sallet left for the US and she was fired. Several months later she gave birth to a mixed-race child.[84]

Kitabayashi Yoshiko worked for a couple of months from April 1946 as a typist at one of the base camps of the US occupation forces in Kanagawa prefecture. Among the typists and "maids" working at the camp were many women from Nagoya. The women had come from Nagoya when the men of the unit had been transferred to Kanagawa. The women totally depended on the US troops for meals and income; they had become virtual "camp followers."[85]

With reference to a couple of the cases above, one may question why a woman would return to an office after she had been sexually abused by one of the staff there, or why a woman would continue to consent to sex with an officer because he had forced her to sleep with him the first time. To understand the patterns of rape and sexual exploitation in the early occupation of Japan, it must be remembered that the economic conditions in immediate postwar Japan were appalling and most Japanese civilians were desperately struggling to survive from day to day. Many families lost their breadwinners – fathers or young able-bodied sons – in the war, leaving mothers or daughters of poverty-stricken families to seek any means to earn a living. In these circumstances, to be employed by the occupation forces was an extremely attractive option. Salaries were relatively high compared to those of ordinary Japanese workers and "free lunch," which was provided, was particularly attractive, given the general food shortage.[86] The following extracts from a letter home from an Australian soldier of the BCOF, who traveled from Hiroshima to Osaka during leave in 1946, clearly illustrate this point:

> Up in Osaka some thousands of people sleep in the enormous central railway station, and each morning half a dozen stiffs are carted off to the potter's field, or its Jap equivalent . . . It is a pathetic sight to see women with breasts little thicker than paper trying to nurse babies who themselves look like skeletons. There is nothing one can do, personally, to alleviate the position. Money wouldn't help because all that one could afford would be a drop in the bucket and the odd scrap of food that one could smuggle from the kitchen would probably be vomited up again . . . I was talking in Osaka to a Christian, English-speaking Jap who is assistant managing editor of the Osaka 'Mainichi', an English language newspaper. He told me that each Jap is allowed 500 yen monthly plus 100 yen for each member of his family. This bloke gets 800 yen. He had that day bought 4 cho (about 10 lbs) of rice which, if spun out, would last the family ten days. And the cost? 400 yen. . . . Until the rice came to light his family had no food for two days.[87]

Plate 5.6 Even in October 1950, five years after the war, widespread poverty was a serious national problem in Japan, as seen in this photo of a group of homeless people gathering in an underground causeway near Ueno Railway Station in Tokyo.
Source: Mainichi Shimbun

We must not forget the economic and social situation in which rape and other forms of sexual abuse of Japanese employees was committed by female workers' "supervisors" and other "employers" of the occupation forces. This sexual abuse suffered by Japanese women at the hands of the occupation troops can be seen as violence on two levels: one being direct physical (military) violence and the other psychological violence, in other words, "economic exploitation." Poverty can be described as one of the worst forms of violence.

The grim reality of this two-tiered violence further unfolds in the next chapter, which examines the historical process of the establishment and expansion of the Japanese sex industry to cater to the demand of the occupation troops in the immediate postwar period.

6 Japanese comfort women for the Allied occupation forces

The Japanese government creates a comfort women system for the occupation forces

In the week following its surrender, and before occupation forces arrived, the Japanese government had discussed ways of dealing with the anticipated problem of sexual violence by occupation forces. On August 21, Prime Minister Prince Higashikuni Naruhiko called a special meeting of several of his ministers. The subject of discussion was the various demands put forward by the Allied forces regarding the actual procedures for ending the war. The details of these demands were brought back by Lieutenant-General Kawanabe Torashirō, an envoy extraordinary, who had just returned to Tokyo that morning from a meeting with the military commanders of the Allied forces in Manila in the Philippines.[1]

At this cabinet meeting, Prince Konoe Fumimaro, then Deputy Prime Minister, who had served as Prime Minister three times during the Asia-Pacific War, expressed grave concern about the possibility of "mass rape" of Japanese women by Allied troops. He suggested setting up a comfort women system to protect Japanese women and girls. The suggestion seemed to come out of his anxiety over the possibility of "mass rape" such as that committed by Japanese troops against civilians in occupied territories during the war.[2] It was during Konoe's first term as Prime Minister that Japanese troops committed mass rape in Nanjing city – the so-called "Rape of Nanjing."

Lieutenant-General Kawanabe by contrast praised the strict morals of the Allied forces. He told the cabinet members that the Allies probably would not accept a scheme of military-controlled prostitution, even if offered by the Japanese.[3] However, after a long discussion, Konoe's proposal was endorsed by the attending cabinet members. In fact, the government had already taken the first step towards establishing such a system four days earlier – the day that Prince Higashikuni formed the new government. This comfort women scheme was probably initiated by Konoe, together with Prime Minister Higashikuni and the Minister of Home Affairs, Yamazaki Iwao, without consulting other cabinet members, as it was regarded an urgent matter.

On August 18, the Police and Security Department of the Ministry of Home Affairs telegraphed the following instructions to the governors and police chiefs of all prefectures:

With regard to the comfort facilities in areas where the foreign troops are going to be stationed:

In the areas where foreign troops will be stationed, the establishment of comfort facilities are necessary as outlined in the following separate notation. As the handling of this matter requires circumspection, please take every possible precaution by paying attention particularly to the following items.

1   It is still beyond speculation where the foreign troops will be stationed and when they will arrive. Therefore, do not cause public unrest by forming a hasty conclusion that it is inevitable for those troops to advance to your prefecture.
2   Make preparation of such facilities now confidentially as their prompt establishment is required in the case of the troops' station, but ensure that the information not be revealed to the outside.
3   In carrying out this plan, avoid arousing misunderstanding among local people by explaining to them that this scheme will be implemented for the purpose of protecting Japanese citizens.

[Separate Notation]
The outline of the preparation for the establishment of comfort facilities for the foreign troops:

1   Allow the business for the foreign troops within limited quarters, regardless of existing regulations of control.
2   The above-mentioned limited quarters should be determined by the [prefectural] police chief, and prohibit Japanese subjects from using the facilities.
3   The police chief should actively give guidance in management of the following facilities and promote their rapid expansion.
    •   Sexual comfort facilities
    •   Eating and drinking facilities
    •   Recreation centres
4   Recruit the women required for the business from geisha, licensed and unlicensed prostitutes, waitresses, barmaids, habitual illicit prostitutes and the like.[4]

Before and during the war, Japan had a licensed prostitution system under which the Metropolitan Police Headquarters in Tokyo and each prefectural police division had the authority to regulate prostitution in its own area by issuing licences to brothel owners and prostitutes and at the same time suppressing unlicensed prostitution. The above-mentioned document, therefore, clearly indicates that prefectural police chiefs were now instructed to recruit unlicensed prostitutes rather than cracking down on their clandestine business. Towards the end of the Pacific War, due to the government policy of promoting nationwide sumptuary regulations, each prefectural police division was not only tightening the control of clandestine operations but also encouraging licensed brothel owners and prostitutes to change their occupations. Yet, just three days after Japan's surrender, they were told the opposite – to secure enough comfort women for the expected Allied troops.

The reaction of each prefectural police division to this government instruction can be found in the official history of various prefectural police forces.[5]

In Hokkaido,

> the recruitment [of comfort women] was carried out mainly through labor brokers, but as it was a matter of great account, police officers were also directly engaged in this task. In other words, officers checked the names and addresses of former licensed prostitutes from the list held in the police stations, visited the villages in the mountain and seacoast areas where these women lived, gave them blankets, socks and sugar, and asked their cooperation by persuading them to work again for the sake of the nation and for the [safety] of the Japanese people.[6]

By early October, more than 320 former prostitutes, as well as more than 450 working prostitutes were mobilized as comfort women in Hokkaido. The author of the official history of the Hokkaido police proudly stated:

> Thus the special comfort stations for the occupation troops, set up as an emergency measure, was utilized to maximum degree, and the number of women victims of [sexual violence committed by the occupation troops] in the general population was therefore kept to the minimum.[7]

The Hokkaido police were also involved in setting up "beer halls" (i.e. bars), restaurants and dance halls for the occupation troops. The total number of women employed at these facilities, including comfort women, was 2,391.[8]

In Akita and Toyama prefectures the police had difficulty in securing enough comfort women within their own districts. Thus, in Akita, in collaboration with the police force, some staff members of the public relations department of the prefectural government were dispatched to neighboring Aomori and Iwate prefectures to recruit women there.[9] In Toyama, the prefectural police office assisted the labor brokers to recruit women from Kyoto and Osaka. By the end of October, when the occupation troops arrived in Toyama, 251 "restaurants," each staffed with about 50 comfort women, had been set up in various places in the prefecture.[10] In the Tsuchiura district of Ibaragi prefecture, no appropriate building could be found for use as a comfort station. Thus, as a last resort, the chief of the Tsuchiura city police station, Superintendent Ikeda Hirohiko, decided to convert the single policemen's dormitory into a comfort station. The dormitory was quickly vacated and renovated, and bedding was brought in from a

Japanese Navy-Air Force compound in Kasumigaura, another city in the same prefecture. This unusual "brothel," made up of police accommodation and navy equipment started its business in late September with 20 comfort women.[11]

In Hyōgo prefecture, 15 officers under the supervision of the chief of the Public Security Section, Okamoto Takeshi, were assigned to set up comfort stations and recruit comfort women. They summoned the representatives of licensed brothels, nightclubs, and restaurant owners in Kobe city, and instructed them to recruit 1,000 comfort women. At the same time they assisted these businessmen to secure several major buildings in the city to convert them into "leisure centres," each of which would accommodate a comfort station, a dance hall, a bar, a cabaret, a coffee shop, a Western-style restaurant, a Japanese/ Chinese restaurant, a games room, and a souvenir shop. Soon five such "leisure centres" were established in Kobe city. The largest among them was set up in the Nishi Nissan-kan Building, where 260 comfort women were employed. Small-scale facilities were also set up in Nishinomiya, Takarazuka, and Himeji as soon as the police authorities found out that occupation troops were due in these cities as well. In total, 1,182 comfort women were mobilized in Hyōgo prefecture by the end of September. According to an official account of the Hyōgo prefectural police office, "all comfort stations were doing a roaring business."[12]

Even in Hiroshima prefecture, where the prefectural capital, Hiroshima city, was completely destroyed by an atomic bomb, the police force made a great effort to find and recruit as many women as possible. However, probably due to post-nuclear chaos, the Hiroshima prefectural police office was a month later than other prefectures in dealing with the matter. On September 20, the police called a meeting of representatives of businessmen from all over the prefecture and asked them to set up comfort stations, promising money and materials. These representatives were also informed that the recruitment of comfort women would be carried out by the police. The initial funding was provided by the prefectural government. With this financial assistance several factories and factory-workers' dormitories in Hiro, Funakoshi, Yoshiura, and Itsukushima were converted to comfort stations.[13] These towns, all some distance from Hiroshima city, had escaped the A-bomb attack.

From September 24, many police officers were mobilized to locate both licensed and unlicensed prostitutes within Hiroshima prefecture and call on them to co-operate. As most of these women were extremely reluctant to work for foreigners, the police had to lure them by guaranteeing – free of charge – sufficient daily food provisions, such as rice, beef, sugar, and cooking oil. This was an extraordinarily attractive offer at a time when the entire population of Japan was suffering from acute food shortages, and malnutrition and starvation were widespread. By the end of September, about 500 women had been recruited and sent into newly established comfort stations. These comfort stations were opened on October 7, the day that the first contingent of the US occupation troops arrived in Hiroshima. According to the official account, "as expected, as soon as they were opened, all comfort stations were crowded with clients" and soon "tickets were issued to the soldiers in order to control their visits." By the end of November, new comfort stations had been set up in Fukuchiyama, Ōtake, Kure, and Edajima as well. By this stage the total number of comfort women had increased to 725.[14]

As it was almost certain that two major ports, Yokosuka and Yokohama, were to be the landing places for the Allied occupation troops, the Kanagawa prefectural police division started organizing facilities immediately on receipt of the government instructions. Yokosuka city had not suffered war damage as badly as some and, being one of the main naval ports, had had a relatively large number of brothels serving the members of the Imperial Naval Force throughout the war. Therefore, it was relatively easy for the police there to organize comfort stations. On August 18, only a few hours after he had received the instruction from the Ministry of Home Affairs, the chief of Yokosuka Police, Yamamoto Yoshiji visited prostitutes in the red-light district of the city and urged them to "contribute to building peace in Japan by softening the American soldiers' wild feeling." A large naval shipyard workers' dormitory with 208 rooms was converted to a comfort station and named Yasu-ura House. About 400 prostitutes were mobilized for Yasu-ura House and a few other facilities.[15]

In Yokohama, on the other hand, the police had difficulty finding enough women. Most prostitutes had left the city due to heavy bombing. The police issued a "free transport pass for public duty" to labor suppliers who travelled to country areas to recruit the women. Police cars were used to transport bedding, blankets, towels, sanitary goods and the like to a newly established comfort station. By the end of August, the police had managed to recruit about 100 women and placed them in a comfort station called Goraku-sō (Mutual Pleasure House), which had been an old apartment-house. On August 30, only a day after the arrival of the US occupation troops in Yokohama, a few thousand GIs had already visited Goraku-so. However, this comfort station was closed one week later after GIs had fought over women and the police had been unable to control them.[16] The official police account suggests a possible link between a lack of comfort women and a higher rate of crimes committed by GIs in Yokohama compared with that in Yokosuka in the early stage of occupation.[17] However, by the end of 1945, nine comfort stations with 355 comfort women were operating – two of them guarded by the military police 24 hours a day.[18]

In almost every prefecture throughout Japan the police played a crucial role in setting up comfort stations and recruiting comfort women to serve the occupation troops. It should be noted that the police were actually breaking the law by introducing unlicensed and illicit prostitutes into the sex industry and by allowing the establishment of comfort stations, which were really special military "brothels" operating without the owners being licensed. Some senior police officers were clearly aware of the fact that their conduct was against the law, made worse by the fact that the instruction had originated from the Police and Security Department of the Ministry of Home Affairs. For example, the above-mentioned Superintendent Ikeda Hirohiko, who converted the single police-men's dormitory into a comfort station in Tsuchiura, looked back on those days by saying that:

Plate 6.1 A large number of US sailors gathering in front of a comfort station, Yasu-ura House, in Yokosuka. Date unknown.
Source: Yokosuka City Council

> Although it was a sort of overstepping the bounds of the Police Act, I thought that, even if I had requested further instructions from Headquarters, I would not have got anything at all. Therefore I made up my mind to deal with the matter by myself, on my own responsibility, without making any queries to my superiors. I was prepared to stand between the occupation forces and the Japanese people for general good in maintaining peace and order, and, if necessary, to bear any reprimand.[19]

Moreover, the official historical account by the police gives the false impression that those recruited as comfort women for the occupation troops were all professional prostitutes, whether licensed or unlicensed. In reality, some non-professional women, notably high-school students who had been put to work in munitions factories towards the end of the war as members of the Women's Volunteer Corps, were recruited. It seems that some *Yakuza* (Japanese mafia) groups, who were closely linked with extreme right-wing, fascist organizations controlled by prominent political fixers such as Kodama Yoshio and Sasagawa Ryōichi, were closely involved in "recruiting" from the Women's Volunteer Corps.

For example, although the war had ended, about 10 high-school students were still staying at a dormitory of one of the arsenals in Kawasaki city in

Plate 6.2 During the war many high-school students were mobilized as members of the Women's Volunteer Corps and worked in munitions factories. After the war, some of those students ended up as comfort women serving the Allied soldiers.
Source: Mainichi Shimbun

Kanagawa prefecture. The students had lost their families due to bombing and had nowhere to go. One day, a certain Yoneyama Saburō came to this dormitory in a truck carrying the sign "Re-born Public Enterprise, Leisure Division." He introduced himself as the Chugoku District Manager of the Peace Maintenance Association, an organization formed by the Ministry of Home Affairs. Yoneyama told these students that they would be drafted into the "special volunteer task." He took them away in the truck.[20] It is almost certain that these girls did not know what sort of "task" they were "volunteering" to carry out.

A dozen high-school students, who were members of the Women's Volunteer Corps, were staying at a dormitory of one of the arsenals in Kure, a major naval port in Hiroshima prefecture. They had become war orphans when, on August 6, 1945, their families had perished and their homes had been destroyed by the atomic bomb. (Shortly after the bombing of Hiroshima, the younger sister of one of the dormitory students, Momoyama Chikako, had made the trip from Hiroshima to Kure on foot, only to fall dead in front of the factory gate on arrival due to radiation exposure.) As the students had nowhere to return to, they stayed at the dormitory, doing domestic work for the factory manager's family. One day, the above-mentioned Yoneyama appeared at the factory, and gave the factory manager several tins of sugar and some packets of foreign-made cigarettes. Then the factory manager took Yoneyama to the dormitory. Yoneyama told the students about a "task" – the same "task" about which he had told the students in Kawasaki. They were put into a truck and taken away. First they were taken into a house in an unknown place where they were gang-raped by a number of GIs, then they were taken by the same truck to a building in another place, where they were again gang-raped by a different group of GIs. Eventually they were taken to a comfort station and attended by a medic of the occupation troops. A few days later all were found to be infected with V.D.[21]

Very little information is available about the cases of high-school students who were deceived or forced to become comfort women. Nor is there much information on the related criminal activities of the gangsters. However, the Tokkō, Special Japanese Police Force, was aware of the fact that some leaders of the popular fascist organizations, which were closely interconnected with the gangsters, were heavily involved in procuring comfort women and setting up comfort stations for the occupation troops. For example, according to the information gathered by the Osaka office of Tokkō in late September 1945, Sasagawa Ryōichi, the president of one of the largest wartime fascist organizations, Kokusui Dōmei ("National Virtues Federation"), set up a new company in Osaka called "American Club," which was nothing but a comfort station. He posted his own brother, Sasagawa Ryōhei, as president of this company, with Okada Tasaburō and Matsuoka Yōji, both former executives of Kokusui Dōmei, as managers of this new club. Kokusui Dōmei had been dissolved when Japan surrendered to the Allied nations, but Sasagawa set about restructuring the organization into a new political party called "Nippon Kinrōsha Dōmei" (Japan Workers' Federation). Sasagawa ordered Okada to "leave the movement [setting up a new political organization] to somebody else and to concentrate on the establishment and management of a comfort station as this business is a big project in which the capital of several million yen has been invested."[22] Several million yen was a huge sum of money at that time, but there is no detailed information available about the "American Club", which was apparently opened on September 18.

According to a report by Iwate prefecture's governor on September 26, a man called Hishitani, the head of the Iwate branch of another nationwide fascist organization called "Sekisei Kai" (Sincerity Association) led by a well-known right-wing ideologue, Hashimoto Kingorō, was working hard setting up a comfort station in a red-light district called Ueda. An article which appeared in one of the local newspapers in Kobe, *Kobe Shimbun*, on September 20 implied the involvement of dubious organizations in setting up comfort stations. It reported that "many so-called grafters are visiting the Public Security Section of the Kobe Police Office, carrying letters of introduction from some members of the city council."[23] Considering how difficult it was to "recruit" even professional prostitutes at the time, it was quite possible that these former fascist organizations, which kept close ties with *Yakuza* groups, used gangsters to hunt and procure comfort women. It is well known that Sasagawa and another right-wing leader, Kodama Yoshio, made a fortune operating the black market in the immediate postwar period, but little is known about their activities in the field of comfort stations.

Such was the reality in the aftermath of the war that even the most ardent nationalists like Sasagawa, who had led a popular anti-American movement during the war, quickly became flattering sycophants of the US occupation forces as soon as the war ended. We find Japanese politicians who had procured tens of thousands of non-Japanese comfort women during the war quickly turning to the procurement of their own women for the benefit of soldiers who had only recently been their enemies. It is obvious that, for people like Sasagawa, political ideologies were simply tools of self-promotion; they were ready to change their hats according to the political conditions of the time.

The Recreation and Amusement Association

The largest private enterprise for the purpose of rendering sexual and other recreational services to the occupation troops was set up in Tokyo.

On August 18 the Police and Security Department of the Ministry of Home Affairs telegraphed the governors and police chiefs of all prefectures regarding comfort stations for the occupation forces. The newly appointed Superintendent-General of the Metropolitan Police Headquarters, Saka Nobuya, was summoned by the Deputy Prime Minister, Prince Konoe. Saka was told to act on the instructions in order to protect "respectable women." Immediately after the meeting with Konoe, Saka summoned the deputy chairman of the Tokyo Metropolitan Association of the Restaurant and Bar Industry, Nomoto Genjrō, the owner of an exclusive Japanese restaurant, *Saganoya*, and asked for his co-operation. As Saka often dined at *Saganoya*, he and Nomoto were already acquaintances. At the same time, Saka assigned the project to the head of the Public Peace and Security Section, Takanori Shakutoku, and his subordinate, Ōtake Bungo. The Public Peace and Security Section of the Metropolitan Police Office was responsible for controlling prostitution in Tokyo. Takanori and Ōtake received instructions not to make any official documents on this matter, as this work would be "outside of the police duty." They were told that all messages should be conveyed verbally.[24]

It is interesting to note that Saka sought the co-operation of the restaurant and bar industry for setting up comfort stations rather than approaching the Tokyo Metropolitan Association of Licensed Brothels, and that the staff of the Public Peace and Security Section were instructed not to produce any paperwork on the matter. This indicates that the Superintendent-General of the Metropolitan Police Headquarters himself was clearly aware of the fact that the police were about to launch illegal clandestine operations. It seems that Saka could not openly encourage the licensed brothel owners to break the law by recruiting unlicensed women or even habitual illicit prostitutes in order to secure sufficient numbers.

Both the chairman of the Tokyo Metropolitan Association of the Restaurant and Bar Industry, Miyazawa Hamajirō, and his deputy, Nomoto, felt that they were in the wrong industry to properly respond to Saka's request. As expected, most members of their Association, owners of top-class Japanese traditional restaurants in places like Ginza and Shinbashi, refused to join such a project. As a result of these refusals, Miyazawa and Nomoto had to use their personal connections to make contact with representatives of the owners of nightclubs, saloons, coffee shops, and popular cheap restaurants, and representatives of licensed brothel proprietors and geisha-house owners. On August 21, Takanori summoned the representatives, with whom Miyazawa had managed to make contact, to the Metropolitan Police Headquarters in Tokyo. Takanori explained the purpose of the project to them, repeatedly emphasizing that he was asking their co-operation in his "private capacity." He said they were not required to report to the police about the details of their business operations, although he guaranteed sufficient financial support from the appropriate authorities. Miyazawa asked for their help "in order to protect 40 million Japanese women." In return, these representatives requested police permission to openly recruit women in and around the Tokyo area because there were far too few existing sex workers. This request was immediately accepted without the issuing of any official document.[25]

On the morning of August 23, these representatives gathered again and officially established the organisation called Tokushu Ian Shisetsu Kyōkai (the Special Comfort Facilities Association), which was soon renamed the Recreation and Amusement Association (RAA). Takanori, Ōtake and two other officers from the Metropolitan Police Headquarters also attended this meeting. Miyazawa was elected director, Nomoto and two other men were elected deputy-directors, three others managing directors and 15 others members of the board. On August 28 the executives of the RAA gathered in front of the Royal Palace, where an "inauguration ceremony" was held involving a group of distinguished guests, government bureaucrats and top-ranking police officers. Director Miyazawa made a speech and said that he had decided to sacrifice himself in order to contribute to laying the foundation for rebuilding the new Japan and for protecting the "purity of all Japanese women." This ceremony was concluded with three cheers of "Long live the Emperor!"[26] It seems that these people were truly proud of their patriotic "enterprise" aimed at protecting innocent Japanese women and contributing to the well-being of the nation and the emperor.

Financial aid was given by the Ministry of Finance of the Japanese government through Nippon Kangyō Ginkō (the Japan Industrial Development Bank) – a quasi-governmental bank. The executives of the RAA were ordered by the Minister of Finance, Tsushima Toshiichi, to see the Director of the Tax Bureau in the Ministry of Finance, Ikeda Hayatato, later Prime Minister between 1960 and 1964. Ikeda told them that he would make sure that up to 100 million yen would be available for the newly established organization. The executives could not believe the astronomical sum that Ikeda was offering for setting up comfort stations. At that time the average monthly salary of a factory worker was 166 yen. It is said that Ikeda told the RAA executives that 100 million yen was cheap if it would provide good protection for Japanese women. Nippon Kangyō Ginkō offered a scheme whereby the first installment of 50 million yen would be given to the organization at low interest. As the bank had to take the formality of lending money on security, it was decided that the fire-insurance of each RAA member would be mortgaged. As fire-insurance had been frozen during the war by the government, in reality, this meant an unsecured loan. The bank eventually loaned 30 million yen (approximately US $2 million at current value) to the RAA on September 6, and a further 3 million yen on January 10 the following year. The shares, valued at 10,000 yen each, were acquired by individual members of the RAA, and according to Mark Gayn, a Canadian correspondent posted in Tokyo shortly after the war, "some shares were presented, as a mark of esteem and appreciation, to high Japanese officials." [27]

Although the 100 million yen that Ikeda had promised was never fully to materialize, 30 million yen was more than sufficient capital to start the RAA. The initial idea was to buy out the entire building of the Mitsukoshi department store in the middle of Ginza and convert each floor to accommodate a comfort station, dance-hall, beer-hall, various restaurants, and the RAA's main office. However, the police authorities probably thought the site too conspicuous and the plan was not approved by the Metropolitan Police Headquarters.[28] Instead, the RAA was advised to set up comfort stations along the Keihin National Highway in the Ōmori and Ōi areas in Shinagawa ward of south Tokyo, a traditional red-light district since the feudal Edo period. Here there were a number of brothels, large restaurants, and inns. Towards the end of the war they had been closed and used as dormitories for the members of the Women's Volunteer Corps who were working at nearby arsenals. It was also expected that the highway would be the route by which the US occupation troops landing at Yokohama and Yokosuka would get to Tokyo. The RAA managed to secure several former Japanese restaurants in this location and quickly converted all of them to comfort stations. [29]

Although the RAA gave up the initial plan to set up a large-scale "entertainment complex" in Tokyo's expensive shopping district of Ginza, it did locate its head office in a Chinese restaurant in Ginza, called Kōraku, and managed to set up a few cabarets, a beer hall, a dance hall and the like in the area. With police protection and strong government financial backing, the RAA had, by the end of November 1945, set up a range of facilities in Tokyo, Chiba, and Atami, a hot-spring resort town in Shizuoka prefecture. The facilities were available only for members of the occupation forces; use by Japanese clients was totally banned. The facilities included:[30]

Ginza & Marunouchi area
- Cabaret:
  1   Oasis of Ginza with 400 dancers
  2   Senbiki-ya with 150 dancers
  3   Kōichiro with 20 dancers
  4   Ryokuryoku-kan with 50 dancers
  5   Ginza Palace [number of dancers unknown]
- Beer hall: Tōhō beer hall

- Dance hall: Itō-ya with 300 dancers
- Bar: Bordeaux
- Billiard parlour: Nishō-kan
- Restaurant (for officers): Kōgyō Club

Shinagawa area
- Cabaret: Paramount with 350 dancers

Shibaura area
- Cabaret and comfort station: Tōkō-en with 30 dancers & 10 comfort women

Mukōjima area
- Banquet house (for high-ranking officers): The Ōkura Villa

Itabashi area
- Comfort station: Narimasu comfort station with 50 comfort women

Akabane area
- Cabaret: Kozō-kaku with 100 dancers

Koishikawa area
- Cabaret: Hakusan cabaret [number of dancers unknown]

Plate 6.3 Tōhō Beer Hall in Ginza was a popular attraction for the Allied servicemen. During the Korean War this place was also frequented by US and Australian soldiers on Rest and Recreation leave.
Source: Australian War Memorial, transparency number 044191

Keihin area
* Comfort stations:
  1 Komachien with 40 comfort women
  2 Miharashi with 44 comfort women
  3 Yanagi with 29 comfort women
  4 Hamakawa with 54 comfort women
  5 Gokūrin with 45 comfort women & 6 dancers
  6 Otome with 22 comfort women
  7 Rakuraku-en with 20 comfort women
  [in addition, three sub-contracted comfort stations – Matsuasa, Sawadaya and Fukuryō]

Santama area
* Comfort stations:
  1 Chōfuen with 54 comfort women
  2 Fussa with 57 comfort women
* Cabaret and comfort stations:
  1 New Castle with 100 comfort women & 150 dancers
  2 Rakuraku House with 65 comfort women & 25 dancers
  3 Tachikawa Paradise with 14 comfort women & 50 dancers
  4 Komachi with 10 comfort women & 10 dancers

Sangenjaya area
* Officers' club: Comfort station exclusively for officers (comfort women were sent from other comfort stations as required)

Ichikawa city (Chiba prefecture)
* Cabaret for officers : Dream Land

Atami (Shizuoka prefecture)
* Hotel: Tamanoi Bekkan
* Hotel & cabaret: Fujiya Hotel
* Cabaret & dance hall: Ōyu

Given the severe economic depression, it was not difficult for the RAA, which was set up with an extraordinarily large sum of capital, to purchase suitable properties and convert them for use as comfort stations, cabarets, dance halls and the like. Various types of properties were available cheaply immediately after the war. The RAA's initial difficulty was to secure enough comfort women. Many parts of Tokyo had been burnt out in US napalm attacks, including those in red-light districts. Moreover, the Tokyo Metropolitan Police Headquarters had issued an order in March 1944 for all brothels, bars, geisha houses, and high-class restaurants to stop business. By mid-1944 most sex workers in Tokyo had left. Thus, the RAA had to use labor brokers to recruit former prostitutes from Tokyo's neighboring prefectures and encourage them to work as comfort women for the occupation troops.[31]

At the same time the RAA tried to recruit women through newspaper advertisements. For example, both *Yomiuri Hōchi* and *Mainichi Shimbun* carried the following advertisement on September 3 and September 5.[32]

> Urgent Notice
> Special female workers wanted
> Free meals & accommodation, high salary, advance payment also available
> Travel expenses paid for applicants from countryside
> Tokyo, Kyōbashi, Ginza 7-1
> The Special Comfort Facilities Association
> Phone: Ginza 919-2282

The RAA could provide free meals to its employees with food supplied by the Metropolitan Government Office as arranged by the police authorities.[33] This supply had probably been built up on rationing control during the war.

The RAA put up a large recruitment poster in front of its office in Ginza, which said:

> Announcement to New Japanese Women! We require the utmost co-operation of new Japanese women who participate in a great project to comfort the occupation forces, which is part of the national emergency establishment of the postwar management. Female workers, between 18 and 25 years old, are wanted. Accommodation, clothes and meals, all free.[34]

Although these advertisements avoided the words "comfort women," most people who read them would have been clear about what sort of work was being advertised. It is said that many "taxi dancers" were recruited through newspaper advertisements. As the condition of "free meals and free accommodation" was extremely attractive, the jobs enticed not only previous entertainers but young women who had become war orphans and young widows who had lost their husbands in the war. They were attracted to work as a "dancer." However, as time passed, the boundary between "dancers" and "comfort women" became blurred; many "dancers" were gradually dragged into the prostitution business as well.[35]

It is not surprising that this kind of blatant advertising upset some nationalists. For example, one day, a surviving former *Kamikaze* pilot stormed into the RAA office in Ginza, holding a drawn sword, and shouted: "I am going to kill the traitors to the nation!" The workers in the office somehow managed to calm him down by saying that they were doing the work purely out of patriotism, to protect the majority of Japanese women, and that really they deeply resented the Americans.[36]

On August 29 a group calling itself the National Salvation Party put up leaflets at various places in Shinbashi railway station near Ginza, which said:

> Notice to the Women of the Japanese Imperial Nation!
> The women of our imperial nation must not have intercourse with the

black race. Those who violate this order deserve the death sentence. Therefore make absolutely sure to keep the purity of the Yamato race![37]

It is interesting to note that this propaganda identified only the black race as the foreign group that would contaminate "the purity of the Japanese blood," not white men – perhaps a reflection of popular Japanese feelings of inferiority towards Caucasians.

Despite having given the RAA initial verbal permission for "open recruitment," two months later the police issued an instruction warning the RAA and its labor brokers not to "unfairly recruit women by using exaggerated or false expressions or by suppressing the names of employers."[38] The existence of this police document strongly suggests that many of those employed by the RAA had been deceived or trapped into the prostitution.

According to the memoirs of Kaburagi Seiichi, who was a public relations officer for the RAA, it was Komachien (which loosely translates as "The Babe Garden") in the Ōmori district of the Keihin area which was first opened as a comfort station. It opened on the morning of August 28, the day that the RAA's inauguration ceremony was conducted in front of the Royal Palace.[39] This was also the day that 46 planes of the advance party arrived at Atsugi airbase on the outskirts of Tokyo. Indeed, some GIs from this advance party visited Komachien that very evening.[40] It is probable they found the comfort station on the way from Atsugi to Kanagawa prefecture, where they had to inspect the port facilities of Yokosuka in preparation for the landing of US marines a few days later. The selection of the site – on the highway linking Tokyo, Yokohama and Yokosuka – was a deft business decision by the RAA.

By the time the occupying forces landed, the RAA had managed to set up only Komachien. As a result this comfort station was flooded with GIs from as early as August 30. There were only 38 comfort women in the station. Given the demand, they hardly had time to rest or have a meal. Shortly thereafter, the RAA recruited new women, managing to increase the number of comfort women at the station to 100. Even then, it is said that the minimum number of clients that each comfort women had to serve each day was 15. One woman was said to have served 60 GIs a day.[41]

GIs paid their money at the front desk and received a ticket and a condom. They gave the ticket to the comfort women who served them.[42] This procedure replicated that used at the Japanese military comfort stations during the war.

The physical hardship that these Japanese comfort women faced was strikingly similar to that endured by Asian comfort women during the war. The only difference was that these Japanese comfort women were paid properly, in most cases, whereas the former had received hardly any payment. The tariff was 100 yen for a so-called "short service." The women collected the tickets that GIs handed to them and then, on the following morning, took the tickets to the accounting office of the comfort station. Each comfort woman received half of the tariff – 50 yen – for each ticket. The other half went into the RAA's coffers. The RAA provided the women with the necessary clothes and toiletries, and with free meals.⁴³ This arrangement was considerably better than that experienced by prostitutes, not to mention comfort women, before and during the war. Under the old regulations, the employing brothel owner took 75 percent of the tariff, the prostitute having to use her 25 percent to cover the costs of clothes, cosmetics and meals, which were deducted.⁴⁴ It was conceivable that, given the general economic situation at the time, many newly recruited comfort women borrowed money in the form of advanced payment.

In order to meet the heavy demand, the RAA purchased several large Japanese restaurants in the district and converted them to comfort stations over the following two months or so. At the same time the RAA quickly expanded its business operations, eventually owning and operating "entertainment facilities" in Atami and all over the metropolitan area.

Another area where the RAA concentrated the establishment of its comfort stations, on the advice of the metropolitan police authorities, was in the Santama area, particularly Tachikawa and Chōfu districts. To accommodate the US occupation forces who advanced to Tachikawa airbase after September 3, a comfort station called Fussa was opened there on September 5. This station was set up in the building used as a dormitory for the riggers at the Tachikawa Imperial Army airbase. Within a short time comfort stations were opened one after another in this district.⁴⁵ According to Mark Gayn, correspondent for the *Chicago Sun*, who was sent to Japan to report on the occupation, the RAA brought a truck full of comfort women to the unit stationed near Chōfu, a neighboring town of Tachikawa, on September 9. The following is what Gayn heard from an officer of the US occupation troops:

> Long after night fall, GIs heard the sound of an approaching truck. When it was within hailing distance, one of the sentries yelled "Halt!" The truck stopped, and from it emerged a Japanese man, with a flock of young women. Warily, they walked towards the waiting GIs. When they came close, the man stopped, bowed respectfully, swept the ground behind him with a wide, generous gesture, and said: "Compliments of the Recreation and Amusement Association!"⁴⁶

At times the RAA had to confront various problems caused by GIs. Comfort stations were often visited by groups of drunken GIs in the middle of the night, after a station had closed. When they were refused entry, GIs committed abuses. For example, on November 8, 1945, about 60 GIs came to a comfort station, Miharashi, in Ōmori district. When they found that it was closed, they went on a wild rampage, setting fire to the kitchen. At many comfort stations, GIs demanded refunds, claiming that the service was poor; others robbed the cash by holding a manager at gunpoint. Some military police who patrolled the district of comfort stations demanded "free service" almost every night.⁴⁷

"Taxi dancers" also became victims of sexual violence committed by GIs. Rape by GIs drove many "taxi dancers" into "prostitution." Typically, they were taken out by GIs on a date and then raped or forced to consent to sexual intercourse. According to a survey conducted in 1949 by Itsushima Tsutomu on 500 prostitutes specializing in services for GIs, 26.8 percent said that they had become prostitutes in order to earn a living – the most common reason. The second most common reason (22.8 percent) was the despair that women experienced as a result of rape by GIs.[48] As we have seen in the previous chapter, many of these victims of rape were not "entertainers" but ordinary civilians.

Comfort women were subject to numerous instances of sexual violence. For example, on the evening of September 4, three Australian soldiers visited a comfort station at Higashiyama in Kyoto. They were apparently former POWs who had been released from a POW camp somewhere in Japan and were staying at a hotel in Kyoto, waiting to be repatriated. After they were entertained at this station, they insisted on being accompanied by three comfort women to their hotel, where their fellow Australian soldiers were staying. The manager of the station refused the request. However, they forcibly took the women away, shouting at the manager that "Japan lost the war and your police have no power at all!" At the hotel, the women were confined to one room and gang-raped by seven drunken former POWs. In the following morning these women were sent back to the comfort station. The Australian men apparently kept the women's underwear kimonos.[49]

For some newly recruited comfort women, who had not been previously associated with the business, it must have been an unbearable experience. For example, Takita Natsue, a 19-year-old girl who had lost all her relatives to bombing, was one of the new comfort women at Komachien. Only a few days after the opening of the station she committed suicide by jumping in front of a train.[50]

Some of the RAA's facilities were set up specifically to entertain high-ranking officers of the occupation forces and top delegates of the US government's missions. These facilities included the Ōkura Villa in Mukōjima of Asakusa ward, the Officers' Club in Sangenjaya of Shibuya ward, and Dream Land in Ichikawa, Chiba prefecture. The Ōkura Villa was a grand mansion on the bank of the Sumida River. The RAA had purchased it from the original owner, Baron Ōkura Kihachirō, and used it mainly as a banqueting hall. A large house in Sangenjaya, owned by the president of a large marine transport company, was also purchased and used as a special comfort station exclusively for the high-ranking officers. Dream Land was set up as a cabaret in a former Japanese restaurant, Hōrai-en, in Ichikawa city, near the border between Tokyo metropolitan area and Chiba prefecture.[51] According to Kaburagi, a former RAA public relations officer, the RAA always kept about 20 top geisha in the head office for dispatch whenever high-ranking officers had a dinner party. These geisha were not prostitutes. The RAA also selected some women from "dancers" at its own cabaret, Oasis of Ginza, to attend the dinner parties held in the Ōkura Villa or the Officers' Club when requested. It seems that some top officers in GHQ were regular clients of these "dancers."[52]

Japanese government officials also used these facilities to entertain delegates sent from Washington, DC. For example, Edwin Pauley visited Japan in November

Plate 6.4 A US soldier patrolling the red-light district in Sasebo in October 1945. Some milit-
     ary police who patrolled the district of comfort stations demanded "free service."
Source: Mainichi Shimbun

1945 in order to write a recommendation report to the US President regarding
Japan's war reparations to the Asian nations occupied by Japan during the war.
Five delegates of this mission, including Pauley himself, were taken to Dream
Land by staff of the Japanese Ministry of Foreign Affairs. The RAA staff were
instructed by the ministry to attend well to these delegates who would determine
the amount of war reparations that Japan had to pay. Kaburagi arranged to
send to Dream Land 10 top "dancers" (selected from various dance halls), 10
geisha from the head office and the 10 most beautiful looking waitresses from
RAA's restaurants. At the dinner party the "dancers" sought to seduce the
delegates, but Pauley and his associates were not drawn in. They left Dream
Land after the two-hour dinner and dance entertainment without accepting the
offer of sexual service.[53]

Occupation policies and the spread of prostitution

On September 13, the Governor of Kanagawa prefecture, Fujiwara Takao,
submitted a secret report to the Minister of Home Affairs, Yamazaki Iwao. In it

he reported what one of the high-ranking officers of the 11th Airborne Division of the US 8th Army had told a Japanese police officer shortly after his arrival in Atsugi. The US officer had said:

> It is expected that women in our home country would blame us, if we asked you to set up pleasure facilities. Therefore we cannot request you to do so . . . However, if you do not provide us with such facilities voluntarily, many troubles tend to occur. As far as these kinds of facilities are concerned, our MP [military police] is prepared to co-operate with you if necessary. I presume that the occupation of Japan by our troops will be about three years at maximum if no trouble occurs, but if there are many troubles, I am afraid that it might be 10 to 15 years.[54]

This "suggestion," which was in reality nothing but naked blackmail, was reported to the Kanagawa prefectural government by Nagai Kiyoshi, a Japanese interpreter for the American officer.

In Chiba prefecture, between September 3 and 5, General Cunningham, commander of the US occupation forces stationed in this prefecture, issued daily orders to the Chiba prefectural government to put up noticeboards declaring the brothel districts within the prefecture "off limits." However, on September 14, he personally asked the governor of Chiba prefecture to establish military brothels for his troops as they were soon to be granted leave.[55] Similar requests from occupation officers were recorded in other prefectures. Therefore, it seems that the expectations of both sides were one on the issue of provision of this kind of "amenity" for US forces.

In fact, independent of the Japanese scheme, US occupation forces from the beginning planned not only to tolerate organized prostitution but to regulate it in ways that would satisfy their troops. Soon after the first contingents landed in Japan between late August and early September 1945, US Army officers inspected red-light districts and set up prophylactic stations. The following memo of September 30, 1945, written by Lieutenant Colonel James Gordon (Public Health and Welfare Section, GHQ) verifies this point:

> Subject: Conference with Major Phillip Weisbach, M.C., C.O. 15th Med Squadron, 1st Cavalry Div.
>
> 1 Major Weisbach reported that he had surveyed the major prostitution area of Tokyo shortly after the arrival of troops in the city and had set up four prophylactic stations as follows:
>   a) Senju area
>   b) Mokojuna [sic] area
>   c) Yokohama road
>   d) 1st Brigade area.
> These stations are giving 7,000–10,000 pros a week in addition to distributing uncounted individual items.

2   He stated that the supply of prophylactic materials, sulfathiazole, calomel ointment, pratorgol, and paper towels is running critically low. Several attempts to obtain additional supplies of these items through 8th Army supply have to date been unavailing.

3   He stated that it is his impression that the 1st Cavalry's V-D rate is relatively low.

4   He was informed of the contemplated projects to re-establish the system of regulation of prostitution. He offered to cooperate in every way possible with any plan which might be adopted.[56]

The words "individual items" used in this report probably mean condoms. It is clear that as many as 10,000 soldiers – just from the 1st Cavalry Division alone – were associating with Japanese prostitutes every week. It is not surprising that the stock of condoms and other prophylactic materials was running low within one month of the landing. It is clear that the US command applied the same method of military-controlled prostitution that had operated widely during the war to its occupation of Japan.

The above document also verifies the fact that US soldiers utilized not only the RAA's facilities but also brothels in traditional red-light districts in Tokyo, such as Senju and Mukōjima. According to a Japanese source, this began as early as September 5 – 12 days before the GHQ office was moved from Yokohama to Tokyo. On September 5 eight soldiers of the 1st Cavalry came to Terashima district near Mukōjima, where five brothels operated illegally using a total of 12 prostitutes. On the following day, 20 GIs visited these brothels. The number of GIs using the brothels increased exponentially, until a few weeks later about 1,600 soldiers a day were visiting them. By then, with "assistance and encouragement from the supervising authorities," the number of brothels was increased to 13, employing a total of 60 prostitutes. This meant that, on average, one prostitute served about 27 GIs a day. By November 1945, the district had expanded to become a large red-light district containing 97 brothels and 230 prostitutes.[57] Behind this rapid expansion was a close collaboration between the police authorities, the proprietors, and the occupation forces.

On October 14, 1945, the Metropolitan Police Headquarters issued a statement reversing the order that it had issued in March 1944 prohibiting brothels, bars, night clubs, expensive restaurants and the like. This legalization of the "entertainment business" gave endorsement to the widespread clandestine prostitution industry for the occupation troops in Tokyo and neighboring areas. The police force itself had helped develop and expand these facilities, which were in addition to the facilities run by the RAA. According to one of the documents prepared by the Public Health and Welfare (PHW) Section of GHQ, by the third week of October there were 23 red-light districts in Tokyo used extensively by GIs, including traditional brothel quarters such as Mukōjima, Hakusan, and Yoshiwara, and central shopping towns like Shibuya and Ikebukuro.[58]

Within just a few months, the sex industry spread quickly and widely in Tokyo. While ostensibly the services were set up for use by Japanese clients as well as the US troops, some brothels adopted the same policy as the RAA and operated for the occupation troops only. Indeed, given the economic hardship faced by the Japanese at that time, the prostitution industry immediately after the war can be said to have serviced almost exclusively US troops.

The largest facility outside the RAA organization was the International Palace, in Koiwa in the east end of Tokyo. This brothel was set up in five of the female workers' dormitories of the munitions plant that the Seikō Company had operated during the war. With advice from the Tokyo Metropolitan Police Headquarters, a certain Harada Gennosuke set up the brothel. He purchased the dormitories from Seikō and converted them into the "world's largest brothel." He enlisted the help of 100 proprietors, or chaperones, from the neighboring downtown red-light districts, each of whom brought three or four girls.[59] The following is an extract from the diary of Mark Gayn, who visited the brothel with Colonel Logie, Deputy Provost Marshall for Tokyo, and a few other Americans in May 1946, three weeks after it had been placed off-limits.

> Only Allied trade was permitted, and when the turnover became heavy the irreverent Americans began to call it "Willow Run" [i.e. a Ford automobile factory in Detroit] – because . . . it processed its product on such a huge scale. . . .
>
> We could see, rising out of the paddies, a series of two story buildings with a sign in English, "Off Limits – VD." . . .
>
> Our first stop was at the infirmary. It was a huge, bare room, lined with tatami (straw mats). There were about dozen girls lying on the floor, under thick comforters. . . .
>
> A Nisei lieutenant and I began to question a girl in a corner. She said she was nineteen, and never been a prostitute until she joined Willow Run five months ago. She now owed the company ¥10,000 (about $660), mostly for the clothes she bought at the brothel store. We got similar stories from the other girls. Most of them had lost their families in the American fire raids. Some had lost jobs in the war industries.
>
> . . .
>
> We entered the "ballroom," in which about a hundred girls, most of them in ugly Occidental gowns – with nothing underneath – danced with each other. . . .
>
> From the ballroom, we walked to the girls' room. There were fifty cubicles to a building, each tiny room separated by a low partition, and a thin curtain for a door. Each entrance had a crayon-coloured sign reading, "Well Come, Kimi," or "Well Come, Haruko," those being the names of the occupants.
>
> . . .
>
> Off the stairway we saw a long, narrow room with the sign "PRO Station" painted out lightly. This was the room where the Army supplied prophylactics for the GIs until it put the place off limits. . . .
>
> Every twenty-four hours a woman "processed" an average of 15 GIs, each of whom paid ¥50, or $3.30. Of this amount, half went to the management,

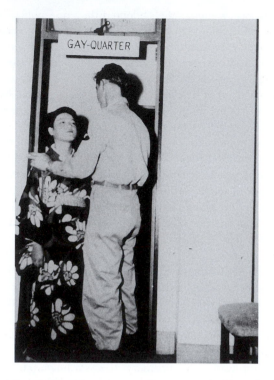

Plate 6.5 A US soldier visiting a Japanese comfort woman in Kyoto in October 1945.
Source: Mainichi Shimbun

and the other half was kept by the women. Out of their income, the women paid for their food, medical expenses, cosmetics and clothes. I did a rapid bit of calculating. Among them, the 250 women "processed" 3,750 GIs every twenty-four hours. This meant a daily income of $6,200 for the International Palace.[60]

There is also a document prepared by the PHW Section of the GHQ which briefly refers to this large brothel complex. According to this document:

- The price of "Short Time" at the International Palace is now 50 Yen. A patron staying after 12 midnight, usually stays all night and must buy four 50 Yen tickets. . . .
- There are many girls who desire to keep on in this business. Most have lost one or both parents in the bombing, and have no funds and no means of livelihood otherwise.
- In the "International [Palace]" the fee is divided as follows: 10 percent to the House; 45 percent to the "Chaperone"; 45 percent to the girl. Girls pay about 10 Yen per day for food. Clothing is very expensive but the exact price and the arrangement for procuring it were not know to the informants. . . .

- Some of their girls came from Ut[s]unomiya, near Nikko. "We had one girl there who served 50 men in one night. She was very busy and the American soldiers stood in line to get to her. . . ."[61]

In the same document dated December 29, 1945, the PHW Section estimated that the total number of prostitutes in the Tokyo area at that time was 6,000, and all of them were "within communicating distance of American troops." It also estimated that the total number of prostitutes in all Japan was 150,000. However, the PHW Section acknowledged that this "estimate does not take into consideration any number of street prostitutes."[62]

According to one Japanese source, by the end of November, apart from RAA facilities, 25 new comfort stations had been set up in various places in Tokyo, employing a total of more than 1,500 comfort women.[63] The number of comfort women and "taxi dancers" employed by the RAA was well over 2,000 at that time.[64] Thus, in the Tokyo area alone, it can be estimated that the total number of comfort women and prostitutes serving the occupation troops at the end of 1945 was 10,000.

It is no exaggeration to say that it was not the textile, chemical or other industries that were rehabilitating the immediate postwar Japanese economy but the sex industry, and that this came at the expense of the physical and psychological health of tens of thousands of Japanese sex workers. According to the survey conducted by the Tokyo Metropolitan Police Headquarters, in 1948 (that is three years after the war) 77.5 percent of prostitutes had become sex workers due to poverty.[65] According to a similar survey conducted by the Yokohama City Police Office in 1950 – five years after the war – more than 43 percent of the 584 prostitutes who were interviewed cited poverty as the main reason they had become prostitutes. Apart from poverty, these women had suffered in other ways. The above survey noted that 13 percent of the interviewed prostitutes had lost their parents either during or immediately after the war.[66] In addition, a large number of the women suffered further with venereal disease contracted through their work.

VD problems and the failure of GHQ's VD prevention policies

The Allied troops suffered VD problems from the start of the occupation. Within a short time VD had become the most serious health issue that GHQ had to confront. This was despite the establishment of a number of VD preventive prophylactic stations in red-light districts.

For example, the VD ratio for the 8th Army troops more than doubled from 26.84 per 1,000 in early September to 56.39 per 1,000 in late October, 1945. The VD rate for the entire US occupation forces during the first three months of 1946 rose as high as 233 per 1,000. The rate was astonishingly high among the US Navy and Marine troops – 476.12 per 1,000 for the troops in Yokosuka and 574.84 per 1,000 for the troops in Sasebo in Nagasaki prefecture in June 1946.[67]

In other words, in some cases, at least half the US Navy and Marine troops were suffering from VD, in particular gonorrhea.

At the same time in Hiroshima and other prefectures of the Chūgoku region of southwest Japan, the British Commonwealth Occupation Forces (BCOF) faced a far more serious VD problem. Between their arrival in Japan in early February 1946 and that June, the VD rate for the 34th Australian Infantry Brigade was 550 per 1,000. According to one of the Brigade's official reports, during this period, at least three men from the brigade were diagnosed with "latent gonorrhea," which meant that they were almost incurable. More than 50 soldiers from the brigade had become neurotic cases as a result of the disease and some had to be sent back to Australia. By September 27, 1946, a total of 5,823 BCOF members were suffering from VD, of which 3,491 were Australian soldiers.[68] Many of these Australian men were infected with syphilis. The headquarters of the brigade adopted a conspiracy theory in order to explain the extraordinarily high incidence of the disease. They claimed that "there may be some substance in the charge that the health of our force is being deliberately destroyed."[69]

In order to combat widespread VD problems among the US occupation troops, Lieutenant-Colonel James H. Gordon, a VD control medical officer in the PHW Section of GHQ, planned to introduce more rigorous VD examinations of the comfort women and prompt treatment for those infected. This plan was devised in September 1945, less than one month after the landing of the troops in Japan. With this aim, Gordon had a series of meetings with Ishibashi Ukichi, head of the Preventive Health Department of the Ministry of Health and Public Welfare of the Japanese government. On October 3, 1945, he summoned Dr. Yosano Hikaru, Chief of the Preventive Medical Section of the Tokyo Preventive Health Department and Dr. Fukai Katsu, superintendent of Yoshiwara City Hospital (a special VD hospital in one of the traditional brothel districts of Tokyo). He wanted to find out about the VD clinics in the metropolitan area and to discuss with the doctors how to control VD among those women in the "service industry."[70] From that point on, the two doctors, and other Japanese VD specialists, were often summoned to the PHW Section and their cooperation sought in implementing the US examination and treatment measures that were new to Japan at the time.

Under existing Japanese law at the time, licensed prostitutes were liable for VD examinations. They were examined once a week by government health personnel and compelled to undertake hospital treatment if found to be infected. On October 16, 1945, GHQ issued an ordinance to the Japanese government not only to enforce this law rigidly but to expand the periodic VD examination system from licensed prostitutes only to "all individuals whose occupations or activities subject them to serious hazard of venereal disease transmission." Through the Japanese government, governors of all prefectures were ordered to enact this ordinance from October 23. At the same time, the PHW instructed the Ministry of Health and Public Welfare to investigate the situation of medical supplies, particularly penicillin and condoms, in each prefecture "as to the amount of such supplies on hand and amounts needed."[71]

According to Gordon's memorandum on October 26, the Tokyo metropolitan government also published the new VD examination requirements. The brothels were often inspected by medical officers, and prophylactic stations were set up in almost all red-light districts. However, he realized that there was a lack of laboratories to perform VD tests in the metropolitan area. On October 27, Gordon met Dr. Ichikawa Tokuji, Professor of Urology at Tokyo Imperial University and an executive member of the Japanese Association for Control of Venereal Disease. Through Ichikawa and his organization, Gordon tried to re-establish and expand clinics and organic laboratories for VD diagnosis in Japan. Many of these had presumably been destroyed by bombing during the war. Gordon also asked Ichikawa to provide a list of competent venerealogists in Tokyo, expecting that he would utilize their services to conduct VD examinations on women in the "service industry." Ichikawa also promised Gordon that he would submit a roster of about 1,500 qualified dermatologists and urologists in Japan.[72]

Despite the new regulations adopted throughout Japan and the continuous efforts to implement a thorough VD examination system, the problem worsened rather than improved. Many brothels in Tokyo, for example, in particular those which were not operated by the RAA, had to be placed "off-limits." In order to tackle this ever-growing problem, the 8th Army – the core body of the US occupation forces – authorized the use of drugs from its stocks for the treatment of "Japanese civilians" i.e. "the women who were a potential source of VD."[73] Drugs, in particular penicillin, a new and effective antibiotic, were not readily available in Japan at that time. From early November, the 8th Army released not only penicillin but various other anti-VD drugs to Japanese health agencies. The following strict order from the PHW Section made sure that the drugs provided by the US forces would not be utilized for anyone but the women who were providing sexual service to the US occupation troops:

Plans for the Use of Anti-Venereal Drugs Released to Japanese from US Army Stocks.

1   The Prefectural Health Office will be held accountable for the proper use of materials supplied from US Army stocks.
2   These supplies will be used only in the treatment of individuals who represent a potential source of venereal disease to personnel of the occupational forces, that is, women infected with gonorrhea, chancroid, lymphogranulom verereum or early syphilis.
    . . .
7   In the event of failure of the Prefectural Health Officer or a subordinate health agency to comply with the requirement set forth herein (or such other restrictions as may be set up) the stock of drugs supplied and remaining on hand will be recaptured by the Surgeon of the military command concerned and additional supplies will be released in that Prefecture only upon further authorization by the Supreme Commander for the Allied Power.[74]

On December 22, 1945, however, GHQ received instructions from Washington, DC that "in view of the recent development of an acute shortage of penicillin for US civilians, US-produced penicillin should not be used for Japanese or Koreans except in extreme emergency as a life saving measure."[75] GHQ ignored this instruction and continued to use penicillin predominantly as an anti-VD medicine. GHQ administered a large quantity of penicillin and other anti-VD drugs to the Japanese women in the early stage of occupation at a time when penicillin was highly sought after as an effective drug for TB and when ordinary people could not afford to purchase it. The Japanese local governments gratefully accepted massive provisions of these drugs and issued them free to infected women. After the San Francisco Peace Treaty was signed in 1951, the US government sought payment for a large amount of drugs, including penicillin for treatment of VD – even where the Japanese had not asked for them. Eventually, the Ministry of Finance agreed to pay on behalf of the local governments.[76]

Together with the provision of new drugs, GHQ introduced a rigorous examination program and VD control laws. On November 22, 1945, the "Complementary Regulation for the Venereal Disease Prevention Law" was issued. This law made it compulsory for any doctor who diagnosed VD in a patient to report all the personal details of the patient such as name, address, and occupation to a local government. Local governments were mandated to order an infected person "whose occupation naturally involves liability of spreading venereal disease to be admitted to a hospital." Furthermore, without a health certificate issued by a local government, a woman was not allowed to "engage in the business of receiving a guest." Proprietors and managers of brothels were also liable to furnish "necessary equipment for the prevention of venereal disease in accordance with the instruction given by a local government." Proprietors were not allowed to operate a business unless they equipped it with appropriate disinfectant equipment. The law also stipulated that anyone who violated the regulations would be fined.[77] As for the enforcement of this law, instructions were sent to every prefectural governor saying in part that if the patient was unable to pay, local government should make sure the woman received adequate medical treatment free of charge.[78] This instruction clearly indicated that both GHQ and Japanese government officials knew that many "service women" were too poor to pay the cost of medical treatment.

In his memorandum on December 6, 1945, Lieutenant-Colonel Hugh McDonald, Chief of the Legal Subsection of PHW briefly analyzed the "practice of procuring girls" for brothels in Japan and wrote:

> The girl is impressed into contracting by the desperate financial straits of her parents and their urging, occasionally supplemented by her own willingness to make such a sacrifice to help her family.
>
>   . . .
>
> It is the belief of our informants, however, that in urban districts the practice of enslaving girls, while much less prevalent than in the past, still exists . . .[79]

Yet, for most of the staff of the PHW Section, whatever their thoughts on the plight of the women, their most important task was quickly to reduce a high VD rate among their own men by administering effective medical VD control methods among the Japanese sex workers.

The contemporary Japanese situation, which was one of the major contributing factors to the boom in prostitution during the occupation, did not really concern the medical specialists. For them, the main concern was the health of their own men and not the health and welfare of the Japanese "service women." GIs saw the Japanese women in the sex industry as a mere "outlet" for their carnal desire and the lust for male domination. Many called Japanese sex workers a "yellow stool." The attitude of medical officers of the PHW Section towards these women was fundamentally little different from that of the GIs. To medical officers of the PHW section, the Japanese women infected with VD were also seen as mere "defective sexual commodities" that had to be fixed in order to satisfy the customers. Throughout the vast number of documents prepared by the PHW Section, any consideration for the women's humanity is totally lacking. In this sense, there is a striking similarity between the medical officers of the US occupation forces in Japan and their counterparts in the Japanese Imperial forces who had been in charge of the VD problems of Asian comfort women during the war.

The provision of "free medical treatment" did not alleviate the difficulty of the women's lives. This is clear from the following memorandum of Major Philip Bourland, one of the staff of the PHW Section. It relates what two of his VD control officers in the Tokyo area reported to him after visiting some hospitals:

> These officers were particularly concerned with the problems and difficulties in maintaining segregation and quarantine in hospitals, of civilian female disease cases under treatment, in the face of present food shortages and the inability to obtain adequate rations for hospital patients.
>
> . . .
>
> Col. Ridgely was consulted in regard to the above problems but was unable to offer any encouragement or any suggestion as to how any additional food might be procured for subject patients.[80]

This report reveals that the women were admitted to the hospital free of charge but were provided inadequate food while there. The natural consequence was that they ran away from the hospital before the disease was completely cured and slipped back into the same old business that provided their only source of income.

The US military clergymen of the occupation forces were also concerned about widespread, military-controlled prostitution and with the VD problems of their troops. In December 1945 the Tokyo–Yokohama Chapter of the Army and Navy Chaplains Association had a conference at which they discussed this matter. On January 11, 1946, this Association submitted its recommendation to the Supreme Commander for the Allied Powers, General MacArthur. In it the chaplains severely condemned the widespread practice of military-controlled prostitution in Japan. They pointed out that it was against the War Department policy. However, for them too, the overriding concern was the "moral degradation," which was "exceptionally widespread and unusually ruinous to the character of American troops."[81] Here too, any thoughtful concern about the Japanese women, who were in their eyes the source of "these evils," was totally absent.

The PHW Section reacted negatively to the chaplains' recommendation that they suppress military-controlled prostitution. The section's opinion was that VD was controllable only by tight regulation of the prostitution system, not by the suppression of prostitution. The staff of the PHW Section felt that this had been repeatedly demonstrated in the "experience of the Army."[82] Thus, the PHW Section basically ignored the chaplains' recommendation. Instead, it continued to apply more rigorous VD examinations and treatment of the Japanese women working in the sex industry. On February 18, 1946, the PHW Section introduced yet another VD control plan. This involved the military police tracking down women who had been in contact with diagnosed patients, i.e. members of the occupation troops, and then forcing them to undergo examination and hospitalization, if required. If a sex worker refused to co-operate, the plan was to make the police invoke their legal authority to isolate her.[83]

Despite their knowledge of the factors related to the spread of the disease, both the staff of the PHW Section and the military chaplains shared the same belief that the source of "evil VD" was the Japanese women. Their own men were seen as clean, innocent and vulnerable to having their high morals corrupted and their health destroyed. The Australian military officers entertained the same ideas. This is clear from the following examples of some comments made by these officers in their own reports:

- Japan offers abnormal temptation.
- It is to be appreciated that among Japanese women no shame attaches to the prostitute whose trade is recognised as honourable and legitimate.
- In consideration of the whole problem there exists a divergence of opinion as to whether prostitutes, part-time street-walkers or "amateurs" were mainly responsible for the incidence of disease among the troops. There was general opinion, however, that action is necessary relative to all three categories . . .[84]

As many as 200,000 VD cases, mainly women in the sex industry, were recorded in Japan in 1946.[85] Yet, it must not be forgotten that the majority of their clients were occupation troops and that the systems of prostitution they patronized were established and sanctioned by both the Japanese and Allied occupation authorities. Therefore, responsibility lay with the occupation troops rather than "shameless Japanese women." There is no doubt that many Japanese women contracted VD from members of the occupation forces. One BCOF report admits that "some (soldiers) had 2 or 3 attacks but still continue having intercourse."[86]

Other Japanese women also contracted VD from GIs. One of the Japanese Central Liaison Office's reports submitted to the GHQ complains that many of the low-paid Japanese employees of the occupation forces, in jobs like telephone operators, contracted VD from GIs.[87]

There is no doubt that MacArthur was embarrassed by the chaplains' report, and he must have felt that some action was necessary. Indeed, by the time that the chaplains met on the issue, GHQ staff were already preparing to take measures to head off any criticism. GHQ came up with the idea of abolishing Japan's "licensed prostitution system," and recommended the Metropolitan Police Headquarters in Tokyo advise licensed brothel owners and their prostitutes to voluntarily give up their business. GHQ also recommended the annulment and abrogation of all the existing contracts in which women had been indentured to serve a certain period as prostitutes as a form of repayment of loans made to themselves or to their parents. Almost all the licensed brothel proprietors and their prostitutes accepted these recommendations in advance of an official order by GHQ on January 21, 1946 (SCAPIN 642), which forced them to do so. However, the order only outlawed "enslaved prostitution" – the practice of "voluntary prostitution" was still permitted under SACPIN 642.[88] Therefore, in reality, nothing changed and the brothel proprietors continued to operate their businesses by "lending out rooms" to "newly liberated voluntary prostitutes." Moreover, unlicensed prostitution organizations, such as the RAA and other newly established comfort stations like "restaurants" and "bars," were never affected by this order because a license had never been issued to them anyway. Likewise, the women working at these places had never been licensed either and were thus unaffected by the new law.

However, the news of the "abolition of Japan's feudalistic licensed brothels" and the "emancipation of women from the enslaved prostitution business" was widely reported back in the US. It gave a false impression to US citizens that all forms of prostitution in Japan had been outlawed. This ruling together with the negation of the Emperor's divinity, announced on January 1, 1946, and the order to purge Japanese militarists from public positions, issued on January 4, were exploited by GHQ as examples of the great success its policies were having in the "democratization of Japan." Yet, in reality, a vast number of comfort women and unlicensed prostitutes continued to be enslaved by loan arrangements. The Japanese police authorities were also aware of the real consequence of this hypocritical "emancipation order." In his report on May 28, 1946, the Director of the Police Affairs Bureau, Ministry of Home Affairs, wrote:

> As regards similar contracts with service women in restaurants, eating-and-drinking-houses, houses of private prostitution, to whom the system of licensed prostitution was not applicable, efforts will be made to persuade and guide the proprietors of the business to voluntarily abandon all such contracts as are likely to be binding the freedom of the service women or their free will.[89]

Regardless of the PHW Section's introduction of VD control regulations in the months following the start of the occupation, the problem continued to worsen. In March, 1946, the average VD rate for the entire US occupation troops was 274 per 1,000; in other words, more than one in every four GIs was suffering from some form of VD.[90] The cost of medical treatment to the US occupation forces must have been high. The facts behind the failure of the "abolition of licensed prostitution" were mounting. Unless VD rates were reduced, the problem would become publicly known and taken up by the media, to the great embarrassment of occupation authorities. This dilemma can be clearly seen in the letter that James Gordon wrote to General MacArthur on January 22, 1946, a day after the above-mentioned order, SCAPIN 642, was issued. In it, he wrote:

> It is reasonable to assume that back-home news accounts of increasing VD rates, licensed prostitution (or perhaps, its abolition), "temporary wives", fraternization and related subjects will create considerable demand from official and domestic sources for special consideration and action on the problem. The probable result will be an increase of critical visitors unless their demands for information are anticipated and forestalled.[91]

As a last resort, on March 25, 1946, GHQ adopted a drastic, nationwide measure. It placed "off-limits" all brothels, comfort stations, houses of private prostitution, and "restaurants and bars" that operated prostitution.[92] Comfort stations which were operated by the RAA were not exempt. Yet this order too failed to result in the total abolition of prostitution. The question remains: Why did the GHQ not suppress prostitution in Japan completely? If they had wished, General MacArthur and his staff of the GHQ could have issued a "Potsdam Ordinance," whereby GHQ could have issued a law directly to the Japanese people which would have bypassed the Diet, the Japanese parliament. Indeed, the above-mentioned "Complementary Regulation for the Venereal Disease Prevention Law" was a Potsdam Ordinance. It is difficult to find a definitive answer to this question, as the available PHW Section's documents do not refer to this particular issue.[93] However, it can be speculated that GHQ was clearly aware that a total ban of prostitution would not stop their men from associating with clandestine prostitutes. Probably the nationwide "off-limits" measure was implemented more as a stern warning to take health precautions to those who chose to indulge.

The nationwide "off limits" policy suddenly put more than 150,000 Japanese women out of a job. Desperate to survive the extreme poverty, many women left red-light districts to become "streetwalkers," loitering around US bases and city centers frequented by GIs. In Tokyo, for example, the main shopping quarters of Ueno, Shinjuku, Yūrakuchō, Shinbashi, and Ikebukuro were flooded with the so-called "Yōpan" – "hookers specializing in Westerners."[94] As "voluntary prostitution" was not illegal, neither the Japanese police nor the MPs could make arrests to control the sudden rise of "open market prostitution." As one Australian soldier later claimed, in the eyes of the men of the occupation troops Japan became "one big brothel."[95] This put GHQ in a position in which it could not control the GIs' sexual activities, which hitherto had been confined to limited quarters. Prostitutes suddenly became conspicuous to many ordinary Japanese citizens and visitors from the US and other Allied nations. Thus, both GHQ and the Japanese authorities faced a far more difficult situation in controlling VD.

In response, GHQ firstly tried to repress the situation by adopting the "non-fraternization policy." Finding almost immediately that this policy had no effect at all, GHQ instructed the Japanese police to "round up" streetwalkers under the auspices of the law by which suspected VD patients could be forced to undergo VD examinations and medical treatment. Thus, on August 20, the first nation-wide "round up" was implemented using the pretext of "VD check-ups." This involved a large number of Japanese police and MPs of the occupation forces. It is reported that 15,000 Japanese women were "rounded up" on this day alone.[96] These "round up" operations were carried out a number of times each month until September 1949. One of the results, however, was that many girls and young women who were just passers-by were caught up in "round up" operations, forcibly taken to the hospital, and detained at the hospital for three days until the result was known. For them it was an extremely humiliating experience. This "violation of civil rights" became a serious controversy and enraged some women politicians and members of various women's organizations.[97] Yet the Japanese government and GHQ ignored the criticism and continued the operation.

This "nationwide off-limits" program, however, provided little reduction in VD rates. The following extract from a letter sent by Lieutenant-General R. L. Eichelberger, then the Commander of the 8th Army, to MacArthur, on January 4, 1947, clearly confirms the point:

> The venereal disease rate in the Eighth Army is of deep concern to me. I have utilized every facility at my command within the Army and firmly feel that a reduction of venereal disease in the civilian population is the only remaining factor which will contribute materially to further reductions.[98]

The commander of the occupation forces, remaining blind to the agency of his own men, continued to insist that it was still the Japanese women who were primarily responsible for the VD problems of the occupation troops.

It was around this time that a second wave of sexual violence by GIs against civilian women hit various parts of Japan. Shortly before the introduction of the nationwide "off-limits," the number of reported cases of sexual crimes commit-ted by GIs in Japan was down to about 40 per day. It is said that the number suddenly jumped to about 330 cases per day from late March 1946.[99] The most well-known case was an incident that occurred on April 4, 1946, at Nakamura Hospital in Ōmori district, not far from the RAA's comfort station quarter. At around 11:30 at night, three military trucks stopped in front of the hospital, throwing their headlights upon the hospital building. Then, at the signal of a whistle, about 50 US soldiers dashed out of the trucks and invaded the hospital from various directions, breaking windows and doors. They raped all 17 nurses on night duty, about 20 nursing assistants, and more than 40 female patients, including a woman who had just delivered a baby. A two-day-old baby was thrown out of the mother's bed onto the floor and killed. There were some male patients in the hospital, but two who tried to protect the women were shot. The soldiers left the hospital after about an hour's sexual orgy.[100]

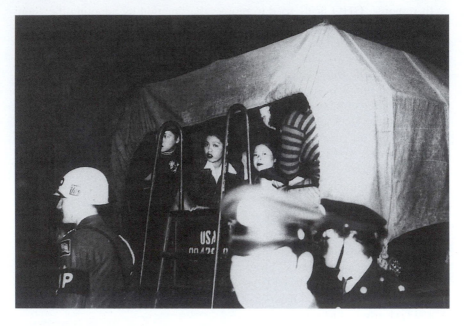

Plate 6.6 Japanese prostitutes in Tokyo who were rounded up by Japanese policemen
and military police of the occupation forces and brought to a hospital for VD
check-ups in November 1948.
Source: Mainichi Shimbun

There were many other reported cases of rape committed by GIs in this and
other districts, such as Kamata and Haneda, between April and June that year.
In most cases, the perpetrators were never identified.[101]

Another large-scale organized rape occurred in Nagoya. At midnight on April
11, one of the blocks in Naka ward of Nagoya city was surrounded by US
soldiers (said to have been between 30 and 60 in number). They had come in a
jeep and a truck. They cut off the telephone lines of the entire block and intruded into a number of houses simultaneously, raping many girls and women
between the ages of 10 and 55 years.[102]

Also at this time the number of so-called "special maids," working for officers
of the occupation forces, greatly increased. In October 1945, fewer than 3,000
were employed as "special maids" throughout Japan. By June 1946 more than
19,000 women were working as "special maids." According to Itsushima Tsutomu,
52 percent of these women were former employees of the occupation troops, 17
percent had been working at dance halls, cabarets, nightclubs and the like, and
the rest – 31 percent – were women whom the officers had met in town or
through organized activities, such as Christian church functions.[103]

Of course, some women among them eventually married the officers and
migrated to the US, Australia, and other Allied nations. These women num-
bered less than 5 percent of the "special maids," the majority performing a role

as "temporary wives" while the officers were stationed in Japan.[104] With officers' privileges and salaries, it was quite easy for them to have such "temporary wives" and thus avoid the prostitution restrictions. Some low-ranking officers rented apartments in order to keep "temporary wives" and commuted to them almost every day. These women were called "only-san," as each of them was paid to serve only one particular man. According to a survey conducted by Yokohama city police office in late September 1951 (several months before the occupation officially ended), 1,186 out of 3,895 prostitutes in the city – more than 30 percent – were "only-san." In addition, 680 (17.5 percent) were so-called "butterflies" – women who entered verbal contracts with several GIs at the same time and served them individually at different times or on different days. The "contracted clients" of these "butterflies" were mainly rank-and-file soldiers of the occupation forces, who could not afford to keep "only-san." There were also 221 "Yōpan", prostitutes serving only GIs.[105]

Some years later, during the Korean War, Japan served as the military work-shop for the US and Australian forces fighting in Korea. It was also used for rest and recreation (R&R) for the soldiers. Soldiers were entitled to five days' holiday for every six weeks' combat duty in Korea. During these times GIs utilized the services provided by Japanese sex workers. For these soldiers, this holiday scheme was called "I&I" (intercourse and intoxication) instead of R&R. According to one informed estimate, in 1952, there were between 70,000 and 80,000 "Yōpan" in Japan. In Yokosuka city alone, in that year, the total revenue from prostitu-tion serving the US troops was estimated at between 200 million and 300 million yen.[106] In his speech at the graduation ceremony of Tokyo University in March 1952, following the end of occupation, Professor Yanaihara Tadao, then the President of Tokyo University and a well-known historian, stated that the US troops' exploitation of postwar prostitution had affected Japanese society "no less than that of the destructive power of the A-bombs" dropped on Hiroshima and Nagasaki.[107]

There is no doubt that the US occupation forces led by General MacArthur brought various progressive policies to Japan, including polices that directly advanced political, educational, social, and job opportunities for women. In the end, they reformed the semi-feudalist and undemocratic social and economic institutions of Japan to a considerable degree. Yet, as far as the prostitution business and the plight of tens of thousands of Japanese women working in this industry are concerned, the occupation forces, far from implementing "demo-cratization policies," actively participated in their subjugation. Not only did they fail in this regard, but, as we have seen, their VD prevention policies failed both GIs and the women who served them. In this sense, the Allied forces who participated in the occupation of Japan, from ordinary soldiers up to the staff of the PHW Section of the GHQ and the Supreme Commander of the Allied Powers himself, were all responsible for the tribulation that many Japanese women experienced. As this study has shown, some Japanese men – politicians, policemen, brothel proprietors and the like – who collaborated with the occupation forces behind the excuse of "protecting Japanese women," were also accountable.[108]

During the Asia-Pacific War, the comfort women system was established wherever Japanese troops were based across the length and breadth of the Asia-Pacific region. That system was maintained both to prevent rape of local women by Japanese troops and to provide controlled forms of entertainment for millions of draftees fighting and dying far from home. Yet the scheme was a miserable failure in many of its goals. Tens of thousands of Asian women became the victims of systematic military sexual violence, i.e. crimes against humanity, which were fraudulently described as "comforting" Japanese soldiers. Thousands more were subject to rape and abuse in military campaigns in contested areas that took women as well as men as the targets for attack and killing.

A system with striking similarities to that of the wartime comfort women system was hastily set up as soon as the war was brought to an end – this time targeting not Asian women but Japanese "prostitutes" for the purpose of "protecting Japanese women and girls" or, stated differently, in order to attempt to control and limit the anticipated rapacious activities of occupying forces. As we have seen, however, the result was a rapid propagation of the sex industry throughout Japan with many unintended consequences, including an uncontrollable VD epidemic. In this system many Japanese women and girls were recruited and harshly exploited. Large numbers of men from the Allied nations took advantage of the socio-economic and power imbalance conditions at the time in order to "comfort" themselves, and some Japanese men benefited by victimizing Japanese women. Such were the grim realities of the comfort women system, about which most of our fathers – not only the Japanese, but also those in the US, Australia, and other Allied nations – have kept silent so long. It would seem, therefore, that from the perspective of these women, both those men who raped them and those who supposedly protected them became exploiters.

Epilogue

From karayuki-san to comfort woman

The comfort women system that the Japanese Imperial forces established originally in China in the early 1930s quickly expanded to almost every corner of the
Asia-Pacific region following the attack on Pearl Harbor in December 1941. It
became the largest and most elaborate system of trafficking in women in the
history of mankind, and one of the most brutal.

The scale of the operation was unprecedented in several ways: the number of
women involved, the international scope of the operation, the scale of the military-
organized system required for procuring women, the length of time over which
the system operated, and the geographical breadth of Japan's wartime empire
wherein the system was administered.

But this was not the first time that Japan had engaged in widespread trafficking
in women in the Asia-Pacific region for the purpose of sexual exploitation. From
the final years of the Tokugawa regime in the mid-nineteenth century, the authority
of the Shogunate over daimyo (feudal lords), then in decline, finally collapsed
over the long-standing policy of national isolation. This was due to the increasing
number of foreign ships that visited Japanese ports and the pressure to open up
the country for trade. It was around this time that young women began to be
smuggled out of Japan and sold to brothels in neighboring countries, in particular China and the east coast of Russia. These women were called karayuki-san,
which literary means "a person travelling to China." Originally coined by the
people of northern Kyushu to refer to those who sought work overseas, the term
came to be applied specifically to the impoverished rural women sold into prostitution far from home.

Shortly after the Meiji Restoration – the establishment of the modern Japanese
state in 1868 – the number of karayuki-san increased rapidly. Within the following few decades, their destinations included various parts of Southeast Asia,
India, Australia, Hawaii, the east coast of the US, and even as far as Cape Town
in South Africa. However, the major business centers for this Japanese sex industry in the late nineteenth and early twentieth centuries were Vladivostok, Shanghai, and Singapore.[1]

When a Japanese government trade representative, Sewaki Kazuto, first visited Vladivostok in 1875, only eight years after the new Meiji government was

established, he found a brothel run by a Japanese proprietor in which Japanese prostitutes served Russian clients. By 1887, the number of Japanese residents in Vladivostok had increased to between 4,000 and 5,000, over 200 of whom were karayuki-san. Many of these women were from Shimabara in Kyushu, one of the most impoverished regions in Nagasaki prefecture.[2] In the late Tokugawa period, Nagasaki was one of several Japanese ports of call for foreign ships, including Russian navy ships. There brothels were frequented by foreign visitors. It seems that brothel proprietors in Nagasaki soon found that operating the business for foreigners, in particular Westerners, was far more profitable than serving domestic clients. Thus they took their business off-shore to port cities like Vladivostok, Shanghai, and Singapore.

From the mid-nineteenth century, prostitution began to thrive in the foreign settlements of Shanghai, where mainly Chinese prostitutes served Westerners, in particular sailors from Britain, the US, and France. As a result, Shanghai was selected as a major destination for Japanese brothel owners. By 1882 the population of karayuki-san in Shanghai was as high as 800.[3] The Japanese consulate in Shanghai regarded this sudden increase in Japanese prostitutes as "a national disgrace." As a consequence, in 1883, the Japanese Ministry of Foreign Affairs adopted a policy of cracking down on the prostitution business in Shanghai in order to force karayuki-san to return to Japan. Following this, more than 500 karayuki-san were sent back to Japan in the years 1884 and 1885. However, about 200 women remained in the city, secretly engaging in the business. Later, in the mid-1910s, recognizing the difficulty of suppressing Japanese prostitution, the Japanese consulate in Shanghai changed its policy to one of "control" and introduced a licensing system.[4] As mentioned in Chapter 1, it was some of these government-regulated Japanese brothels operating in Shanghai that were used by the Japanese Imperial Navy as *Ianjo* (comfort stations), shortly after the Shanghai Incident in 1938.

It seems that in the latter half of the 1880s karayuki-san, forced out of Shanghai by the above mentioned policy of the Japanese consulate, moved to other parts of China and Asia. Karayuki-san were soon found in places like Hong Kong, Ningbo, Chongging, British Malaya, and Singapore. By the early twentieth century, Singapore had become the center of overseas Japanese prostitution. At the time of the Russo-Japanese War (1904–1905), about 6,000 Japanese prostitutes were working in Southeast Asia, 700 of them in Singapore. Among the 1,835 Japanese residents in the Straits Settlement in 1906, 852 were karayuki-san and 113 were brothel-keepers.[5] In other words, more than half of the Japanese residents there were engaged in prostitution. A Japanese government survey conducted in January 1910 found that the largest number of business premises operated by the Japanese in Singapore and its neighboring towns were brothels – a total of 188 brothels staffed by 1,048 Japanese women.[6]

Clients of these Japanese prostitutes in British Malaya included not only Caucasians, who were mainly engaged in various kinds of business or colonial government administration, but also Asian migrants, particularly Indian and Chinese workers employed at rubber plantations, in mining or in construction.

Because of its ideal location – surrounded by the hinterlands of the Malay peninsula, Thailand, and the Dutch East Indies – Singapore became a vital trade center. In the second half of the nineteenth century, Singapore prospered as the main port of entry for exports of Southeast Asian natural resources to the West and for the import of European industrial manufactured goods. Prostitution developed apace, serving a growing number of young male migrant workers in Singapore and throughout the region. Over 90 percent of licensed prostitutes in Singapore in the late nineteenth century were Chinese, but they mainly served Chinese clients. A small number of European prostitutes catered solely to Caucasians. Japanese prostitutes, however, entertained customers irrespective of race or nationality.[7] As a result of this non-discriminatory attitude, the karayuki-san became popular and business prospered.

Due to this rapid expansion of Japanese prostitution overseas, by 1910 the number of Japanese women registered as overseas prostitutes increased to more than 19,000, compared with 47,541 officially registered prostitutes within Japan. The Japanese government had already prohibited women from leaving the country to engage in prostitution abroad by promulgating a law in 1896. However, the government effort to reduce the number of Japanese prostitutes working outside the country failed, just as it had done in Shanghai in 1883. This was partly because of the existence of well-established organizations smuggling young women out of Japan. It was also due, however, to the Japanese government's half-hearted effort to crack down on the trafficking of women, as it was well aware that the overseas prostitution business was an important source for the acquisition of much needed foreign currency at the time.[8]

Many young women were kidnapped and smuggled out of Japan by "labor brokers" who specialized in trafficking women, particularly in the early karayuki-san era. These "labor brokers" also deceived young women, and sometimes their parents, with false promises of employment overseas, promising jobs such as shop assistants in Japanese retail stores. There were highly organized Japanese groups trafficking in women both within and outside Japan, each controlled by a kingpin.[9] One such group was controlled by a man called Muraoka Iheji, a resident of Singapore. Muraoka later claimed that he had set up his own group in July 1889, recruiting a few dozen men with criminal records as "labor brokers." These men were assigned to travel to various parts of Japan and procure young women. Between 1889 and 1894, Muraoka's men reportedly smuggled 3,222 women out of Japan to Singapore and sold them to brothels.[10] Although much of Muraoka's autobiography is thought to be exaggerated and unreliable,[11] there were many "labor brokers" of dubious character like Muraoka, who made a fortune by trafficking in young women in the late nineteenth and early twentieth centuries.

Among karayuki-san there were also those who were sold to procurers by their own poverty-stricken parents. As time passed, some women chose to become karayuki-san in order to earn money quickly. Indeed, a few returned home with substantial assets. However, most karayuki-san ended up destitute and in ill-health. Many died overseas without ever seeing their families again.[12]

Each woman was sold to a brothel for between $500 and $600, which was levied upon her as a "debt" by her brothel keeper. Even in the case of kidnappings, a levy was imposed for "travel expenses." As a result, almost all karayuki-san were financially bound to their brothels for years until this "debt" was paid off. Generally, the debt also included the cost of bedding, clothes, furniture and the like. Half of their daily earnings went to a brothel keeper as his income, leaving the other half for the prostitute, from which was deducted the debt and other living expenses, including the full cost of periodic medical check-ups. After these necessary "expenditures," very little money was left for the karayuki-san. If she became ill and could not work for any period, her debt would multiply, thus prolonging the bondage period. Such conditions caused many deaths from sickness and drove many karayuki-san to suicide.[13] It is indisputable that the comfort women system was essentially based on this karayuki-san system.

Most Japanese residents in Singapore who were not directly involved in prostitution were, however, initially dependent upon the Japanese sex industry that operated in the city. Various goods and services were required by prostitutes and brothels, such as sundry retail dealers, drapers, photographers, doctors, and brothel keepers. As karayuki-san usually wore kimonos, a reliable supply from Japanese drapers was particularly important.[14] It can be said that Japan's modern international trade developed from such small-scale retail trade beginnings which followed the expansion of the traffic in Japanese women in the Asia-Pacific region. The following remarks made by two Japanese men in 1919 clearly support this point:

> It is true that five-*shaku* men ["men of 150 cm in height" – a Japanese expression in those days for "adult Japanese men"] followed the Japanese prostitutes and then spread everywhere [in Southeast Asia]. . . . The Japanese prostitutes needed Japanese food, Japanese beverages, Japanese clothes and many other Japanese goods. Their demand was met by queer Japanese sundry-goods traders who dealt in a wide variety of goods, ranging from Japanese clothing to canned food. As the Japanese goods were also sold to non-Japanese customers by such traders, their business became widely known. The prosperity of Japan's trade in Southeast Asia today is not thanks to Mitsui & Co and some other large merchants. But the trade was in fact developed by these sundry-goods retailers, behind whom there was the shadow of the Japanese prostitutes.[15]

It seems that the foreign currencies that these Japanese brothel keepers and traders (as well as some karayuki-san) saved and sent back to their homes in Japan played an important role in developing Japan's modern economy. For example, it is said that of a total of one million yen that Japanese residents in Vladivostok remitted home to Japan in 1900, 630,000 yen was from earnings in the sex industry.[16] The acquisition of foreign currency was one of the most urgent tasks for the new Meiji regime in order to lay the foundations of its capitalism. In early Meiji, apart from a few semi-processed manufactured goods, such as silk yarn, Japan did not have many export staples to aid the speedy accumulation of foreign money. Many contemporaries in the early Meiji era were aware of the indispensable contribution of Japan's overseas sex industry to securing foreign currency. For example, the philosopher and educator Fukuzawa Yukichi – who promoted Western ideas of individualism, equality between men and women, and national independence – argued against some of the domestic criticism of Japan's large-scale overseas prostitution business. In January 1896 he wrote:

> In human society prostitutes are necessary. . . . As the work by women away from home necessarily follows the migration of people, it would be wise to openly permit [the business of prostitution]. . . . It is economically necessary to promote migration and at the same time to allow women to freely work away from home.[17]

This was the opinion of one of the most prominent educators in the early Meiji period, a man heavily influenced by seemingly "progressive" Western ideas. It seems, however, that Fukuzawa misunderstood the situation. The above remarks create the false impression that Japanese prostitutes left Japan, seeking business opportunities created by Japanese men who were migrating overseas. In fact, it was the other way around, as we have seen – in many instances it was men who followed the karayuki-san.

Thus, by the outset of the Russo-Japanese War, a large number of Japanese brothels were being operated in various parts of Asia and Oceania – from Khabarovsk in the north to Perth, Western Australia in the south, and from China in the west to insular Southeast Asia in the east. Shortly before the war began, almost all of the Japanese brothel keepers and karayuki-san in Russian territories moved out. As soon as the war broke out, many Japanese brothel keepers in Russia decided to move to the major cities in South Manchuria, where Japanese Imperial Army troops were stationed. They brought a large number of karayuki-san with them.[18] This was the origin of the close relationship between Japanese prostitutes and Imperial Army forces abroad.

When the war ended in September 1905, there were more than 1,400 Japanese prostitutes in Kwantung province in Manchuria – 54.3 percent of the Japanese civilian resident population of the province at that time. In the city of Yingkou, about 400 Japanese prostitutes were staying at several inns which were frequented by members of the Japanese Army. Concerned about the spread of VD among the troops, the military authorities quickly introduced a licensing system and imposed regular medical check-ups on the prostitutes. This was the origin of the direct role of military authorities in organizing and controlling military prostitution to service Japanese forces abroad. These military regulations were also applied to Chinese prostitutes. In some places, the kempeitai (military police) were mobilized to enforce these regulations. In Andong, under the instruction of the military authorities, a brothel named Yūenchi was opened in December 1904. It was also open for civilian clients. However, in February 1905, the

Japanese Restaurant and Bar Business Association of the city voluntarily established a new brothel called Suiraitei, reserved exclusively for the use of members
of the Imperial forces.[19] However, generally speaking, the military authorities
were not directly involved in setting up and operating brothels.

From this perspective, the brothels that operated in South Manchuria during and
immediately after the Russo-Japanese War, despite the close regulation by military
authorities, differed from the future "comfort stations." They were independently
established and managed by civilian brothel keepers. They differed, too, in that
the facilities also usually catered to non-military personnel as well, although in
reality most of the clients were members of the Japanese forces. The control that
the military authorities exercised over the brothels at that time was limited,
mainly to that of VD. In this regard, it was similar to the control that the Allied
forces exercised over privately-operated brothels during World War II.

This small boom in the sex industry and the emergence of military-controlled
prostitution in South Manchuria was short-lived. Following Japan's victory in
the Russo-Japanese War, the major component of the troops soon returned to
Japan and the number of brothels and karayuki-san decreased. However, there
is no doubt that the frequent use of Japanese brothels by the military in South
Manchuria during and after the Russo-Japanese War period laid the foundation
for the subsequent spread of Japanese prostitution in north-eastern China and
beyond. For example, in December 1907 a Japanese newspaper reported that
one out of every two or three Japanese business premises in the city of Lushun
(Port Arthur) was a brothel. An official survey conducted in Dalian in May 1907
found 630 sex workers, of whom 554 were Japanese and the rest Chinese. In
May of the following year, the number increased to 883 (790 Japanese, 81
Chinese, and 12 Russians). By the end of 1911, a red-light district was set up in
this city, and prostitution outside the district was prohibited by the Japanese civil
administrative bureau. Japanese brothels were also established in many places
along the South Manchurian Railway line between Lushun and Changchun,
which Japan acquired from Russia at the end of the war. For example, in
February 1906, it is reported that there were 156 prostitutes and 34 Japanese
restaurant-brothels in Changchun. In Jinling, in early 1906, there were 74 brothels.
Of the 907 Japanese residents in this town 466 were engaged in the sex
industry. From September 1906, these Japanese brothels in Manchuria came
under the control of the office of the Japanese consulate of each major city of the
region. This government supervision allowed the continuation of regular VD
inspections for Japanese prostitutes. From 1918, the Japanese Ministry of Foreign
Affairs adopted a new policy to prohibit Japanese prostitutes in Manchuria from
serving non-Japanese clients.[20]

Japan's colonization of Korea officially took place in 1910. From the 1920s
onward many Korean women were procured as prostitutes and sent to Manchuria.
Gradually karayuki-san were replaced by Korean women to work at Japanese
brothels in Manchuria and in other places in China, like Shanghai.[21] Therefore,
by the time of the Shanghai Incident in 1938, certain basic elements of the
comfort women system were already in existence in parts of East Asia where the

Japanese government, military and business organizations were established. It remained for the Japanese military authorities to take direct control and to create a more systematic and comprehensive structure of military sexual slavery. The karayuki-san system was undoubtedly a repressive system of sexual exploitation. The methods of procuring young women were clearly unlawful and morally unjustifiable. In this sense, they were little different from the methods that were used for the later procurement of comfort women. In both cases, serious criminal acts were involved. The source of karayuki-san was mainly impoverished families in the lower strata of Japanese society. For political, diplomatic, security, medical, and other reasons, the Japanese military authorities changed the supply source for the comfort women system from the homeland to Japan's colonies and occupied territories, and adopted methods of direct enslavement to secure the system.

Sexual slavery, social death, and military violence

Japan's military leaders, the administrators of the comfort women system, viewed it as an extension, indeed a rationalization of the karayuki-san system, in essence comparable to a widely sanctioned system of prostitution elsewhere. Thus, despite the methods used, which included kidnapping and sexual slavery, Japanese military leaders certainly did not regard the establishment of the comfort women system as an organized crime against humanity. The sexual service rendered by women ostensibly took the form of a "commercial transaction" – "an exchange in equal value" between sexual service and financial reward. At times unconsciously and at other times intentionally this "business formality" was used to blur the criminality and coercion of sexual slavery inherent in the military comfort women system. The personal history and social background of individual women behind these "commercial transactions" was equally irrelevant to the brothel keepers, "clients," and military organizers. In other words, from the perspective of the authorities, it was irrelevant whether or not a woman was forcibly pressed into prostitution, and whether or not she lived as a slave under military discipline. She was simply a "sexual commodity," not an individual with human value and dignity. Military leaders viewed the comfort women as "commodities" supplied by "labor brokers" and managed by brothel keepers to be used as instruments to satisfy the sexual appetites of soldiers and sailors, while securing them from contracting VD and committing rape. The fact that comfort women in transit were often listed in the inventory as "cargo" clearly demonstrated how the top military officers regarded these women.

From the perspective of the client, there were important continuities between the karayuki-san system and the subsequent wartime comfort women system. In the comfort women system, soldiers usually purchased a ticket to receive service from a comfort woman. Entering the woman's room, they personally handed the ticket to her. This action encouraged the belief that their conduct was a legitimate, commercial transaction. Whether or not a woman was properly paid by her "employer" – the brothel keeper – was of no concern to these soldiers, as they had "paid" for the service in any case. Whatever the misery of her existence, they felt entitled to enjoy the service in the exchange for payment. For them, comfort women were not "slaves," but "serving women" who were commercially obliged to "comfort" them. If the service was not to his satisfaction, a service-man might consider himself cheated and therefore assume the right to coerce the comfort woman to satisfy him – after all, he had "paid"! Such an attitude contributed to the frequent violence by soldiers against comfort women. This fraudulent notion of "commercial transaction," which conceals and distorts both the direct role of the military in the system and the elements of coercion, slavery, and deception in which many women were kidnapped or deceived and received little or no payment for their services, even now blurs the perception of former Japanese soldiers and some nationalist historians about the real nature of the comfort women system. The fear of being branded a "prostitute" due to the deceptive nature of this business formality was for a long time a major hindrance preventing former comfort women from coming forward and testifying about their ordeals.

The postwar comfort women system that the Allied occupation soldiers extensively utilized in Japan was based upon the same fraudulent conception of a business transaction. It is therefore hardly surprising to find the behaviour of Japanese soldiers towards Asian comfort women and that of American, British and Australian soldiers towards Japanese comfort women almost identical. Both Japanese and Allied soldiers held comfort women in contempt, calling them "a communal toilet" or "a yellow stool," yet the soldiers did not hesitate at all to use the "service" rendered by these "cheap whores." In this context, each comfort woman was reduced to a sexual object.

However, the commodification and depersonalization of women's sexuality is not unique to the comfort women system. Indeed, it is a universally distinctive characteristic of all forms of prostitution, whether a woman (or, less commonly, a man) is coerced or not. Even when a woman chooses to become a prostitute and is paid the agreed sum by her client, the transaction differs from most other types of commercial business. Being a prostitute means that one's body and sexuality are objectified, impersonalized, and commodified. One's entire body becomes the property of the client, and thus one's personal autonomy is stripped away. In other words, the prostitute is physically alive, but socially dead in each transaction.[22] Yet the paradox is that, by paying the prostitute, the client demands that "the prostitute be a person who is not a person."[23] However, a socially dead person is "a person without power, natality or honour."[24] She is powerless "in the sense that the degraded status of the 'whore' dissolves any entitlement to the protection and respect accorded to non-prostitutes."[25] There-fore, regardless of the circumstances, any person who acts as a prostitute feels vulnerable because she is dominated by and subordinated to her client, not only in the physical sense but also in a profound personal sense. In this context, there is a fundamental similarity between prostitutes and slaves. The comfort women system and the more recent Bosnian case of "rape factories" are often described as systems of "sexual enslavement." It can be said, however, that all forms of prostitution basically share the universal characteristics of enslavement, although the comfort women system and the Bosnian case greatly deepen the alienation and exploitation of women as systems of a particularly brutal sexual enslavement.

While noting the fundamental, universal characteristics shared by various types of broadly defined "prostitution," we emphasize the fact that the exploitation of women's sexuality by military men is particularly notable and for the frequent association with intense violence. We should ask the basic question: Why does sexual exploitation of women invariably increase and take on more terrible forms during wartime?

Sexual activity provides human beings not only with physiological pleasure, but also with an escape from reality – psychological joy – no matter how momentary that joy is. At the same time, through intimate and affectionate physical contact, one rediscovers one's existence and reaffirms the value of one's life. Thus, sexual joy is the joy of deep and strong mutual reaffirmation in the lives of two people. Drinking alcohol is another human activity which has the function of helping one escape from reality, but it lacks the function of reaffirming the value of life's existence. In war, when facing imminent death, and far removed from home and family, it is not surprising that many men are drawn to strongly seek sexual gratification.

The more dangerous a battle, the more intense a soldier's sexual desire may become. The following account by an American Vietnam War veteran vividly illustrates the psychological state that many soldiers confront:

> A man and a woman holding each other tight for one moment, finding in sex some escape from the terrible reality of war. The intensity that war brings to sex, the "let us love now because there may be no tomorrow" is based on death. No matter what our weapons on the battlefield, love is finally our only weapon against death. Sex is the weapon of life, the shooting sperm sent like an army of guerillas to penetrate the egg's defenses – the only victory that really matters. War thrusts you into the well of loneliness, death breathing in your ear. Sex is a grappling hook that pulls you out, ends your isolation, makes you one with life again.[26]

It is therefore a common phenomenon through the history of warfare – not only during World War II – that soldiers desperately seek women. In World War I, British soldiers were given bromide to curb their sexual urges. Despite this, one brothel in Rouen set up by the British Army was visited by 171,000 men in the first year of the war alone. A startling number of soldiers – more than 400,000 British and 340,000 US – contracted VD during that war. VD was the cause of hospitalization for over one-quarter of the British army.[27] The medical cost for treating these men must have been astronomical. In the final 11 months of World War II in Europe, one scholar has estimated that the average soldier slept with 25 women, not necessarily all of them professional women.[28] In short, the problem of war is intimately intertwined with the problems of sexuality, and sexuality shapes the conduct of men in war.

The sexual activities of men during war almost always involve heightened violence against women. Soldiers' survival hinges on their violent action in attacking the enemy as well as in defending themselves. The same can be said for the enemy. Therefore, a soldier has to become more violent than his enemy in order to defend his own life. A vicious cycle occurs, in which violence creates more violence, escalates in intensity, and leads to brutality. Once war breaks out, soldiers are quickly caught up in this psychological process, losing their humanity by brutalizing themselves and, at the same time, dehumanizing the enemy. The brutalization of oneself and the dehumanization of the enemy may lead to the dehumanization of third parties, such as civilians, as well. It is under such relentless conditions that soldiers seek sexual intercourse as a means of escaping from the fear of death and to reconfirm the value of their lives. They try to gratify this desire even by violating women's bodies and thus dehumanizing them. For the soldiers involved in a fierce and merciless battle, the dehumanization of women becomes psychologically easier due to the constant and intensive process of dehumanizing "others" and brutalizing oneself on the battlefield. It is a stark irony that, in war, sexual intercourse becomes corrupt and is exploited as a means of dehumanization, while it should provide great joy, reaffirming life, and confirming an intimate relationship with a partner.

Physical domination over women may also spark soldiers' desires to dominate and humiliate the enemy. This is particularly so if the victims of their sexual violence are "women belonging to the enemy." This is one of the major reasons that in wartime women are often raped before the very eyes of their fathers, husbands or brothers. For men in battle, the physical violation of their women by the enemy is a most humiliating act; it serves to reinforce their subjugation to the occupying troops.[29] It is therefore not surprising that certain vocabulary used on the battlefield corresponds to sexual language. For example, an army "penetrates enemy territory" and the Japanese military-supplied condom brand was "Assault No. 1."

The internal power relations of armies constitute a strict class system in which enlisted soldiers are always subject to the orders of officers. This creates a contradiction whereby soldiers whose principal task is to dominate and subjugate the enemy must subordinate themselves to the unquestionable authority of their officers. This contradiction is intensified on the battlefield, where the necessity to dominate the enemy is literally a matter of life or death for the individual soldier, and the need for the officer class to dominate and exercise unquestioned authority over groups of soldiers becomes strategically imperative. Such a contradiction creates both a high degree of tension and a context in which violence is the standard mode for the release of tension. Consequently, the rape of women perceived as being the "enemy," or "belonging to the enemy," becomes a frequently used form of release – an apparently unruly behaviour, escaping the disciplinary matrix, which is really the underbelly of the disciplinary system. The more absolute the relationship of domination between officers and enlisted men within an army, the greater is the contradiction between their relations to the subjugated enemy and their situation within their own force. As a result, their behaviour towards the enemy – soldiers, male civilians and women – becomes more violent. This is one explanation for the comparatively large number of rapes committed by the Japanese troops in the Asia-Pacific War.[30]

Whether or not rape is committed in wartime, one of its major motives is the "conquest of others," a phenomenon which Nicholas Groth calls "power rape."[31] This motive is clearly illustrated in the following confession of a rapist (in this case a civilian):

> In my rapes the important part was not the sexual part, but putting someone else in the position in which they were totally helpless. I bound and gagged and tied up my victims and made them do something they didn't want to do, which was exactly the way I felt in my life. *I felt helpless, very helpless.*[32]
>
> [Emphasis added]

According to Groth, there are two other types of rape – anger rape, in which sexuality becomes a hostile act, and sadistic rape, in which anger and power become eroticized. However, Groth's research shows that more than half (55 percent) of the cases he and his colleagues examined could be categorized as power rapes, while about 40 percent were anger rapes and 5 percent were sadistic rapes.[33] The feeling of helplessness is particularly enhanced while men are involved in fierce combat. In war, soldiers frequently feel that their own fate is beyond their control and that they could be killed at any time. They need to feel powerful and many resort to aggressive behavior in order to overcome this feeling of helplessness. To achieve this goal, sex becomes their weapon and its consequence is the destruction of women. However, the sexual exploitation of women provides only momentary relief from such debilitated feelings, and it does not solve the problem of vulnerability. Thus, soldiers have to continually rely upon these self-deceptive, temporary measures of "power rape." This helps to explain the frequent brutality of Japanese soldiers towards comfort women, particularly after returning from battle. They needed someone to vanquish in order to feel that they were the master of their own fate, although the satisfaction gained from such victimization of women was brief and illusory. In the Philippines and many parts of China, as we have seen in Chapter 2, the comfort women system revealed its real nature – power rape. When it was set up and operated in these places where the Japanese military could not destroy the enemy and control its own fate, it was not even disguised as a "commercial transaction."

For a soldier who is placed in a life-or-death situation, and whose humanity is threatened by merciless war, abstract moral concepts such as "international law" or "crimes against humanity" may have little immediate or effective meaning. It was not only in World War II, but also in Vietnam, the Persian Gulf, Somalia, Rwanda, Bosnia-Herzegovina, Kosovo, and Chechnya, among many others, that international law was ignored and many women were victimized by rape and massacre. This is because, as we have seen, the sexual abuse of women is one of the inevitable aspects of war. In order to prevent military violence and forced prostitution (the Japanese comfort women system providing an extreme example), it is necessary to re-examine the very nature of the organization of military forces and of war in general.

Although military violence against women is heightened to extreme levels during war, such a firm-rooted tendency towards the sexual exploitation of women by military men is not limited to wartime. The fact that soldiers are possessed of a strong propensity to commit sexual violence even in peacetime is well supported by studies of base area prostitution, including numerous criminal cases involving soldiers. For example, it is well known that sexual violence committed by US military personnel was long endemic at its Subic Bay naval base in the Philippines, which it operated until the end of 1992. It remains a serious concern for residents living near the US military bases in Okinawa and Korea. Military violence against Okinawan women continued after the Battle of Okinawa, despite a widespread clandestine prostitution that was regulated by the US military authorities. For example, in 1955, a 6-year-old girl, Nagayama Yumiko, in Ishikawa city, was abducted, raped, and murdered by a GI stationed at Kadena Base. This is only one, if the most shocking, of numerous cases of sexual crimes committed by American soldiers in Okinawa over the past half century.[34] One of the most widely publicized cases was the abduction and rape of a 12-year-old Okinawan girl on her way home from shopping by three US servicemen in September 1995. The incident triggered massive demonstrations against the location of US military facilities on Okinawa.[35] In Korea, too, in the 20 years between 1967 and 1987, there were 72 reported cases of rape, in addition to numerous cases of physical violence against women committed by the members of the US troops stationed there. The most shocking case in Korea is probably the murder of Yun Kumi, a 26-year-old employee at one of the US military recreation clubs. She was killed by a young US soldier in October 1992. Her dead body was covered with heavy bruises, two beer bottles and a coke bottle being inserted in her vagina.[36]

However, the fact that many sex workers serving US soldiers in Okinawa, Korea, the Philippines, Japan and elsewhere are also confronting sexual violence every day receives little public attention simply because they are "prostitutes." Yet, the sex industry around the military bases continues to function with no sign of disappearing. As Cynthia Enloe clearly demonstrated in her study of contemporary military prostitution, military organizations in general require the service provided by prostitutes in order to confirm and reconfirm a militarized masculinity.[37] Soldiers are expected, indeed trained, to constantly demonstrate their masculinity and dominant power over the potential enemy, even in peacetime, and the notion of masculinity naturally involves the expectation of vigorous, even exploitative, sexual activity as a "tough guy." Therefore, military prostitution is different from other types of commercialized sex in the sense that "there are explicit steps taken by state institutions to protect male customers without undermining their perception of themselves as sexualized men."[38] In other words, military and state authorities are predisposed not only to tolerate military-controlled prostitution, but also to encourage soldiers' macho involvement in sexual activity, in order to enhance their aggressiveness. It is not surprising, therefore, to find high levels of sexual violence committed by soldiers against women living near military bases, despite provision of military-controlled prostitution. The fundamental cause of sexual violence committed by soldiers both in war and peacetime is this military culture of sexualized masculinity, a phenomenon common to military organizations regardless of nationality.

Have any military organizations broken the pattern of militarized and sexualized masculinity? Only further research will provide a satisfactory answer to this question. The slender available evidence, however, suggests that some national liberation movements fighting for independence, including China's People's Liberation Army in the anti-Japanese resistance and the civil war of 1937–1939, and the Vietnamese forces resisting the US and its allies in the 1960s and 1970s, worked to curb and punish rape. Cases of serious sexual crimes committed by members of the Chinese and Vietnamese liberation armies appear to have been rare. It may be argued that this is because they were hardly faced with "women belonging to the enemy" given the geopolitical situation of their conflict. Yet it is true that, while a large number of Japanese women left in Manchuria at the end of the Asia-Pacific War were raped by invading Russian troops, very few Japanese women have testified to rape by Chinese soldiers. It also appears that neither the Chinese nor the Vietnamese liberation armies had extensive access to prostitution services, whether organized by the military or the market, in contrast to the Guomindang and South Vietnamese and American forces that were their foes. The limited evidence suggests that the sexual morale and conduct of these national liberation forces were superior to those of their enemies, even in the face of protracted punishment by foes with superior weapons and resources. So, what kept their morale high and their conduct disciplined under punishing conditions? The answer lies in no small part in their nationalist commitment to the cause of resisting the military domination, colonization, and systematic barbarism of the invading forces. Those in the liberation movement were well aware of the consequences of occupation and colonization of their nations. They must have been conscious of what would happen to the women in the course of their nations being colonized or occupied by enemy troops, i.e., the frequently barbarous treatment of their nation's women. The Chinese people were familiar with the plague of rapes committed by the Japanese and their puppet soldiers, though the extent of their familiality with the comfort women system is not certain. So, too, the Vietnamese soldiers and civilians, and especially DRV and NLF forces, knew of the sexual misconduct of American soldiers stationed in Vietnam. In other words, consciously or unconsciously, they perceived the indissoluble link between sexual exploitation and colonization. It is possible that this knowledge of the sexual exploitation of their enemies and the nature of the patriotic independence struggle contributed to the creation and maintenance of an attitude that kept sexual abuse in check at least for the duration of the liberation and independence wars. This is a subject that merits further study.

Imperialism, the patriarchal state, and the control of sexuality

The colonization of one race by another or subordination of one racial group to another frequently involves the sexual exploitation of the women of the subordinated group by the men of the dominant one. For example, in the early stages of the British colonization of Australia, a large number of Aboriginal women were raped by white settlers, which caused widespread VD among the Aboriginal women. This consequently made many young Aboriginal women infertile, which eventually led to a rapid decrease in the Aboriginal population.[39] An almost identical phenomenon can be found in the modern history of the Ainu – the Japanese aboriginal people – whose population quickly declined after the movement of Japanese men – Wajin – from the main island to the Ainu homeland, the island of Hokkaido, in the late Tokugawa era.[40]

Colonization also frequently gives rise to widespread prostitution involving indigenous women. This happened in Korea and Taiwan after Japanese colonization, in India under the British,[41] and in the Dutch East Indies under the Dutch colonial government,[42] to name but a few. These are examples of the interlinkage of political and sexual domination, often with terrible and long-lasting physical and emotional effects on the colonized. The power over female members of a subjugated people is emblematic of the power exercised by colonial administrators to dominate colonial subjects. Japan's seizure of Manchuria illustrates the parallel between changing political and sexual relationships. Before the Japanese gained control, Japanese prostitutes in the territory served non-Japanese as well as Japanese clients. But that changed under Japanese rule, when the authorities prohibited Japanese prostitutes from serving non-Japanese customers. In the eyes of Japanese power holders, the bodies of women of their own racial group should not be penetrated by foreigners – an act symbolizing the invasion and deprivation of the motherland. This is the converse of the phenomenon of the active sexual exploitation of women of an invaded nation by the conquering force. Sexual exploitation affects the psyche of the occupied nation; it becomes de-masculinized, feminized, and subjugated. What the Japanese leaders were really trying to avoid by providing so-called "professional women" for the Allied forces following the end of the Asia-Pacific War was not the loss of the virginity of Japanese young women but the feminization of themselves by the occupation forces. They sought to avoid the humiliation of being feminized by sacrificing a limited number of "prostitutes," i.e. women viewed as marginal to the nation-state. As we have seen in the previous chapter, this scheme to contain the occupying forces failed miserably. Eventually, all of Japan came to be seen by the Allied soldiers as "one big brothel." Surely these patriarchal politicians could not have conceived a more humiliating situation. By corrupting one of the most private and intimate aspects of human life into humiliatingly open and impersonal conduct, the systems of imperialism and militarism establish political authority.

Conversely, therefore, popular slogans of political movements resisting colonization or military occupation by a foreign nation often use rhetorical expressions to symbolize the purity of their nation. For example, in South Korea during the recent campaign against SOFA,[43] i.e. the security agreement with the US, the slogan "Let us keep the virginity of our race" was repeatedly used in order to gain popular support for the movement . When the above-mentioned murder of a Korean sex worker, Yun Kumi, by a US soldier occurred in 1992, condemnation of the crime by the mass media promoted Yun Kumi as a "virgin victim." Thus, the symbolic victim of sexual violence by members of the occupying military forces must not be someone already rendering sexual service to them. She must be an innocent whose virginity embodies racial purity.[44]

Iris Young identifies the following five faces of oppression to which prostitutes are generally subjected: exploitation, marginalization, powerlessness, cultural imperialism, and violence.[45] These five apply not only to all forms of prostitution, but with particular force both to the comfort women system and to rape. Indeed, the comfort women system was a highly organized, systematic form of military rape. In its essence, as I have argued, the comfort women system was no different from any other type of prostitution or rape. However, it was clearly different in degree when measured against the above-mentioned five aspects of oppression. In all the areas where they were used, comfort women undoubtedly experienced the most extreme degrees of oppression. (Another, more recent, group of women who suffered a similar degree of oppression were the rape victims in Bosnia-Herzegovina.)

The comfort women system also differed from many other types of organized prostitution in the sense that it was organized at the highest echelon of the military, which planned and implemented it in co-operation with the state authorities. (In this sense too, the Yugoslavian military forces and the government seem to have organized sexual atrocities as a deliberate policy.) It was indeed different from any other forms of sexual exploitation in the sense that tens of thousands of women – Koreans, Chinese, Taiwanese, Filipinas, and other Asian women as well as some Dutch women – became victims of military rape and were forced to endure intense physical abuse over a long period. In other words, it was an unprecedented case in terms of the violation of the basic human rights of so large a number of women of different nationalities who were violated and abused as "sex slaves" over a considerable period.

The criminal nature of the comfort women system cannot be mitigated by the historical fact that the US and other Allied forces also used military-controlled prostitution. Nor can the crimes be argued away by the theory that all types of prostitution share the fundamental characteristics of oppression and enslavement. The Japanese cannot escape responsibility for these unprecedented violations of human rights by pointing to the common characteristics that the comfort women system and other types of prostitution share. Rather, it is essential to recognize the extreme levels to which rape and sexual slavery were carried out in the comfort women system.

For Japanese historians, including myself, one way to contribute towards accepting responsibility for this national crime committed by our fathers is to record honestly and to analyze systematically the extraordinary ordeals experienced by comfort women and to critically examine the historical processes of Japan's development as a nation-state that led to the formation of the comfort women system. We need to assess the socio-political and value structures that made it possible to perpetrate such a vast scheme of military-organized sexual exploitation. A comprehensive treatment of this issue would be a massive undertaking, and it would require a long-term, co-operative work between a number of Japanese historians (in particular feminist historians) specializing in various aspects of modern and contemporary Japanese history.

However, the key to finding the answer to this question may lie in an examination of the historical course of Japan's modernization. This has been characterized by an extraordinarily speedy transition from feudalism to capitalism, without a bourgeois revolution. This shift took place while maintaining some feudal elements, particularly the patrimonial socio-economic systems and the patriarchal ideologies. The transition also required the exploitation of women's labor in order to accumulate sufficient capital to develop modern industries. In recent times, Japanese historians, especially economic historians, have paid attention only to the contribution made by the female workforce in basic industries, such as agriculture, the textile industry, and coal mining. Although, as early as the late 1950s, a small number of Japanese feminist historians, such as Takamure Itsue, had pointed out the economic role of "the export of the sex industry" (in this case the karayuki-san system) in the formation of Japanese capitalism,[46] this aspect of Japan's modernization process has been long neglected. Modern Japan's domestic licensed prostitution industry, on which high tax rates were levied, also played an important role in raising public money when the government needed large sums to build the basic economic infrastructure.[47] As we have seen in the previous chapter, Japanese sex workers serving the GIs also contributed by earning vital foreign currency in the immediate postwar period, when Japan faced acute shortages of food and capital. In this way, Japan's sex industry has been closely intertwined with its accumulation of national capital from the very early stages of Japanese capitalism in the Meiji era. While it is not peculiar to Japan that the female workforce was, and still is, exploited for the development of a modern economy, it may be unusual to find another nation that exploited women for sex to that extent.

The socio-economic and cultural climate of Japan provided the environment for Japanese men – our fathers and grandfathers – to create an extraordinary military machine whose organization was deeply intertwined with sexual enslavement. This book is an initial step in the journey of research, which, I hope, will eventually lead Japanese men (and here I include myself) – the sons and grandsons of Japanese Imperial soldiers – to critically and productively re-examine our own history and culture.

Notes

Introduction

1 Maria Rosa Henson, *Comfort Women: A Filipina's Story of Prostitution and Slavery Under the Japanese Military* (Rowaman & Littlefield, Maryland, 1999) pp. 36–37.
2 Pak Kyeong sik, *Chōsenjin Kyōsei Renkō no Kiroku* (Mirai-sha, Tokyo, 1965).
3 Jonathan Glover, *Humanity: A Moral History of the Twentieth Century* (Jonathan Cape, London, 1999) p. 404.
4 Primo Levi, *The Drowned and the Saved* (Michael Joseph, London, 1988) pp. 169–170, cited by Jonathan Glover, op. cit., p. 402.

Chapter 1: The origins of the comfort women system

1 Yoshimi Yoshiaki ed., *Jūgun Ianfu Shiryō-shū* (Ōtsuki Shoten, Tokyo, 1992) Document No. 34, pp. 183–185. *Jūgun Ianfu Shiryō-shū* (hereafter *JIS*) is a collection of extracts of relevant parts from 106 items of official documents related to the comfort women issue. They were found mainly at the Archives of the Defense Research Institute (hereafter ADRI) in Tokyo between the late 1980s and early 1990s.
2 Ibid., Document No. 34, p. 184.
3 Ibid., Document No. 34, p. 185.
4 Ibid., Document No. 4, pp. 100–101.
5 Inaba Masao ed., *Okamura Yasuji Taishō Shiryō Vol. 1* (Hara Shobō, Tokyo, 1970) p. 302.
6 I will analyze the history of karayuki-san in more detail in the conclusion of this book in relation to the development of the comfort women system. For details of the history of karayuki-san, see, for example: Morisaki Kazue, *Karayuki-san* (Asahi Shinbun-sha, Tokyo, 1980); Yamazaki Tomoko, *Sandakan Brothel No. 8: An Episode in the History of Lower-class Japanese Women* (M. E. Sharpe, New York, 1999); James Warren, *Ah Ku and Karayuki-san: Prostitution in Singapore 1870–1940* (Oxford University Press, 1993); and Bill Mihalopoulos, "The Making of Prostitutes: the *Karayuki-san*" in *Bulletin of Concerned Asian Scholars*, Vol. 25, No. 1, 1993.
7 Okabe Naozaburō, *Okabe Naozaburō Taishō no Nikki* (Fuyō Shobō, Tokyo, 1982) p. 23.
8 Senda Kakō, *Jūgun Ianfu, Seihen* (Sanichi Shobō, Tokyo, 1978) pp. 26–29; Yoshimi Yoshiaki, *Jūgun Ianfu* (Iwanami Shoten, Tokyo, 1995) pp. 17–18.
9 Yoshimi Yoshiaki, *Jūgun Ianfu*, pp. 18–19.
10 Japanese National Public Record Office (hereafter JNPRO) Collection, *Konsei Dai 14 Ryodan Shirēbu, Eisei Gyōmu Junpō*, March 21–March 31, April 11–April 20, April 21–April 30, May 1–May 10, 1933; Rikugun Shō, *Manshū Jihen Rikugun Eisei-shi, Vol. 4* (Rikugun Shō, Tokyo, 1935) June 1933 Section.
11 JNPRO Collection, *Konsei Dai 14 Ryodan Shirēibu, Eisei Gyōmu Junpō*, July 21–July 31, 1933.

12 Nakayama Tadanao, "Manshū no Tabi" in *Tōyō* (Tōyō Kyōkai, Tokyo, 1933), November 1933 issue.
13 For details of various war crimes committed by Japanese troops in Nanjing, see, for example: Hora Tomio ed., *Nitchū Sensō Shiryō, Vols. 8 and 9* (Kawade Shobō, Tokyo, 1973); Nankin Jiken Chōsa Kenkyū Kai ed., *Nankin Jiken Shiryō-shū* (Aoki Shoten, Tokyo, 1992); and Honda Katsuichi, *The Nanjing Massacre: A Japanese Journalist Confronts Japan's National Shame* (M. E. Sharpe, New York, 1999).
14 Nankin Jiken Chōsa Kenkyū Kai ed., op. cit., pp. 211, 220, and 280.
15 Ibid., p. 411.
16 Yoshimi Yoshiaki, *Jugun Ianfu*, p. 25; Hata Ikuhiko, *Shōwa-shi no Nazo o Ou, Vol. 2* (Bungei Shunjū-sha, Tokyo, 1993) p. 327.
17 26 Kai Senyū-kai ed., *Hohē Dai 26 Shidan Shireibu Sen-shi* (private publication, 1988) p. 99.
18 Ho 104 Monogatari Kankō-kai ed., *Ho 104 Monogatari* (private publication, 1969) p. 425.
19 Asō Testuo, "Hanayagi-byō no Sekkyokuteki Yobō-hō" (June 26, 1939). This report written by Dr. Asō was reproduced in his autobiography, *Shanhai yori Shanhai e: Heitan Byōin no Sanfujinkai* (Sekifū-sha, Fukuoka, 1993) pp. 214–230.
20 Senda Kakō, op. cit., pp. 31–36.
21 Ōbayashi Kiyoshi, *Tamanoi Banka* (Sēchūbō, Tokyo, 1983) pp. 194–239.
22 *JIS*, Document Nos. 34, 36, 37, 53, 54, 55, 57, and 58, pp. 186–192, 258–263, and 266; Yoshimi, *Jūgun Ianfu*, p. 28.
23 *JIS*, Document No. 42, pp. 209–210.
24 Yoshimi Yoshiaki, *Jūgun Ianfu*, pp. 30–31.
25 *JIS*, Document No. 44, pp. 214–216.
26 ADRI Collection, Kimbara Setsuzō, *Rikugun Gyōmu Nisshi Tekiroku*, Part.1, 1-I. For a detailed analysis of these documents, see Yoshimi Yoshiaki, "Rikugun Chūō to Jūgun Ianfu Seisaku: Kimbara Setsuzō Gyōmu Nisshi o Chūshin ni" in *Kikan Sensō Sekinin Kenkyū*, Vol. 1, No. 1, 1993, pp. 4–11.
27 Shimada Toshihiko, *Kantōgun: Zaiman Rikugun no Dokusō* (Chūkō Shinsho, Tokyo, 1965) p. 176.
28 Jūgun Ianfu 110 Ban Henshū Iinkai ed., *Jūgun Ianfu 110 Ban* (Akashi Shoten, Tokyo, 1992) pp. 43–45.
29 Fujii Tadatoshi, "Chūgoku Senryōchi ni okeru Chōshu to Ianjo" in Yoshimi Yoshiaki and Hayashi Hirofumi eds., *Kyōdō Kenkyū: Nippongun Ianfu* (Ōtsuki Shoten, Tokyo, 1995) Chapter 4, pp. 71–97.
30 Okabe Naozaburō, op. cit., p. 23; Inaba Masao, op. cit., p. 302.
31 Nankin Jiken Chōsa Kenkyū Kai ed., op. cit., pp. 211, 220, and 280.
32 *JIS*, Document No. 42, pp. 209–210.
33 Senda Kakō, op. cit., pp. 103–105.
34 For details of the organizational structure of the Japanese Imperial forces, see US War Department, *Handbook on Japanese Military Forces* (Presidio Press, California, 1991) Chapter III.
35 Yoshimi Yoshiaki, "Gun Ianfu Seido no Shiki Mērei Kētō" in Yoshimi and Hayashi eds., op. cit, Chapter 2, pp. 15–28.
36 Mizobe Kazuto ed., *Doku San Ni: Mōhitotsu no Sensō* (private publication, 1983) p. 58.
37 *JIS*, Document No. 6, pp. 105–107.
38 Ibid., Document No. 28, pp. 164–172.
39 Sakurada Takeshi and Shikauchi Nobutaka, *Ima Akasu Sengo Hiwa, Vol. 1* (Sankei Shuppan, Tokyo, 1983) pp. 40–41.
40 For details of statistical data on condoms used by the Japanese Imperial forces during the Asia-Pacific War, see Hayashi Hirofumi, "Rikugun Ianjo Kanri no Ichi Sokumen: Eisei Sakku no Kōfu Shiryō o Tegakari ni" in *Kikan Sensō Sekinin Kenkyū*, Vol. 1, No. 1, pp. 12–19.
41 Yoshimi Yoshiaki, "Gun Ianfu Sēdo no Shiki Meirei Keitō" in Yoshimi and Hayashi eds., op. cit, pp. 24–25.

42 *JIS*, Document No. 5, pp. 102–104.
43 Mun P'ilgi, "I so much wanted to study" in Keith Howard ed., *True Story of the Korean Comfort Women* (Cassell, London, 1995) p. 81.
44 Mun Okuchu, *Biruma Sen-sen Tate Shidan no Ianfu datta Watashi* (Nashinoki-sha, Tokyo, 1996) p. 28.
45 *JIS*, Document No. 16, pp. 130–138.
46 ADRI Collection, Kimbara Setsuzō, *Rikugun Gyōmu Nisshi Tekiroku*, Part 1, July 26, 1941.
47 *JIS*, Document No. 18, pp. 142–143.
48 Ibid., Document Nos. 19 and 20, pp. 144–146.
49 Ibid., Document No. 29, pp. 171–172.
50 ADRI Collection, Kimbara Setsuzō, *Rikugun Gyōmu Nisshi Tekiroku*, Part 2, September 3, 1942.
51 Shigemura Minoru, "Tokuyōin to iu Na no Butai" in *Tokushū Bungei Shunjū*, No. 1 (Bungei Shunjū-sha, Tokyo, 1955), pp. 224–225.
52 *JIS*, Document No. 83, pp. 365–375.
53 Cited by Yoshimi Yoshiaki in his book, *Jūgun Ianfu*, p. 44.
54 This statistical data appears in the report entitled *The Roll of Court-Martialled Personnel, Compiled in 1942*, which was submitted by Ōyama Fumio, head of the Legal Affairs Bureau of the Japanese Imperial Army, to the prosecutors at the Tokyo War Crimes Tribunal after the war. See Utsumi Aiko, "How the Violence against Women were Dealt with in War Crime Trials" in Indai L. Sajor ed., *Common Grounds: Violence Against Women in War and Armed Conflict Situations* (Asian Centre for Women's Human Rights, Quezon, 1998) p. 191.
55 Ibid., p. 192.
56 *JIS*, Document No. 47, pp. 224–233.
57 Cited by Yoshimi Yoshiaki in his book, *Jūgun Ianfu*, p. 45.
58 *JIS*, Document Nos. 48 and 49, pp. 234–247.
59 Ibid., Document No. 60, pp. 273–277.
60 Yoshimi Yoshiaki, *Jūgun Ianfu*, p. 51.
61 Suzuki Yoshio, "Kagaisha no Shōgen: Ianfu kara Minoue-banashi o Kiita" in *Sekai* No. 637 (Iwanami Shoten, Tokyo, July 1997) pp. 120–121.
62 This estimate is based upon a report that the Kuwantung Army of 800,000 men planned to mobilize 20,000 Korean comfort women during the so-called "Kuwantung Army Special Maneuvres" in July 1941.
63 For details of Japan's eugenic policy during the Asia-Pacific War, see Matsunaga Ei, "Nippon no Yūsei Seisaku: Nachisu Doitsu to no Hikaku"; and Yonemoto Shōhei, "Yūseigaku: Nippon to Doitsu to no Hikaku" in Kanagawa University ed., *Igaku to Sensō* (Ochanomizu Shobō, Tokyo, 1994) pp. 24–43, 137–154.
64 Wakakuwa Midori, *Sensō ga Tsukuru Josei-zō* (Chikuma Shobō, Tokyo, 1995) pp. 66–67.

Chapter 2: Procurement of comfort women and their lives as sexual slaves

1 For details of the history of Korea and Japan's intervention in Korean affairs between the late nineteenth and early twentieth centuries, see, for example, Peter Duus, *The Abacus and the Sword: the Japanese Penetration of Korea, 1895–1910* (University of California Press, Berkeley, 1995) Part One; and Bruce Cumings, *Korea's Place in the Sun: a Modern History* (W. W. Norton, New York, 1997) Chapter 2.
2 Recently, some Korean and Japanese historians have cast doubt on the legality of the Second as well as the Third Japan–Korea Conventions in the light of the contemporary international law. For details of their arguments see Unno Fukuju ed., *Nikkan Jōyaku to Kankoku Hēgō: Chōsen Shokuminchi Shihai no Gōhōsei o Tou* (Akashi Shoten, Tokyo, 1995). In fact, even by 1906, a French professor of international law, Francis Rey, had pointed out the illegality of the "Second Convention" in his article "La Situation

Internationaie de la Coree", published in *Revue Generale de Droit International Public*, Vol. 13.

3 For details of the Japanese colonial administration in Korea, see, for example, Unno Fukuju, *Nippon no Rekishi, Vol. 13: Nisshin, Nichiro Sensō* (Shūeisha, Tokyo, 1992) Chapter 8.

4 P. Duss, op. cit., pp. 364–396; B. Cumings, op. cit., pp. 148–152.

5 Higuchi Yūichi, "Senjika no Chōsen Nōmin: Rison o Chūshin ni" in *Kikan Sensō Sekinin Kenkyū*, No. 7, 1995, pp. 55–63; Yun Myeongsuk, "Nicchū Sensō-ki ni okeru Chōsenjin Guntai Ianfu no Keisei" in *Chōsen-shi Kenkyūkai Rombun-shū*, No. 32, 1994, pp. 91–93.

6 For details of this massacre of Korean residents in Japan shortly after the Great Kantō Earthquake, see Kan Tokuso and Kum Byondon eds, *Gendai-shi Shiryō Vol. 6: Kantō Daishinsai to Chōsenjin* (Misuzu Shobō, Tokyo, 1963).

7 Ajia Minshū Hōtei Jumbi-kai ed., *Shashin Zusetsu: Nippon no Shinryaku* (Ōtsuki Shoten, Tokyo, 1992) pp. 80–82. For details of the history of Korean migrant workers in Japan, see Pak Kyonshiku, *Chōsenjin Kyōsei Renkō no Kiroku* (Mirai-sha, Tokyo, 1965).

8 Yun Myeongsuk, op. cit., pp. 93–94.

9 Ibid., p. 94.

10 Ibid., p. 94.

11 A Korean historian, Song Youn-ok, reports that the majority of Korean prostitutes in this period were married women. See her article, "Japanese Colonial Rule and State-managed Prostitution: Korea's Licenced Prostitutes" in *Positions: East Asia Cultures Critique*, Vol. 5, No. 1, 1997, p. 189.

12 Yun Myeongsuk, op. cit., p. 95.

13 Ibid., p. 95.

14 Ibid., pp. 96–97.

15 Song Youn-ok, op. cit., p. 182.

16 Ibid., pp. 181–182.

17 Yun Myeongsuk, op. cit., pp. 100–102.

18 *JIS*, Document No. 54, pp. 260–262.

19 Ibid., Document No. 11, pp. 118–120.

20 As Bruce Cumings suggests, the fact that many Korean men were involved in recruiting comfort women and running comfort stations may well have been one of the factors that hindered the South Korean Government from investigating this matter for so many years. See B. Cumings, op. cit., p. 179.

21 See, for example, testimonies of former comfort women, Yi Yongsuk, Yi Yongsu, Yi Sunok, Yi Tugnam, Yi Yongyo, and Kim T'aeson, which are all included in Keith Howard ed., *The Stories of the Korean Comfort Women* (Cassell, New York, 1993).

22 Jong Jinsong, "Nippon-gun no 'Ianfu' Seisaku no Keisei to Henka," paper presented at the Second Japan–Korea Joint Research Conference in Seoul in December 1993.

23 Keith Howard ed., op. cit., p. 42.

24 Ibid., p. 117.

25 Ibid., p. 81.

26 Ibid., p. 186.

27 Yoshimi Yoshiaki, *Jūgun Ianfu*, p. 100.

28 Ibid., p. 101; Pak Kyonshiku, op. cit., pp. 54–55; and Miyata Setsuko, "Chōsen ni okeru Kōmin-ka Seisaku" in *Kikan Sensō Sekinin Kenkyū*, No. 7, 1995, pp. 45–46.

29 See her testimony, "Silent Suffering" in Keith Howard ed., op. cit., pp. 168–176.

30 Yun Jeongok et al., *Chōsenjin Jōsei ga Mita "Ianfu Mondai"* (Sanichi Shobō, Tokyo, 1992) p. 13–14; Yoshimi Yoshiaki, *Jūgun Ianfu*, p. 101.

31 Keith Howard ed., op. cit., pp. 151–152.

32 The US National Archives (hereafter USNA) collection, United States Office of War Information, Psychological Warfare Team Attached to US Army Forces India–Burma Theater, *Japanese Prisoner of War Interrogation Report, No. 49*.

33 USNA collection, South-East Asian Translation and Interrogation Center, *Psychology Warfare: Interrogation Bulletin, No. 2.*

34 Taipei-shi Fujo Kyūen Shakai Fukushi Jigyō Kikin-kai, *Taiwan-chiku Ianfu Hōmon Chōsa Kobetsu Bunseki Hōkokusho* (June 1993) pp. 8–14.

35 Ibid., p. 12; Yoshimi Yoshiaki, *Jūgun Ianfu*, p. 111–112.

36 Taipei-shi Fujo Kyūen Shakai Fukushi Jigyō Kikin-kai, op. cit., pp. 15–17.

37 Ching-Feng Wang and Mei-Fen Chiang, "Japan Should Bear Full Legal Responsibility for Compensation – An Account of Taiwanese Comfort Women's Quest", paper presented at the International Conference on Violence Against Women in War and Armed Conflict Situations, held in Tokyo in November 1997, p. 3; Itō Takashi, "Kokoro no Itami wa Wasurenai: Taiwan Senjūminzoku no Nippon-gun 'Ianfu'-tachi" in *Shukan Kinyōbi*, No. 230, August 1998, pp. 70–73.

38 Itō Takashi, op. cit., p. 72.

39 An exceptional case was that of Mun Okuchu. In one of her testimonies, Mun claims that, one autumn evening in 1940, she was kidnapped by a Japanese military policeman on her way home from a friend's house. In another testimony, she claims that she was kidnapped by three men – a Japanese military policeman, a Korean military policeman, and a Korean police detective. See her testimonies, "Back to my wretched life" in Keith Howard ed., op. cit., pp. 106; and Mun Okuchu, *Biruma Sensen Tate Shidan no "Ianfu" datta Watashi* (Nashinoki-sha, Tokyo, 1996) p. 28.

40 Su Zhiliang, "The Nanking Massacre and the 'Comfort Women' System of the Japanese Military," paper presented at the International Conference on Violence Against Women in War and Armed Conflict Situations, held in Tokyo in November 1997, p. 5.

41 There is some evidence to indicate that, towards the end of the war, some Chinese women were sent from Guangzhou to various comfort stations in Southeast Asia, in particular Burma. But detailed information about these women is not available. See Fujii Tadatoshi, op. cit., pp. 91–92.

42 For details of atrocities that Japanese men committed against Chinese civilians under the name of the "scorched-earth strategy" in various places in China, see, for example: Kasahara Tokuji, "Chūgoku Sensen ni okeru Nippon-gun no Seihanzai" in *Kikan Sensō Sekinin Kenkyū*, No. 13, 1996, pp. 2–11; Fujiwara Akira, "Sankō Sakusen to Kita Shina Hōmen-gun" Part I and Part II, *Kikan Sensō Sekinin Kenkyū*, No. 20 (pp. 21–29) and No. 21 (pp. 68–75), 1998. A collection of confessions of some former Japanese soldiers who committed atrocities in China is also available in Japanese. See Chūgoku Kikansha Renraku-kai ed., *Watashitachi wa Chūgoku de Nani o Shitaka: Moto Nipponjin Senpan no Kiroku* (Sanichi Shobō, Tokyo, 1987).

43 Ōmori Noriko, "Chūgokujin 'Ianfu' Soshō: Torikumi no Kēi to Genjō" in *Kikan Sensō Sekinin Kenkyū*, No. 15, 1997, pp. 66–69; Kang Jian, "Chinese Women War Victims and the Legal Responsibilities of the Japanese Government", paper presented at the International Conference on Violence Agaianst Women in War and Armed Conflict Situations, held in Tokyo in November 1997, p. 1.

44 Li Xiumei's testimony is available in Japanese in *Kikan Sensō Sekinin Kenkyū*, No. 15, 1997, pp. 72–75.

45 Ibid., p. 74.

46 Liu Mianhuan's testimony was also published in *Kikan Sensō Sekinin Kenkyū*, No. 15, 1997, pp. 75–77.

47 *JIS*, Document Nos. 67–74.

48 Ibid., No. 67.

49 For details of her experience as a comfort woman, see R. Henson, op. cit.

50 A summary of these 51 testimonies, as well as the complete record of several of them, are now available in Japanese. See *Firippin no Nippon-gun Ianfu: Seiteki Bōryoku no Higaisha-tachi*, compiled by the Panel of Japanese Lawyers Working for the Filipina Comfort Women (Akashi Shoten, Tokyo, 1995). Eighteen of these testimonies are also available in English under the title of *Philippine "Comfort Women" Compensation Suit: Excerpts of*

the Complaint published by the Task Force on Filipino Comfort Women and the Japanese Committee for the Filipino Comfort Women (Manila, 1993).

51 Satō Yoshitsugu, "Firippin Senryōshi" in the Panel of Japanese Lawyers Working for the Filipina "Comfort Women" compiled, op. cit., p. 143.

52 Ibid., p. 52.

53 *Philippine "Comfort Women" Compensation Suit: Excerpts of the Complaint*, p. 17.

54 Ibid., p. 53.

55 For details of sexual violence at "rape camps" in Bosnia-Herzegovina during the Bosnian War, see, for example, Alexandra Stiglmayer, "The Rape in Bosnia-Herzegovina" in Alexandra Stiglmayer ed., *Mass Rape: The War against Women in Bosnia-Herzegovina* (University of Nebraska Press, Lincoln, 1992) pp. 82–169.

56 Keith Howard, ed., op. cit., p. 90. English translations of the Japanese words in brackets were added by Yuki Tanaka to the original text.

57 As few former Japanese comfort women have so far come forward, it is difficult to draw a general picture of their life during the war. In the late 1960s and early 1970s, a Japanese freelance writer, Hirota Kazuko, conducted extensive interviews with a former Japanese comfort woman, Kikumaru, who served at a navy comfort station on Truck Island. According to Kikumaru's testimony, she served only the officer-class men and was comparatively well treated. Yet she committed suicide at 48 years old in April 1972, having spent most of her postwar life as a sex worker. See, Hirota Kazuko, *Shōgen Kiroku: Jūgun Ianfu, Kangofu – Senjō ni Ikita Onna-tachi no Dōkoku* (Shin Jimbutsu Ōrai-sha, Tokyo, 1975) pp. 11–115.

58 Testimony of Nishihira Junichi cited by Fukuchi Hiroaki in his book *Okinawa-sen no Onna-tachi: Chōsen-jin Jūgun Ianfu* (Kaifū-sha, Naha, 1992) p. 73.

59 Keith Howard ed., op. cit., pp. 53–54.

60 Ibid., p. 45.

61 Ibid., p. 37.

62 Ibid., pp. 84 and 155.

63 Ibid., p. 74.

64 Stated in her compensation suit against the Japanese government, which was submitted to the Tokyo District Court in April 1993, p. 44.

65 USNA collection, Allied Translation and Interpreter Section Research Report No. 120, *Amenities in the Japanese Armed Forces* (November 1945), p. 12. "Chinese" in this chart probably means "Taiwanese." According to available information and testimonies of former comfort women, it can be confirmed that some Taiwanese women were sent to the Philippines, while so far there is no document or testimony which refers to any Chinese woman from mainland China who was sent to the Philippines.

66 Ibid., p. 10.

67 Yoshimi Yoshiaki, *Jūgun Ianfu*, p. 145.

68 Keith Howard ed., op. cit., p. 137.

69 Ibid., p. 129.

70 Ibid., pp. 112–113.

71 Ibid., pp. 118–119.

72 Ibid., p. 85.

73 Ibid., p. 85.

74 *JIS*, Document No. 92, pp. 413–416.

75 Keith Howard ed., op. cit., p. 36.

76 Ibid., p. 62.

77 Kawada Fumiko, "Gun Ianjo ni okeru Seikatsu Jittai" in Yoshimi Yoshiaki and Hayashi Hirofumi eds., op. cit., Chapter 6, pp. 163–164. The widespread use of drugs by comfort women was also testified to by a former Japanese soldier, Suzuki Yoshio. See Suzuki Yoshio, op. cit., p. 119.

78 Kawada Fumiko, op. cit., pp. 164–166. Some former comfort women talked about their colleagues who had committed suicide. See, for example, Yi Yongnyo's testimony, in

which she refers to a few such cases, including one who committed suicide by taking *sake* mixed with opium, in Keith Howard ed., op. cit., pp. 143–150.

79 A Japanese film-maker, Yamatani Tetsuo, recorded several interviews with Pe Pongi, conducted between 1977 and 1979, and produced a documentary film entitled *Okinawa no Harumoni*. The full transcript of these interviews is included in the book which Yamatani edited under the same title, *Okinawa no Harumoni* (Bansē-sha, Tokyo, 1979).

80 Ibid., pp. 92–121.

81 Keith Howard ed., op. cit., p. 140.

82 Ibid., p. 92.

83 There are anecdotes that, in some remote places such as Sakhalin and the Solomon Islands, Japanese troops killed all the remaining comfort women shortly after the surrender was announced. However, to date I have not obtained any concrete evidence or reliable testimony to confirm such claims.

84 Keith Howard ed., op. cit., p. 86.

85 From 1994, the Korean Council for the Women Drafted for Military Sexual Service by Japan, a Korean organization led by Professor Yun Jeongok, started investigating former Korean comfort women who stayed on in China after the war. They have so far located 10 such women who are still alive in China, mainly in Hankou and its neighboring regions. The testimonies of these 10 women are now available in Korean and Japanese. The Japanese edition is: Kankoku Teishintai Mondai Taisaku Kyōgi-kai, Tēshintai Kenkyū-kai ed., *Chūgoku ni Renkō sareta Chōsenjin Ianfu* (Sanichi Shobō, Tokyo, 1996). In 1997, a Korean woman living in Kampuchea named Hun came forward and stated that she was a comfort woman.

86 With regard to comfort women and comfort stations in Southeast Asia, see the following work by Hayashi Hirofumi, "Marē Hantō no Nippon-gun Ianjo" in *Sekai*, No. 579, 1993, pp. 272–279; "Ajia Taiheiyō Senka no Ianjo no Tenkai" in Yoshimi Yoshiaki and Hayashi Hirofumi eds., op. cit., Chapter 5, in particular pp. 99–114; "Shingapōru no Nippon-gun Ianjo" in *Kikan Sensō Sekinin Kenkyū*, No. 4, 1994, pp. 34–43; "Shiryō Shōkai: Biruma Mandāre no Nippon-gun Inajo Kitē" in *Kikan Sensō Sekinin Kenkyū*, No. 6, 1994, pp. 74–79.

Chapter 3: Comfort Women in the Dutch East Indies

1 Harada Katsumasa ed., *Shōwa: Niman Nichi no Zen Kiroku, Vol. 6, Taiheiyō Sensō* (Kōdansha, Tokyo, 1990), pp. 142–143.

2 For details of the Japanese military occupation of the Dutch East Indies, see Sato Shigeru, *War, Nationalism and Peasants: Java Under the Japanese Occupation, 1942–1945* (M. E. Sharpe, New York, 1994), in particular, Part I "The Military Administration for Total Mobilization."

3 The International Military Tribunal for the Far East (Tokyo, 1946; hereafter *IMTFE*) p. 13,639.

4 Ibid., pp. 13,639–13,642.

5 Ibid., p. 13,638.

6 *Report of a Study of Dutch Government Documents on the Forced Prostitution of Dutch Women in the Dutch East Indies during the Japanese Occupation* (Amsterdam, 1994; hereafter *The Dutch Government Report*) p. 4.

7 Ibid., p. 4.

8 Ajia Minshū Hōtei Jumbi-kai ed., Nippon no Shinryaku (Ōtsuki Shoten, Tokyo, 1992) pp. 228–229.

9 See note 6 this chapter. This report was presented to the Lower House of the Dutch Parliament by the Dutch Minister of Foreign Affairs on January 24, 1994. The report contains basic errors in reference to Japanese history. It claims, for example, that prostitution was illegal in pre-war Japan. On the contrary, Japan had a long history of regulated prostitution before World War II. In addition, the 7th Army of the Japanese

Imperial forces at Singapore was not directly under the command of the Headquarters in Tokyo as stated here but under the control of the South Army.

10 *The Dutch Government Report*, p. 2.

11 This extract from Nakamura Hachirō's memoirs in his book *Aru Rikugun Yobishikan no Shuki* (Gendai-shi Suppan-kai, Tokyo, 1978) was reproduced in Takasaki Ryūji ed., *Hyakusatsu ga Kataru Ianjo: Otoko no Honne* (Nashinoki-sha, Tokyo, 1994) pp. 74–75.

12 An extract from Kuroda Toshihiko, *Gunsei* (Gakufu Shoin, Tokyo, 1952) appeared in Takasaki Ryūji ed., op. cit., pp. 72–73.

13 An extract from Gotō Motoharu, *Kaigun Hōdō Senki* (Shin Jimbutsu Ōrai-sha, Tokyo, 1975) appeared in Takasaki Ryūji ed., op. cit., pp. 73–74.

14 John Ingleson, "Prostitution in Colonial Java" in D. P. Chadler and M. C. Ricklefs eds., *Nineteenth and Twentieth Century Indonesia: Essays in Honour of Professor J. D. Legge* (Centre of Southeast Asian Studies, Monash University, Melbourne, 1986) pp. 126 and 134. For details of the history and the contemporary situation of the prostitution industry in Indonesia, see also G. W. Jones, E. Sulistyaningsih and T. H. Hull, *Prostitution in Indonesia*, Working Papers in Demography No. 52 (Research School of Social Sciences, the Australian National University, Canberra, 1995).

15 J. Ingleson, op. cit., p. 137.

16 Tio Biauw Sing, *De Syphilis in het Regentschap Bandoeng*, p. 51, cited by J. Ingleson, op. cit., p. 136.

17 J. Ingleson, op. cit., p. 138.

18 For details of the worsening living conditions in the internment camps, see Nell van den Graaff, *We Survived: A Mother's Story of Japanese Captivity* (University of Queensland Press, Brisbane, 1989), in particular, Chapters 4–10. At the International Military Tribunal for the Far East in Tokyo, a British officer, Lieutenant-Colonel Nicholas Read-Collins, testified to the appalling physical and mental conditions of the Dutch female internees whom he met and interviewed during his trip to Java shortly after the war. His testimony appears in *IMTFE*, pp. 13,528–13,553. He stated, for example, in Batavia, "the main diseases were malnutrition, edema from beriberi, dysentery and a variety assortment of nervous disorders." He also claimed that "practically every women bore the marks of tropical ulcers and some still had an extreme wasting of various parts of the body, of the arms and of the legs, and in one instance I saw a woman whose legs had been eaten away to the bone by a tropical ulcer." See, *IMTFE*, p. 13,541.

19 *IMTFE*, pp. 13,487–13,488.

20 For details of the changes in Japanese policies concerning the internment of Dutch civilians during the war, see Utsumi Aiko, "Sumaran Ianjo Jiken" in *Indonesia*, Nos. 5/6, 1995, pp. 5–6.

21 Ibid., p. 7; *The Dutch Government Report*, p. 12.

22 The Dutch National Archives (Algemeen Rijksarchief) Collection, Algemene Secretarie 5200 (hereafter AS 5200). A Japanese freelance journalist, Kajimura Taichirō, who resides in Berlin, translated this document into Japanese in 1992, with assistance from Koen Mathot. I obtained a copy of the Japanese translation through a Japanese Publishing House, Ōtsuki Shoten, to which the translation manuscript was submitted for consideration for publication. Unfortunately, the Japanese translation of this document has not yet been published. The document contains interrogation texts of the Japanese suspects in war crimes committed against Dutch women, those of some victims of Japanese sexual violence, as well as of camp leaders and other internees of several camps in Java. It also contains court proceedings of War Crimes Tribunals on comfort women cases conducted by the Dutch military forces in Batavia. The page numbers of the Japanese translation are believed to differ from those of the original documents, and therefore I do not specify page numbers when referring to this document in footnotes.

23 Chaen Yoshio ed., *Horyo ni kansuru Sho-hōki Ruishū* (Fuji Shuppan, Tokyo, 1988) pp. 85–90.

24 Utsumi Aiko, op. cit., p. 6.
25 AS5200.
26 AS5200 and *The Dutch Government Report*, pp. 13–14. There are some discrepancies in the details of the account of this event among testimonies given by some camp leaders and internees of the Muntilan Internment Camp. I reconstructed the whole event by relying upon a few camp leaders' testimonies which seem to be the most reliable information collected by the Dutch military authorities after the war.
27 Ibid.
28 Ibid.
29 *The Dutch Government Report*, pp. 19–20.
30 Ibid., pp. 20–21.
31 Utsumi Aiko, op. cit., p. 9.
32 AS5200.
33 Ibid.
34 Ibid.
35 Testimony of E. van der Plog, the Japanese translation of which was published in *Kikan Sensō Sekinin Kenkyū*, No. 6, 1994, pp. 69–71.
36 AS5200; Jan Ruff-O'Herne, *50 Years of Silence* (Edition Tom Thompson, Sydney, 1994) pp. 64–72.
37 AS5200.
38 Ibid. According to Jan Ruff-O'Herne, who was taken to a comfort station directly from Ambarawa No. 6 camp, the paper that they were ordered to sign was written only in Japanese, and a Japanese army interpreter orally translated the gist of its content into English for the Dutch women. This information was given to me by Ruff-O'Herne in her letter addressed to me in August 1997. However, several other Dutch victims, who were interrogated by the Dutch military authorities after the war, testified that the paper was written both in Indonesian and Japanese. Incidentally, Ruff O'Herne and some others from the same internment camp refused to sign the paper.
39 AS5200; Jan Ruff-O'Herne was also raped by this doctor at each medical inspection. See J. O'Herne, op. cit., pp. 94–96.
40 AS5200; J. Ruff-O'Herne, op. cit., pp. 93–94, 102–103.
41 J. Ruff-O'Herne, op. cit., pp. 82–89.
42 An extract from the testimony of J. Ruff-O'Herne, published in *The Age*, December 11, 1992.
43 Testimony of E. van der Plog. See footnote 35 to this chapter.
44 AS5200; Utsumi, op. cit., pp. 11–12.
45 J. Ruff-O'Herne, op. cit., p. 108.
46 AS5200; Utsumi, op. cit., p. 14. The Japanese translation of the results of this Dutch War Crimes Tribunal was published in *Kikan Sensō Sekinin Kenkyū*, No. 3, 1994, pp. 44–50.
47 AS5200.
48 Ibid. Initially the Japanese treated the Eurasians in the same way as the Indonesians rather than the Dutch, and thus they were not put into the internment camps. However, as anti-Japanese sentiment became stronger among the Indonesians, the Japanese suspicion of the Eurasians' loyalty to Japan also grew stronger. As a consequence they took harsh attitudes towards them from early 1943, although the Eurasians were still free to move around. See H. J. Benda, J. K. Irikura and K. Kishi eds., *Japanese Military Administration in Indonesia: Selected Documents* (Southeast Asian Studies, Yale University, 1965) p. 72.
49 AS5200.
50 Ibid.
51 Ibid.
52 Ibid.

53 Ibid.
54 Utsumi, op. cit., p. 2.
55 This fact is stated by Nakasone himself in his memoir "Nijū-san sai de Sanzen-nin no Sō-shikikan," in Matsuura Takanori ed., *Owari-naki Kaigun* (Bunka Hōsō Kaihatsu Sentā Shuppanbu, 1978) p. 98.
56 For details of this tribunal, see the Japanese National Diet (i.e. parliament) Library (hereafter JNDL) Collection, Microfilm Document No. 5594. For details of the murder of 1,500 civilians in Pontianak, see Izeki Tsuneo, *Nishi Boruneo Gyakusatsu Jiken: Kenshō "Ponteana Jiken"* (Fuji Shuppan, Tokyo, 1987); and Gotō Kenichi, "Ponchanakku Jiken no Shiteki Kōsatsu', in Tanaka Hiroshi ed., *Nippon Gunsei to Ajia no Minzoku Undō* (Ajia Keizai Kenkyūsho, Tokyo, 1983) pp. 21–40.
57 Pramoeda Ananta Tur, "Mencari Jejak Para Perawan Yang Digondol Jepang: 1942–1945" (unpublished paper). A small proportion of this Indonesian manuscript was translated into Japanese and published in *Kikan Sensō Sekinin Kenykū*, No. 16, 1997. For details of Sti Fatima's testimony, see the Japanese translation, pp. 62–65.
58 Ibid., p. 59.
59 Ibid., p. 60.
60 Ibid., p. 61.
61 Ibid., pp. 58–59.
62 Interview with Doug Davey, conducted by the author in August 1992.
63 The Australian War Memorial holds several photos of these Javanese comfort women who were found in Timor when the Australian Forces landed at Kupan (Negative Numbers: 120082–120087). However, apart from short captions for each photo, there is no other information available on these women.
64 A Japanese broadcasting corporation based in Nagoya, Chukyō TV, produced a documentary film on the Indonesian comfort women and broadcast it in May 1997. One of several former Indonesian comfort women who were interviewed in this film testified that she was taken to New Guinea. This film, entitled *Koe Tozasarete Soshite*, was directed by Ms. Ōwaki Michiyo.
65 This information is provided in the above-mentioned documentary film, the source of which is the Indonesian government itself.
66 An article in the Indonesian weekly newsmagazine *Tempo* also suggests that there were probably many women who were "professionals" through both periods of the Dutch and Japanese colonial regimes. See Pandir Kelana, "Kisah Kadarwati yang sebenarnya" in *Tempo*, 25 July 1992.
67 For details of high VD rates among the Dutch forces stationed in the Dutch East Indies before the Pacific War, see John Ingleson, op. cit., pp. 133–136.

Chapter 4: Why did the US forces ignore the comfort women issue?

1 *Amenities in the Japanese Armed Forces*, ATIS Report No. 120 (15 November 1945) pp. 5–20.
2 USNA Collection, RG 165, Entry 79 "P File," Box 254, ATIS Bulletin No. 1483; Box 282, ATIS Current Translation No. 100; Box 320, ATIS Interrogation Report No. 25, Serial No. 35: Report No. 30, Serial No. 42A: Report No. 37, Serial No. 55; Box 321, Interrogation Report No. 57, Serial No. 99: Report No. 104, Serial No. 175.
3 USNA Collection, RG 208, Entry 378, Box 446, "United States Office of War Information, Psychological Warfare Team Attached to US Army Forces India–Burma Theater, Japanese Prisoner of War Interrogation Report, No. 49." Three photos of these Korean women being interrogated by the Nissei members of the Psychological Warfare Team are also held at the US National Archives: their reference numbers are RG 111, SC 267578, 267579, and 267580.
4 USNA Collection, RG 208, Entry 378, Box 446, "South-East Asia Translation and Interrogation Centre, Psychological Warfare, Interrogation Bulletin No. 2."

5 This information was obtained during my interview with Grant Hirabayashi on March 21, 1996, in McLean, Virginia, USA.

6 Fukuchi Hiroaki, op. cit., p. 19.

7 Hoover Research Institute, Stanford University, Collection, "Report of Military Government Activities for October 1945" and "Report of Military Government Activities for November 1945."

8 USNA Collection, RG 331, GHQ/SCAP Box 1967.

9 For example, Pe Pongi was one of a few Korean women who stayed in Okinawa after the war and lived there until she died in October 1991. See note 79 to Chapter 2.

10 USNA, RG 111, SE 4443/LA, 4450/LA, 4522/LA, 4523/LA: SC 230147, 230148, 247386: SC 20812. Australian War Memorial (hereafter AWM) Collection, Neg. Nos. 120082, 120083, 120086, 120087.

11 Yoshimi Yoshiaki, *Jūgun Ianfu*, pp. 175–192.

12 USNA Collection, RG 338, XXIV Corps, Box 8039, "Investigation."

13 See, for example, Tokyo Saiban Handobukku Henshū Iin Kai (ed.) *Tokyo Saiban Handobukku* (Aoki Shoren, Tokyo, 1989) pp. 167–169.

14 See, for example, Cynthia Enloe, *Does Khaki Become You? The Militarization of Women's Lives* (Pluto Press, London, 1983) pp. 27–29; and Susan Brownmiller, *Against Our Will: Men, Women and Rape* (Penguin Books, London, 1991) pp. 92–93.

15 USNA Collection, RG 165, Entry 43, Box 438, "Subject: Facilities for venereal prophylaxis for Air Force Ferry Command. Headquarters, Services of Supply, Washington, D.C., SPOM 726.1., To: The Surgeon General" (August 6, 1942).

16 Ibid., "War Department Headquarters, Services of Supply, Washington, D.C., SPOPM 726, Facilities for Venereal Prophylaxis" (August 6, 1942).

17 Ibid., "SPRMP 726.1, Facilities for venereal prophylaxis for Air Force Ferry Command" (September 19, 1942).

18 Ibid., "War Dept., S.O.S., SPMCE, Washington, D.C.; To: The Assistant Chief of Staff, G–1 (Through the Commanding General, S.O.S.)" (October 15, 1942).

19 Ibid., "Memorandum for the A.C. of S., G-1, Subject: Conditions in the Africa, Middle East and India-China Theaters" (September 18, 1942).

20 Ibid.

21 For details of "Circular 170", see USNA Collection, RG 165, Entry 43, Box 438, "SPGAM/250.1, Memorandum for the Chief of Staff, Subject: Revision of Circular No. 170, War Department, August 16, 1941" (December 30, 1942).

22 A reference to the existence of such stations already appears in the memo dated August 19, 1942, which was sent from 1st Lieut. Philip Grenley, Chief of Urology Section, Medical Corps to the Surgeon of Quarry Heights in the Panama Canal Zone. See USNA Collection, RG 165, Entry 43, Box 438, "Subject: Prophylaxis for Venereal Disease-(Gonorrhoea); To: The Surgeon, Panama Canal Department, Quarry Heights, Canal Zone."

23 USNA Collection, RG 165, Entry 43, Box 438, "War Dept., S.O.S., SPMCE, Washington, D.C.; To: Assistant Chief of Staff, G-1." (September 25, 1942); "Subject: Orders; Thru: The Surgeon General, Washington, D.C.; To: Major William A. Brumfield, Jr, 0226566, MC."

24 Ibid., "War Dept., S.O.S., SPMCE, Washington, D.C.; To: The Assistant Chief of Staff, G-1" (October 15, 1942).

25 Ibid.

26 Ibid., "Personnel Division, G-1 WDGS, WDGAP 250.1"; "SPGAM/250.1; Memorandum for the Chief of Staff, Subject: Letter to President, International Association of Chiefs of Police."

27 Ibid., "SPGAM/250.1, Memorandum for the Chief of Staff, Subject: Revision of Circular No. 170, War Department, August 16, 1941" (December 30, 1942).

28 Ibid., "Invocation of the May Act."

29 Ibid., "M/250.1, Control of Vice in the Area of Army establishments" (April 20, 1943).

30 Ibid.

31 Ibid., "Portland's Fight for Repression of Prostitution." (April 3, 1945). A similar problem of organized prostitution at Fort Huachuca in Arizona was also reported. See, ibid., "Conference on Segregated Prostitution – Fort Huachuca, Arizona – Recommend that no further action be taken" (July 6, 1942).

32 Ibid., "SPGAM/250.1, Memorandum for the Assistant Chief of Staff, G-1, Subject: Improvement of moral conditions in the vicinity of camps and stations" (July 6, 1943).

33 Ibid., "Conduct of Troops at Camp Polk, La." (March 15, 1945).

34 Ibid., "Memorandum for the A.C. of S., G-1, Subject: Medical Conditions in the African–Middle Eastern and India–China Theaters" (October 29, 1942).

35 Ibid., "Subject: Report of Investigation of Venereal Diseases among United States Army Forces in Central Africa, the Middle East, and India; To: Assistant Chief of Staff, G-1, War Department, Pentagon Building, Washington, D.C." (March 2, 1943) pp. 8–10.

36 Ibid., p. 10.

37 Ibid., "Subject: Moral Situation; To: Chief Administrative Services, War Department, Washington, D.C." (December 18, 1942).

38 Ibid., "Subject: Report of Investigation of Venereal Diseases among United States Army Forces in Central Africa, the Middle East, and India; To: Assistant Chief of Staff, G-1, War Department, Pentagon Building, Washington, D.C." (March 2, 1943) pp. 22–23, 35, 37.

39 Ibid., p. 25.

40 Ibid., p. 25.

41 Ibid., pp. 24–25.

42 Ibid., p. 19.

43 Australian Archives (hereafter AA) Collection, MP763/3, G135, *The Management of Venereal Diseases in Egypt during the War* by Sir James W. Barrett (London, 1919) pp. 7–8.

44 AWM Collection, AWM54, 267/6/17, Pt. 6, "The problem of VD in 7 Aust Div During Fifteen Months in the Middle East," p. 3.

45 Ibid., p. 4.

46 Ibid., pp. 4–6.

47 AWM Collection, AWM54, 267/4/11, "Incidence of VD A.I.F. in the Middle East."

48 AWM Collection, AWM54, 267/4/12, "Notifiable Diseases: Comparative Rates for 1,000 of Strength."

49 USNA Collection, RG 165, Entry 43, Box 438, "Subject: Report of Investigation of Venereal Diseases among United States Army Forces in Central Africa, the Middle East, and India; To: Assistant Chief of Staff, G-1, War Department, Pentagon Building, Washington, D.C." (March 2, 1943) pp. 12, 28.

50 Ibid., p. 12.

51 AWM Collection, AWM54, 267/4/11, "Incidence of Particular Diseases in A.I.F. in M.E., 1941."

52 USNA Collection, RG 165, Entry 43, Box 438, "Subject: Report of Investigation of Venereal Diseases among United States Army Forces in Central Africa, the Middle East, and India; To: Assistant Chief of Staff, G-1, War Department, Pentagon Building, Washington, D.C." (March 2, 1943) p. 42.

53 Ibid., pp. 1–2.

54 Ibid., "Memorandum for Assistant Chief of Staff for Personnel, S.O.S., Subject: Venereal Diseases in Overseas Bases." (December 5, 1942).

55 Ibid., "Prostitution and Venereal Diseases in Caribbean Bases"; "IG 333.9 – Caribbean Defense Command (B), Memorandum to the Assistant Chief of Staff, G-1, Subject: Prostitution within the Caribbean area" (April 6, 1943).

56 Ibid., "Prostitution and Venereal Diseases in Caribbean Bases," pp. 1–2.

57 Ibid., "IG 333.9 – Caribbean Defense Command (B), Memorandum to the Assistant Chief of Staff, G-1, Subject: Prostitution within the Caribbean area" (April 6, 1943) p. 3.

58 Ibid., p. 2.
59 Ibid., "Venereal Disease Control in Antigua."
60 Ibid., "Office of the Surgeon, Atkinson Field Air Base, British Guiana" (July 31, 1942). It is not a phenomenon peculiar to the US forces that many soldiers failed to use condoms although they were provided free of charge. A similar situation existed in the Australian forces during the war. According to one official report, only half the soldiers stationed in a particular part of Australia used condoms when associating with prostitutes. One-third of them used neither condoms nor chemical prophylactic at all. For more details, see AA Collection, MP742/1, 211/6/236, "Venereal Disease Survey in Queensland and L of C Area."
61 USNA Collection, RG 165, Entry 43, Box 438, "Letter from Eliot Ness, Director, Division of Social Protection, Community War Services, to Col. H. A. Cooney, G.S.C., Chief, Miscellaneous Branch, G-1 Division, War Department" (October 9, 1943).
62 There are substantial numbers of official documents relevant to V.D. problems amongst the Australian forces as well as civilians during World War II. A detailed analysis of these records would require writing a separate book.
63 AA Collection, MP742/1, 211/6/236, "Venereal Disease Survey in Queensland and L of C Area."
64 AA Collection, B551/0, 1943/110/4772. "Comb-out of Unemployed Women (Camp Followers) in Townsville Area [Prostitution]."
65 Peter Charlton, *Australia At War: War Against Japan 1942–1945* (Time-Life Books Australia, Sydney, 1989) p. 61.
66 Kay Saunders, "In a Cloud of Lust: Black GIs and Sex in World War II" in Joy Damousi and Marilyn Lake eds., *Gender and War: Australia at War in the Twentieth Century* (Cambridge University Press, Melbourne, 1995) pp. 178–190.
67 AA Collection. MP742/1, 65/1/92, "Prime Minister's Committee on National Morale, re Queensland."
68 AA Collection, A816, 37/301/199. "Report on Civilian Morale in North Queensland."
69 USNA Collection, RG 165, Entry 418, Box 465, "Subject: Establishment of Brothels in North African Theater" (November 25, 1943).
70 Ibid., "OPD 250.1, Memorandum for the Chief, Legistlative and Liaison Division, Subject: Establishment of Brothels in the North African Theater of Operation" (December 21, 1943).
71 Ibid., "War Department General Staff, Operation Division, Washington; Memorandum for General Hull" (November 28, 1943).
72 Ibid., "Confidential, War Department Classified Message Center, Incoming Message; From Algiers, No. W 6617" (December 1, 1943); "Confidential, War Department Classified Message Center, Incoming Message; From Cairo, No. AMSME 9923" (December 7, 1943).
73 Ibid., "Opening Brothel for the Soldiers of the 29th Division in France" (November 3, 1944).
74 Ibid., "WDGAP/250.1; House of Ill-Repute" (February 16, 1945).
75 Ibid., "AGOB-C-A Prostitution, House of Ill-Repute" (February 17, 1945).
76 Ibid., "AG726.1, OB-S-A SPGAM, Subject: Prostitution in Overseas Theaters of Operation" (April 24, 1945).

Chapter 5: Sexual violence committed by the Allied occupation forces against Japanese women: 1945–1946

1 For an official account of "Operation Iceberg," see R. E. Appleman, J. M. Burns, R. A. Gugeller, and J. Stevens, *United States Army in World War II, The War in the Pacific; Okinawa: The Last Battle* (Historical Division, Department of the Army, Washington DC, 1948). For a more recent unofficial analysis of this battle, see, for example, G. Astor, *Operation Iceberg: The Invasion and Conquest of Okinawa in World War II – An Oral*

History (Donald I. Fine, Inc., New York, 1995); R. Leckie, *Okinawa: The Last Battle of World War II* (Viking, New York, 1995); G. Feifer, *Tennozan: The Battle of Okinawa and the Atomic Bomb* (Houghton Mifflin, Boston, 1992).

2　Numerous books and memoirs on the battle of Okinawa are available in Japanese, but very few have been translated into English. One interesting Japanese memoir available in English is Colonel H. Yahara, *The Battle for Okinawa: A Japanese Officer's Eyewitness Account of the Last Great Campaign of World War II* (John Wiley & Sons, New York, 1995). Yahara was the senior staff officer of the 32nd Army in Okinawa.

3　Yamada Akira, "Beigun no Jōriku" in Fujiwara Akira ed., *Okinwas-sen: Kokudo ga Senjō ni natta toki* (Aoki Shoten, Tokyo, 1987) pp. 76–78.

4　Ōshiro Masayasu, *Okinawa-sen: Minshū no Me de toraetra Sensō* (Kōbunken, Tokyo, 1994) pp. 172–173.

5　M. Bilton and K. Sim, *Four Hours in My Lai: A War Crime and its Aftermath* (Viking, New York, 1992) pp. 102–162.

6　Takazawa Suzuyo, "Postwar US Military Crimes Against Women in Okinawa", paper presented at the International Conference on Violence Agaianst Women in War and Armed Conflict Situations, held in Tokyo in November 1997, p. 1.

7　Ōshima Yukio, *Genshoku no Nihon-shi: Sengo Nippon-jin wa dō Ikitaka* (Kōdan-sha, Tokyo, 1986) pp. 327–329; Shimabukuro Sōkō and Urashima Etsuko, "Kichi naki Okinawa o" in *Oruta*, No. 218, January 1996, p. 15.

8　Yamada Meiko, *Nippon Kokusaku Ianfu: Senryō-gun Ian Shisetsu, Onna-tachi no Isshō* (Kōjin-sha, Tokyo, 1996) p. 9.

9　"Kikisugita Joshi Sokai: Kanagawa-ken de Kairan-ban kara Konran Maneku" in *Asahi Shimbun*, 19 August 1945.

10　JNDL Collection, *Chian Jōsei* Nos. 8 (August 22, 1945) and 30 (August 31, 1945) in "Chian Jōsei Kempei Shireibu 1945, August–September," Japanese Army and Navy Archives, Reel 229, T1555/f02498-02511; Yamada Meiko, op. cit., pp. 10–11.

11　JNDL Collection, *Chian Jōsei*, No. 10 (August 23, 1945).

12　"Arienu Ryakudatsu Bōkō: Chōshū mo Waga Seifu no Te o Tsūjite Okonau" in *Asahi Shimbun*, August 19, 1945.

13　"Jōriku suru Beihei tachi yo: Mamore Genjū na Kiritsu" in *Asahi Shimbun*, August 19, 1945.

14　Due to this activity, Father Barn was investigated by the US Counter Intelligence Corps (C.I.C.) shortly after US occupation forces landed in Japan. However, he was soon cleared by the C.I.C. and his opinion on Japanese people was often sought by General MacArthur. A few years later he moved to Korea and he died at the beginning of the Korean War while participating in the well-known peace march to the north. See Duus Masayo, *Haisha no Okurimono: Kokusaku Ianfu o Meguru Senryō-ka Hishi* (Kōdan-sha, Tokyo, 1979) pp. 57–61.

15　"Dema ni Odoru wa Gu: Yatarani Konran Sureba Sekai no Monowarai" in *Yomiuri Hōchi*, August 20, 1945.

16　"Rengō-gun Hondo Shinchū Zengo no Kokoroe" and "Hikaeyo Fujoshi no Hitori Aruki: Fushidara na Fukusō wa Tsutsushimō" in *Yomiuri Hōchi*, August 23, 1945.

17　Yamada op. cit., p. 10. A similar notice was also circulated by some neigborhood associations in Yokosuka City. See *Yomiuri Hōchi*, September 2, 1945.

18　"Dai 8-gun to Kihei Dai 1-gun Jōriku" in *Yomiuri Hōchi*, August 31, 1945; "Makkāsā Shireibu: Atsugi Chakuriku, Yokohama e Shinchū" and "Kaihei-tai Zokuzoku Jōriku" in *Asahi Shimbun*, September 3, 1945.

19　Takemae Eiji, *GHQ* (Iwanami Shoten, Tokyo, 1983) p. 44.

20　JNDL Collection, "Rengō-gun Shinchū go ni okeru Jiko Hassei Chōsa-sho" in MOJ 6, *Japanese Police Intelligence Reports* (Naimushō, Keiho-kyoku, 1910–1945) Reel 2.

21　Kanagawa-ken Keistasu-shi Hensan Iin-kai ed., *Kanagawa-ken Keisatsu-shi Vol. 2* (Kanagawa-ken Keisatsu Honbu, Yokohama, 1974) p. 378.

22　Takemae, op. cit., p. 35.

23 Fujiwara Akira, Awaya Kentaro, and Yoshida Yutaka eds., *Shōwa 20 Nen, 1945 Nen* (Shōgaku-kan, 1995) p. 219.
24 Reports on many extortion cases are included in USNA Collection, GHQ/SCAP Records, Box No. 408, Sheet No. AG(a)-00022-00023, and GHQ/SCAP Records, Box 763, Sheet No. AG(d)-03132-03133.
25 Kitamura Yoshiko, "Kizu wa Iezu" in Itsushima Tsutomu ed., *Kuroi Haru: Bei-gun Panpan Onna-tachi no Sengo* (Tōgo-sha, Tokyo 1953) p. 256. Kitamura worked at the Yokohama office of the CLO from late August 1945 until March 1946. In April 1946, she was employed as an office worker at one of the camp bases of the US occupation forces in Yokohama. Her memoirs provide reliable first-hand information on various crimes committed by GIs in and around Yokohama city.
26 Ibid., p. 256.
27 For example, on September 4, 1945 alone, 98 extortion cases were reported to GHQ by the CLO, many involving the extortion of privately owned cars. However, in some cases, even police cars were extorted. See "General Headquarters US Army Pacific, Adjutant General Office, Radio and Cable Centre, Incoming Message: Japanese Government Radio NR C.L.O No. 41 DTD 9 September" in USNA Collection, GHQ/SCAP Records, Box No. 408, Sheet No. AG(a)-00022–00023. Incidentally, on the same day, some US soldiers broke into the official residence of the Mayor of Yokohama, unaware that it was the Mayor's house. Soon they were informed that they were in the Mayor's official residence. The report said that on "breaking into the drawing room, they asked the Mayor to sell the leopardskin hung for ornament on the wall, and upon the latter's refusal, they drove away in a jeep."
28 JNDL Collection, MOJ 38, "Documents on Japanese Police Activities" (Naimushō Keiho-kyoku, 1912–1946) Reel 13.
29 JNDL Collection, *Chian Jōsei* in "Chian Jōsei Kempei Shireibu 1945, August–September," Japanese Army and Navy Archives, Reel 229, T1555/f02498–02511.
30 USNA Collection, GHQ/SCAP Records, Box No. 408, Sheet No. AG(a)-00022–00023, and GHQ/SCAP Records, Box 763, Sheet No. AG(d)-03132–03133.
31 JNDL Collection, MOJ 6, Japanese Police Intelligence Reports, Reel 2, "Report on Incidents that Occurred After the Landing of the Allied Forces"; MOJ 8, "Japanese Government Documents and Censored Publications," Reel 4, "Police Intelligence Reports"; MOJ 38, "Japanese Police Intelligence Reports," Reel 13, "Documents Concerning the Occupation Forces."
32 JNDL Collection, MOJ 38, "Documents on Japanese Police Activities" (Naimushō Keiho-kyoku, 1912–1946) Reel 13, p. 38,3043. This document contains the names of victims and their addresses. However, I have not disclosed them for the sake of the privacy of the victims.
33 Ibid. A letter submitted by the CLO to GHQ on August 31 also refers to this case as well as the first case. See the letter marked as "CLO No. 4b" in USNA Collection, GHQ/SCAP Records, Box No. 408, Sheet No. AG(a)-00022–00023.
34 "General Headquarters US Army Pacific, Adjutant General Office, Radio and Cable Center, Incoming Message: Japanese Government Radio C.L.O–18 Cont'd: 11 cases against women" in USNA Collection, GHQ/SCAP Records, Box No. 408, Sheet No. AG(a)-00022–00023. This document also contains the names and addresses of the victims. However, for the sake of the privacy of the victims and their relatives, I have used only their initials and have deleted the details of their addresses. In fact, throughout this chapter, I have used only the initials of the rape victims, except those where there was an *attempted* rape.
35 "Tokkō Report No. 6478, 24 September 1945" in JNDL Collection, MOJ 8, "Japanese Government Documents and Censored Publications," Reel 4, "Police Intelligence Reports."
36 Ibid.
37 Takemae, op. cit., p. 40.

38 "Tokkō Report No. 7056, 2 October 1945" in JNDL Collection, MOJ 8, "Japanese Government Documents and Censored Publications," Reel 4, "Police Intelligence Reports."

39 The letter addressed "To the Supreme Commander for the Allied Powers from the Japanese Government, Central Liaison Office, Tokyo, Sept. 3rd 1945" in USNA Collection, GHQ/SCAP Records, Box 763, Sheet No. AG(d)-03132.

40 JNDL Collection, *Chian Jōsei*, "Shōgai Jōhō" No. 4 (September 5, 1945).

41 Ibid.

42 The letter from the Yokohama Liaison Office to the GHQ, marked as "YLO No. 21, 10 September 1945" in USNA Collection, GHQ/SCAP Records, Box No. 408, Sheet No. AG(a)-00022–00023.

43 According to one of the US occupation forces' documents, by mid-November 1945, 130 vehicles were reported stolen by GIs in Tokyo and of these 65 were recovered. The author of this report wrote "*only* 130 vehicles have been reported stolen" [emphasis added]. See the document entitled "Crime Held to Minimum in Tokyo During Occupation" in USNA Collection, GHQ/SCAP Records, Box No. 22, MISC-00928, "Allied Council for Japan: Public Information Section."

44 "Tokkō Report No. 7056, October 2, 1945" in JNDL Collection, MOJ 8, "Japanese Government Documents and Censored Publications," Reel 4, "Police Intelligence Reports."

45 JNDL Collection, MOJ 38, "Documents on Japanese Police Activities" (Naimushō Keiho-kyoku, 1912–1946) Reel 13, p. 383,111.

46 Ibid., p. 383,069.

47 Ibid., p. 383,122.

48 Sugita Tomoe, "Tsuma to natta Watashi no Kunō o Koete" in Mizuno Hiroshi ed., *Shini Nozonde Uttaeru* (Tōgo-sha, 1982) pp. 191–205. *Shini Nozonde Uttaeru* was first published in 1952 under the title *Nippon no Teisō*. All the testimonies of victims of rape by GIs included in this book were written under assumed names.

49 Duke University Library Special Collection, "Eichelberger Papers," Box 10: Letters (May–December 1945) September 2, 1945.

50 Ibid.

51 Ibid., September 3, 1945.

52 See note 24 to this chapter.

53 JNDL Collection, MOJ 38, "Documents on Japanese Police Activities" (Naimushō Keiho-kyoku, 1912–1946) Reel 13, p. 382,999.

54 See, for example, "Bei-gun no Miwake-kata" and "Kyōryoku shite Atare Tonari-gumi: Shinchū-gun ni Zettai Suki o Miseruna" in *Asahi Shimbun*, September 4, 1945.

55 See, for example, "Kanagawa-ken no Joseito wa Kyūkō: Kyō-shokuin ga Katei o Junkai Shidō" in *Asahi Shimbun*, and "Shinchū Chiku no Joseito Jugyō Chushi shite yoi: Kanagawa-ken Tōkyoku Kaku Gakkō e Hijō Sochi" in *Yomiuri Hōchi*, September 5, 1945.

56 'Junsatsu-hei o Dashite Keikai: Beigawa mo Hannin no Genjū Shobatsu o Yakusu' in *Asahi Shimbun*, September 5, 1945.

57 "Kempei Gosen-mei ga Shutsudō: Fushōji Bōshi ni Bei-gun Kyōryoku" in *Yomiuri Hōchi*, September 15, 1945.

58 Chiba-ken Keisatsu-shi Hensan Iin-kai ed., *Chiba-ken Keisatsu-shi Vol. 2* (Chiba-ken Keisatsu Honbu, Chiba, 1985) p. 484.

59 "Crime Held to Minimum in Tokyo During Occupation" in USNA Collection, GHQ/SCAP Records, Box No. 22, MISC-00928, "Allied Council for Japan: Public Information Section."

60 "Press Code for Japan" in JNDL Collection, Japanese Army and Navy Archives, Reel 225, T1531/f97699–97698, "Tsūcho Shorui Hensatsu: 1945. 8–10."

61 Takemae, op. cit., pp. 77, 124, and 196. The major English sources on this issue are: Monica Braw, *The Atomic Bomb Suppressed: American Censorship in Occupied Japan* (M. E.

Sharpe, New York, 1991); and John Dower, *Embracing Defeat: Japan in the Wake of World War II* (Norton, New York, 1999), Chapter 14.

62 "Amerika Minshu-shugi no Shinzui" in *Yomiuri Hōchi*, September 23, 1945.

63 "Inochi no Oya: Bē Guni-san" in *Asahi Shimbun*, September 26, 1945.

64 Both the kempeitai and Tokkō were abolished in October 1945, although some members of the Tokkō were subsequently employed by the CID (Civil Intelligence Division) of the US occupation forces.

65 Cited in Duus Masayo, op. cit., p. 75.

66 Chida Takeshi, *Kure-shi Shi Vol 8. Rengō-gun no Shinchū to Kure-shi* (Kure Shiyaku-sho, Kure, 1995) pp. 431–432.

67 Hiroshima-ken Keisatsu-shi Henshū Iin-kai ed., *Shinpen Hiroshima-ken Keisatsu-shi* (Hiroshima-ken Keisatsu Renraku Kyōgi-kai, Hiroshima, 1954) pp. 888–889.

68 Allen S. Clifton, *Times of Fallen Blossoms* (Cassell, Melbourne, 1950) pp. 141–144.

69 Ono Toshiko, "Shini Nozonde Uttaeru" in Mizuno Hiroshi ed., op. cit., p. 16.

70 Ibid., p. 17.

71 Kanzaki Kiyoshi, *Baishun: Kettei-ban Kanzaki Repōto* (Gendai-shi Shuppan-kai, Tokyo, 1974) p. 187.

72 Ono Toshiko, op. cit., pp. 18–23.

73 Kanzaki Kiyoshi, op. cit., p. 188.

74 Mizuno Hiroshi, "Watashi wa Tsūyaku datta" in Mizuno Hiroshi ed., op. cit., p. 287.

75 Regarding various difficulties that the Japanese police faced in investigating crimes committed by members of the Allied occupation forces, see, for example, Kanagawa-ken Keistasu-shi Hensan Iin-kai ed., op. cit., pp. 370–382. Even if a crime case was substantiated and the criminal was found, Japanese authorities lacked jurisdiction over the members of the Allied occupation forces during the occupation period.

76 Kawabe Satoko, "Watashi wa Dare ni Kōgi Sureba Yoinoka" in Mizuno Hiroshi, ed., op. cit., pp. 151–152.

77 Ibid., pp. 153–155.

78 Hamada Mieko, "Watashi no Shōgai o Fuminijitta Mono" in Mizuno Hiroshi ed., op. cit., pp. 232–242.

79 Ibid., pp. 249–253.

80 Itsushima Tsutomu, "Gaitō e no Shinshitsu" in Itsushima Tsutomu ed., op. cit., pp. 81.

81 Ibid., pp. 81–82.

82 Mizuno Hiroshi, op. cit., p. 285.

83 James Bone, "Beyond the Call of Duty" in *The Weekend Australian Review*, December 20–21, 1997, pp. 4–6.

84 Itsushima Tsutomu ed., op. cit., pp. 67–69.

85 Kitabayashi Yoshiko, op. cit., p. 297.

86 Ibid., p. 292.

87 AWM Collection, AWM 267/6/17/Part 17.

Chapter 6: Japanese comfort women for the Allied occupation forces

1 Kobayashi Daijirō and Murase Akira, *Minnawa Shiranai Kokka Baishun Meirei* (Yūzankaku Shuppan, Tokyo, 1992) pp. 3–4; Kaburagi Seiichi, *Hiroku: Shinchū-gun Ian Sakusen* (Shufu to Seikatsu-sha, Tokyo, 1972) p. 11. The original source for this information is the diary of Hosokawa Masasada, who was private secretary to Prince Konoe at the time.

2 Mentioned by Hosokawa Masatada in his diary. See Duus Masayo, op. cit., p. 22, and Kobayashi Daijirō and Murase Akira, op. cit., pp. 4–5.

3 Kobayashi Daijirō and Murase Akira, op. cit., p. 4.

4 Rōdō Shō Fujin Shōnen Kyoku ed., *Baishun ni kansuru Shiryō* (Rōdō Shō, Tokyo, 1955) pp. 12–13.

5 Relevant sections extracted from 17 official history books of 15 prefectural police divisions as well as the Tokyo Metropolitan Police Headquarters were reproduced in *Kikan Sensō Sekinin Kenkyū* Nos. 13 and 14, 1996, under the title of "Nippon Keisatsu no 'Ianfu' Seisaku (1), (2)" (hereafter, NKIS Part I and Part II).
6 NKIS Part I, p. 53.
7 Ibid., p. 53.
8 Ibid., p. 53.
9 Ibid., p. 54.
10 Ibid., p. 55.
11 NKIS Part II, p. 66.
12 Ibid., pp. 62–63.
13 Ibid., p. 63.
14 Ibid., pp. 63–64.
15 Kanagawa-ken Keisatsu Hombu Keisatsu-shi Hensan Iinkai ed., *Kanagawa-ken Keisatsu-shi Ge-kan* (Kanagawa-ken Keisatsu Hombu, Yokohama, 1974) pp. 346–347.
16 Ibid., p. 347–348.
17 Ibid., p. 352.
18 Ibid., pp. 355 and 360.
19 NKIS Part II, p. 66.
20 Yamada Meiko, op. cit., p. 117.
21 Itsushima Tsutomu ed., op. cit., pp. 30–36. The source of information is a testimony by one of the rape victims.
22 Osaka-fu Tokkō Ikka, "Kyū Kokusui Dōmei no Dōsei" (September 19, 1945) and Osaka-fu Keisatsu Buchō, "Nippon Kinrōsha Dōmei no Kanka ni Okeru Kesshū Jumbi Undō Jōkyō ni Kansuru Ken" (September 27, 1945). Both of these documents are included in *Naimu-shō Shiryō* in the collection of the Japanese National Diet Library (JNDL) Collection. See also Awaya Kentarō, *Gendaishi Hakkutsu* (Ōtsuki Shoten, Tokyo, 1996) p. 71.
23 Awaya Kentarō, op. cit., p. 72; *Kobe Shimbun* (September 8, 1945).
24 Duus Masayo, op. cit., p. 30.
25 Ibid., pp. 32–38; Kobayashi Daijirō and Murase Akira, op. cit., p. 9.
26 Kaburagi Seiichi, op. cit., p. 25; Kobayashi Daijirō and Murase Akira, op. cit., pp. 13–14; Duus Masayo, op. cit., pp. 61–63.
27 Kaburagi Seiichi, op. cit., pp. 16–17; Kobayashi Daijirō and Murase Akira, op. cit., pp. 10–11; Duus Masayo, op. cit., pp. 41–45, 51–52; Mark Gayn, *Japan Diary* (William Sloane Associates, New York, 1948) p. 233.
28 Duus Masayo, op. cit., pp. 52–53.
29 Ibid., p. 53; Kanzaki Kiyoshi, *Baishun: Kettei-ban Kanzaki Repōto* (Gendai-shi Shuippan-kai, Tokyo, 1974) pp. 134–136.
30 Kaburagi Seiichi, op. cit., pp. 20–21; Kobayashi Daijirō and Murase Akira, op. cit., pp. 21–23; Duus Masayo, op. cit., pp. 90–96.
31 Kobayashi Daijirō and Murase Akira, op. cit., pp. 26–27.
32 *Yomiuri Hōchi Shimbun* and *Mainichi Shimbun*, September 3 and 5, 1945.
33 Duus Masayo, op. cit., pp. 54–55.
34 Kanzaki Kiyoshi, op. cit., p. 134.
35 Ibid., p. 142; Mark Gayn, op. cit., p. 234.
36 Kanzaki Kiyoshi, op. cit., p. 135; Kobayashi Daijirō and Murase Akira, op. cit., p. 17.
37 JNDL Collection, Kempei Shireibu Jōhō, *Chian Jōsei*, No. 29 (August 30, 1945) in Japanese Army and Navy Archives, Reel 229.
38 Cited in Kobayashi Daijirō and Murase Akira, op. cit., pp. 27–28.
39 Kaburagi Seiichi, op. cit., pp. 25–26.
40 Ibid., p. 26; Kanzaki Kiyoshi, op. cit., pp. 136–137.
41 Kaburagi Seiichi, op. cit., pp. 7–28; Kanzaki Kiyoshi, op. cit., pp. 137–138; Duus Masayo, op. cit., p. 67.

42 Kaburagi Seiichi, op. cit., p. 28.

43 Ibid., p. 28; Duus Masayo, op. cit., p. 54; Kobayashi Daijirō and Murase Akira, op. cit., p. 52.

44 For details of Japan's prostitution industry prior to the end of World War II, see, for example: Yoshimi Kaneko, *Baishō no Shaki-shi* (Yūzankaku Shuppan, Tokyo, 1992) Chapters 1–12; Fujime Yuki, "The Licenced Prostitution System and the Prostitution Abolition Movement in Modern Japan" in *Positions: East Asia Cultures Critique*, Vol. 5, No. 1, 1997.

45 Duus Masayo, op. cit., p. 94.

46 Mark Gayn, op. cit., p. 232.

47 Duus Masayo, op. cit., p. 133; Kaburagi Seiichi, op. cit., p. 30.

48 Itsushima Tsutomu, ed., op. cit., p. 238.

49 JNDL Collection, *Chian Jōsei* No. 394 (September 15, 1945) in "Chian Jōsei Kempei Shireibu 1945, August–September," Japanese Army and Navy Archives, Reel 229, T1555/f02498–02511.

50 Kaburagi Seiichi, op. cit., pp. 50–55.

51 Ibid., pp. 35–36.

52 In his memoirs, Kaburagi mentions "the Admiral of the US Pacific Fleet" who was entertained at the Ōkura Villa one night. A "dancer" called Emiko, from Oasis of Ginza, who served the Admiral, complained to Kaburagi the following morning that she had had to serve him five times during the night and was thoroughly exhausted. See Kaburagi Seiichi, op. cit., pp. 43–44.

53 Ibid., pp. 42–43. In his diary, Mark Gayn, a correspondent for the *Chicago Sun*, also refers to a special club called the Daian Club, at which American guests were treated to "good food, liquor, and women on the house." This club, which was not part of the RAA's organization, was run by a multi-business operator and gangster, Andō Akira. Gayn described Andō's various tactics "of the shrewd, well-organized and well-financed Japanese campaign to corrupt the Army of the United States." He concluded that "the weapons are wine, women, and hospitality, and the objective is to subvert the starch and purpose of the occupation." See Mark Gayn, op. cit., pp. 124–125, 245–246.

54 JNDL Collection, Kanagawa-ken Chiji Fujiwara Takao, "Gaihi Gōgai" (September 13, 1945) in MOJ 8, "Japanese Government Documents and Censored Publications," Reel 4, "Police Intelligence Reports."

55 Duus Masayo, op. cit., pp. 83–84.

56 "Memorandum for the Record by James H. Gordon, Subject: Conference with Major Philip Weisbach" (September 30, 1945) in USNA Collection, RG 331, SCAP, Box 9370, "Venereal Disease Control: 1945–1946," Document No. 3. In this memorandum, "Mokojuna" seems to refer to "Mukōjima," one of the well-known red-light districts in Tokyo.

57 Kanzaki Kiyoshi, op. cit., pp. 144–148.

58 "Record of Health: Examination of the 3rd week of October" in USNA Collection, RG 331, SCAP, Box 9370, "Venereal Disease Control: 1945–1946," Document No. 17.

59 Duus Masayo, op. cit., pp. 153–155.

60 Mark Gayn, op. cit., pp. 212–215.

61 "GHQ Public Health and Welfare Section, Welfare Sub-Section, Memorandum for the Record" (December 29, 1945) in USNA Collection, RG 331, SCAP Box 9370, "Abolition of Licenced Prostitution."

62 Ibid.

63 Kobayashi Daijirō and Murase Akira, op. cit., pp. 21–23.

64 Ibid., pp. 21–23.

65 Cited in Duus Masayo, op. cit., pp. 174–175.

66 Kanagawa-ken Keisatsu Hombu Keistasu-shi Hensan Iinkai ed., op. cit., p. 693.

67 "Commander Naval Activities Japan" (August 2, 1946) in USNA Collection, RG 331, SCAP, Box 9370, "Venereal Disease Control: 1945–1946," Document No. 50.

68 AA Collection, A5954/1886/2 "Report by Commander-in-Chief, British Commonwealth Occupation Force for Month of September 1946: Part IV – 'A' (Personal) Matters, Section 12 – Medical;" AWM Collection, AWM 114/267/6/17 "Notes on VD Control Officers (10 October 1946)" and "Control of VD (12 September 1946)."

69 AWM Collection, AWM 114/267/6/17 "Notes on VD Control Officers (10 October 1946)" and "Control of VD (12 September 1946)."

70 A series of memorandums by James H. Gordon under the title of "Conference with Dr. H. Yosano and Dr. Fukai" in USNA Collection, RG 331, SCAP, Box 9370, "Venereal Disease Control: 1945–1946," Document No. 5.

71 "Memorandum for the Record by James H. Gordon, Subject: Conference with Dr. Yosano, Tokyo Health Department, on Venereal Disease" (October 26, 1945) in ibid., Document No. 19.

72 "Memorandum for the Record by James H. Gordon, Subject: Conference with Dr. T. Ichikawa, Professor of Urology, Tokyo Imperial University" in ibid., Document Nos. 19 and 20.

73 "Memorandum for the Record by James H. Gordon, Subject: Visit to Yokohama" (November 3, 1945) and "Memorandum for the Record by James H. Gordon, Subject: Plan for the Use of Anti-Venereal Drugs Released to Japanese form US Army Stocks" (November 4, 1945) in ibid., Document Nos. 16 and 24.

74 "Memorandum for the Record by James H. Gordon, Subject: Visit to Yokohama" (November 3, 1945) in ibid., Document No. 25.

75 "Incoming Message, Restricted, Routine from Washington (SPMDW) to CINCAFPAC (For Sams Public Health and Welfare Section)" (November 22, 1945) in ibid., Document No. 45.

76 Duus Masayo, op. cit., p. 151.

77 "Regulation No. 45 issued by the Ministry of Health and Social Affairs. The Complementary Regulation for the Venereal Disease Prevention Law in accordance with Imperial Ordinance No. 542" (November 22, 1945) in USNA Collection, RG 331, SCAP, Box 9370, "Venereal Disease Control: 1945–1946," Document No. 28.

78 Ibid.

79 "Memorandum for the Record by Hugh McDonald, Subject: Conference on Venereal Disease and Related Legislation" (December 6, 1945) in ibid., Document No. 32.

80 "Memorandum for the Record by Philip E. M. Bourland, Subject: Venereal Disease Control and Treatment Problems in Tokyo" (June 6, 1946) in ibid., Document No. 50.

81 "Letter from Tokyo–Yokohama Chapter Army–Navy Chaplains Association. to SCAP, General Headquarters" (January 11, 1946) in ibid., Document No. 45.

82 "Memorandums by Public Health and Welfare Section, under the title of 'Control of Venereal Disease'" (January 22, and February 2, 1946) in ibid., Document No. 45.

83 "Memorandum by C. F. Sams, Chief, Public Health and Welfare Section, Subject: Venereal Disease Contact-Tracing in Tokyo" in ibid., Document No. 43.

84 "From BCOF to Army Melbourne, COS 8177. TOP SECRET for JCOSA" (September 12, 1946); "Joint Chiefs of Staff in Australia Agendum. Report by C.N.S. (K) and C.O.S. (I) on their visit to Japan – Subsequent Action. Appendix C, Medical – High Incidence of Venereal Disease Within BCOF" in AA Collection, A5954/1886/2, "British Commonwealth Occupation Forces: Incidence of Venereal Disease" (September 4, 1946–July 27, 1956).

85 "Memorandum by Crawford F. Sams" (December 26, 1946) in USNA Collection, RG 331, SCAP, Box 9370, "Abolition of Licenced Prostitution."

86 AWM Collection, AWM 114/267/6/17 "Duties of Personnel Comprising the Anti-VD Team" (June 28, 1946).

87 "Letter from T. Katsube, Chief of Liaison Section, Central Liaison Office, to GHQ" (July 17, 1946) in USNA Collection, RG 331, SCAP, Box 9370, "Venereal Disease Control: 1945–1946," Document No. 55.

88 "Memorandum sent from H. W. Allen, Colonel, AGD, Asst. Adjutant General to Imperial Japanese Government, Subject: Abolition of Licensed Prostitution in Japan" (January 21, 1946) in ibid., Document No. 37; "Memorandum for the Record by M. H. McDonald, Subject: Elimination of Licensed Prostitution in Japan" (January 7, 1946) in USNA Collection, RG 331, SCAP, Box 9370, "Abolition of Licenced Prostitution."

89 "Memorandum by Director of the Police Affairs Bureau, Ministry of Home Affairs, submitted to Superintendent-General of the Metropolitan Police Board, Subject: Guidance and Control regarding Abolition of the System of Licensed Prostitution" (May 28, 1946) in USNA Collection, RG 331, SCAP, Box 1416 "Japanese Taxes on Prostitution."

90 "Memorandum by Crawford F. Sams" (December 26, 1946) in USNA Collection, RG 331, SCAP, Box 9370, "Abolition of Licenced Prostitution."

91 "Memorandum by James H. Gordon, Subject: Venereal Disease Problems in Japan" (January 22, 1946) in USNA Collection, RG 331, SCAP, Box 9370, "Venereal Disease Control: 1945–1946," Document No. 37.

92 Kobayashi Daijirō and Murase Akira, op. cit., pp. 87–88; Duus Masayo, op. cit., pp. 202–203.

93 Strangely, documents related to the introduction of the nationwide "off-limits" policy are not included in a large volume of files on VD problems prepared by PHW Section, USNA Collection, RG 331, SCAP, Box 9370, "Venereal Disease Control: 1945–1946."

94 Itsushima Tsutomu, ed., op. cit., pp. 76–79; Duus Masayo, op. cit., pp. 223–224.

95 Stated by Bruce Ruxton, a former member of BCOF and presently the president of the Returned Services League (i.e. an Australian veterans organization) in the state of Victoria. The interview appeared in 'RSL denies mass rape in occupied Japan,' *The Australian*, September 24, 1993.

96 Yoshimi Kaneko, op. cit., pp. 206–212; Kanzaki Kiyoshi, op. cit., p. 384; Duus Masayo, op. cit., p. 230.

97 Kanzaki Kiyoshi, op. cit., p. 384; Duus Masayo, op. cit., p. 234.

98 "Letter from R. L. Eichelberger, Commanding General, Eighth Army, to Commander-in-Chief, Far East, Subject: Suppression of Prostitution" (January 4, 1947) in USNA Collection, RG 331, SCAP, Box 9370, "Abolition of Licenced Prostitution."

99 Itsushima Tsutomu, ed., op. cit., p. 80.

100 Ibid., pp. 53–58.

101 Tsutsumi Mineo, "Senryōka no Gunji Saiban" in Shisō no Kagaku Kenkyū-kai ed., *Kyōdō Kenkyū Nippon Senryō* (Tokuuma Shoten, Tokyo, 1972), in particular pp. 347–349.

102 Itsushima Tsutomu, ed., op. cit., pp. 58–62.

103 Ibid., p. 85.

104 Ibid., p. 85.

105 Kanagawa-ken Keisatsu Hombu Keistasu-shi Hensan Iinkai ed., op. cit., pp. 693–696.

106 Duus Masayo, op. cit., p. 292.

107 Cited in Duus Masayo, op. cit., p. 292.

108 It was in 1956 that the Diet finally passed the bill to make illegal any form of prostitution in Japan. Yet, clandestine prostitution has been widely practised all over Japan since the law was enacted. Traditional red-light districts, such as Yoshiwara in Tokyo, are still a Mecca of the sex industry, attracting many Japanese businessmen, bureaucrats, and politicians – often guests of large corporations. For details of Japan's present sex industry, see, for example, Yoshimi Kaneko, op. cit., pp. 216–257.

Epilogue

1 There are a number of publications on the history of the karayuki-san system. The most well known work in Japanese is probably Morisaki Kazue's *Karayuki-san* (Asahi Shimbun-sha, Tokyo, 1977). Some publications on this topic are also available in English, such as Yamazaki Tomoko, *Sandakan Brothel No. 8: An Episode in the History of Lower-class Japanese Women* (M. E. Sharpe, New York, 1999); and Jim Warren, *Ah Ku and Karayuki-san: Prostitution in Singapore 1870–1940* (Oxford University Press, Singapore, 1993).

2 Morisaki Kazue, op. cit., pp. 66–69.

3 Fujinaga Takeshi, "Shanhai no Nippon-gun Ianjyo to Chōsenjin" in Katsura Mitsumasa *et al.* eds, *Kokusai Toshi Shanhai* (Ōsaka Sangyō Daigaku Kenkyūjo, Osaka, 1995) pp. 113–120.

4 Ibid., pp. 120–122.

5 Shimizu Hiroshi, "Karayuki-san and the Japanese Economic Advance into British Malaya, 1870–1920" in *Asian Studies Review*, Vol. 20, No. 3 (Asian Studies Association of Australia, Melbourne, 1997) pp. 107–108.

6 Yoshimi Kaneko, *Baishō no Shakai-shi* (Yūzankaku Shuppan, Tokyo, 1992) p. 10.

7 Shimizu Hiroshi, op. cit., pp. 111–114.

8 Karen Colligan-Taylor, "Translator's Introduction" in Yamazaki Tomoko, op. cit., pp. xviii-xxiv.

9 Morisaki Kazue, op. cit., pp. 22–55.

10 Yoshimi Kaneko, op. cit., pp. 7–8.

11 Yamazaki Tomoko, op. cit., pp. 9–14.

12 Morisaki Kazue, op. cit., Chapters 4 & 5.

13 Shimizu Hiroshi, op. cit., p. 119–120.

14 Ibid., pp. 120–121.

15 K. Tsukuda and S. Kato, *Nanyō no Shin Nihonjinmura* (Nanbokusha, Tokyo, 1919) pp. 101–102, cited by Shimizu Hiroshi, op. cit., p. 107.

16 Yoshimi Kaneko, op. cit., p. 12.

17 Fukuzawa Yukichi, "Jinmin no Ijyū to Shōfu no Dekasegi" in *Jiji Shinpō*, January 18, 1896, cited by Yoshimi Kaneko, op. cit., p. 11.

18 Fujinaga Takeshi, "Nichi-Ro Sensō to Nippon ni yoru 'Manshu' e no Kōshō Seido Ishoku" in *Osaka Sangyo University Research Studies* No. 8 (Osaka Sangyo Daigaku, Osaka, 1998) pp. 63–64; Morisaki Kazue, op. cit., pp. 132–142.

19 Fujinaga Takeshi, "Nichi-Ro Sensō to Nippon ni yoru 'Manshu' e no Kōshō Seido Ishoku" pp. 67–70.

20 Ibid., pp. 73–91.

21 Ibid., pp. 91–92.

22 Julia O'Connell Davidson, *Prostitution, Power and Freedom* (Polity Press, Cambridge, 1998) p. 134.

23 Ibid., p. 134.

24 Ibid., p. 134.

25 Ibid., p. 134.

26 W. Broyles Jr., "Why Men Love War" in Walter Capps ed., *The Vietnam Reader* (Routledge, London, 1991) p. 79.

27 ANA Collection, MP76/3, G135, "Sir James Barret, Medical Control Venereal Diseases"; Richard Holmes, *Acts of War: the Behaviour of Men in Battle* (Free Press, New York, 1985) pp. 95–96.

28 Richard Holmes, op. cit., p. 97.

29 For a more detailed psycho-social analysis of the relationship between sexual violence and war, see Yuki Tanaka, *Hidden Horrors: Japanese War Crimes in World War II* (Westview, Boulder, 1996) pp. 105–109; and Ruth Seifert, "War and Rape: A Preliminary Analysis" in Alexandra Stiglmayer ed., *Mass Rape: The War against Women in Bosnia-Herzegovina*

(University of Nebraska, Lincoln, 1994) pp. 54–72. In particular, the argument in her "Thesis 3" is useful in this context.

30 Y. Tanaka, op. cit., p. 107.

31 A. Nicholas Groth, *Men Who Rape: The Psychology of the Offender* (Plenum Press, New York, 1979) pp. 25–44.

32 Ibid., p. 30.

33 Ibid., p. 58. The power rape is also a widely practised but hidden problem among incarcerated men at penal institutions. Homosexual rape is often used by a kingpin prisoner to feminize other prisoners and to demonstrate his power over them. Very little research has so far been conducted on this topic, but some useful information is available in David Heilpern, *Fear of Favour: Sexual Assault of Young Prisoners* (Southern Cross University Press, Lismore, 1998).

34 For details of sexual crimes committed by American soldiers in Okinawa, see, for example, Takazato Suzuyo, *Okinawa no Onna-tachi: Jyosē no Jinken to Kīchi, Guntai* (Akashi Shoten, Tokyo, 1996)

35 Shimabukuro Sōkō and Urashima Etsuko, "Kichi naki Okinawa o" in *Oruta*, No. 218, January 1996, p. 15.

36 Chūkan Beigun Hanzai Konzetsu no tame no Undō Hombu ed., *Chūkan Beigun Hanzai Hakusho* (Aoki Shoten, Tokyo, 1999) pp. 26–28, 123–133.

37 Cynthia Enloe, *The Morning After: Sexual Politics at the End of the Cold War* (University of California Press, Berkley, 1993), in particular Chapter 5.

38 Ibid., p. 145.

39 Henry Reynolds, *The Other Side of Frontier: Aboriginal Resistance to the European Invasion of Australia* (Penguin Books Australia, 1981) pp. 70–72. For more details of the historical process of the colonization of Australian Aborigines by the Europeans, see, for example, Henry Reynolds, *Dispossession: Black and White Invaders* (Allen & Unwin, Sydney, 1996).

40 Okuyama Ryō, *Ainu Suibō-shi* (Miyama Shobō, Sapporo, 1966) pp. 140–143, 146–155; Sekiba Fujihiko, *Ainu Ijidan* (originally published in 1896 and reproduced by Hokkaidō Shuppan Kikaku Sentā in Sapporo in 1980) p. 165. For example, it is estimated that, between 1822 and 1874, the Ainu population in western Hokkaido decreased by one-sixth, and, according to Dr. Sekiba Fujihiko, a general practitioner who worked in Hokkaido in the Meiji period, syphilis was still one of the most common diseases among his Ainu patients in the mid-1890s.

41 See, for example, Ronald Hyam, *Empire and Sexuality: The British Experience* (Manchester University Press, Manchester, 1990).

42 See, for example, John Ingleson, "Prostitution in Colonial Java" in D. P. Chadler and M. C. Ricklefs eds., *Ninteenth and Twentieth Century Indonesia: Essays in Honour of Professor J. D. Legge* (Centre of Southeast Asian Studies, Monash University, Melbourne, 1986).

43 SOFA stands for Status of Forces Agreement, but the full title of this agreement is "Agreement under Article IV of the Mutual Defense Treaty between the United States of America and the Republic of Korea, regarding facilities and areas and the status of US Armed Forces in the Republic of Korea."

44 This information was provided to the author by Ms. Jeong Yu-jin, Secretary General of the National Campaign for Eradication of Crimes by US Troops in Korea.

45 Iris Young, *Justice and the Politics of Difference* (Princeton University Press, Princeton, 1990) p. 64.

46 Takamure Itsue, *Jyosē no Rekishi, Vol. 2* (Kōdan-sha, Tokyo, 1972) pp. 43–47.

47 For details of Japan's modern history of its licensed prostitution industry and how tax on prostitutes was used to gain government revenue, see Fujime Yuki, "The Licensed Prostitution System and the Prostitution Abolish Movement in Modern Japan" in *Position*, Vol. 5, No. 1, 1997, as well as her Japanese book, *Sei no Rekishigaku* (Fuji Shuppan, Tokyo, 1998). Fujime is one of a growing number of Japanese feminist scholars who are trying to re-examine Japan's modern history from feminist perspectives.

Index

Hospital 163; Preventive Health Department 156;
red-light districts 15, 152, 157; shopping districts
142, 143, 146, 152; University 165; US troops
arrive in 115, 116, 121; Yoshiwara City Hospital
156
Tokyo Metropolitan Association of Licensed Brothels
141
Tokyo Metropolitan Association of the Restaurant
and Bar Industry 141
Tokyo University 165
Tokyo War Crimes Tribunal 29, 61, 62, 84, 87, 64,
67
Tomita Kenji 25
torture by Japanese 50–1, 56, 74
Townsville 102, 103
trafficking in women xvi, 25–6, 33
Trinidad 100
Tripoli 96–7
Tsukada Osamu, Maj-Gen. 20
Tsushima Toshiichi 142

Ulio, Maj-Gen. J. A. 108–9
Umezu Yoshijirō, Lt-Gen. 18, 21, 23
United States of America: black GIs 103; comfort
women 167; 8th Army 123, 124, 151, 155, 157,
163; 1st Cavalry 123, 152; 41st Engineers 92;
G-1 90, 91, 92, 100, 102; G-2 87; General Staff
88; indifference to comfort women 82, 83, 84–7;
Joint Army-Navy Vice Control Board 91; marines
123, 155, 156; military-controlled prostitution 91,
92–8, 101, 106, 107, 108; National Archives 84–5,
88; navy 155, 156, 168; Office of War Information
85; prostitutes sent abroad 101; sailors 168; 24th
Corps 86–7; 29th Division 107; venereal disease
prevention 87–92; War Department 88, 89, 91, 98,
99, 100, 101, 102, 106, 107, 108, 109, 159–61

van Bakerghem, Mrs 62
van der Ploeg, Ellen 75–6
vandalism, Allied 124
'Venereal Disease Control Programs in the Caribbean
Area' 102
venereal disease: Allies 88, 89, 90, 92–8, 99, 100,
101, 102, 140, 152, 155–66, 175, 180; American
policies on prevention 87–92; brothel owners 18;
brothels and prevention 9, 10, 24, 27, 30, 32, 98,
108, 109, 173; Chinese comfort stations 17;
comfort women 18, 30, 44, 53, 57, 74, 77, 101,
153, 156, 172; Dutch army 82; Italian 97; Japanese
11, 22, 27, 30, 67, 72, 171, 172, 180; medical
examinations 9, 11, 51; prophylactic chemicals 30,
78, 88–9, 90, 91, 94, 95, 101, 108, 152, 156;
prophylactic stations 90, 91, 92, 93, 96, 98, 100,
101, 102, 151, 153, 157; uncontrollable 166; *see also*
condoms

Venezuela 100
Verbeek, Mrs 62
Vietnam War xvi, 60, 112, 175, 177, 179
Vladivostok 10, 167–8, 170

Wagner, Robert 106
waitresses 9, 36
Warella, Mrs 62
Weisbach, Maj. Phillip 151–2
Weston, *see* Beaufort
Willow Run, *see* Tokyo: International Palace
Wilson, Maj. 129–30
women's villages 92
Women's Voluntary Labor Service Corps 40, 41
Women's Voluntary Labor Service Law (1944) 40,
41–2
Women's Volunteer Corps 138, 139, 143
Wood, Col. W. A., Jr 88
World War, First 114, 175
Wright, Prof. R. D. 103
Wuhan 15, 28
Wuhu 15
Wusong 15

Xuzhou 15

Yakuza 138, 140
Yamamoto Yoshiji 137
Yamazaki Iwao 119, 133, 150–1
Yamazaki Masao, Maj. 13
Yanagawa Heisuke, Lt-Gen. 20, 21
Yanaihara Tadao, Prof. 165
Yangzhou 14, 15, 45
Yantzi River 13, 16
Yingkou 171
Yokohama 113, 116, 118, 122, 137, 152, 165; Ashina
Bridge 121; City Police 155; earthquake (1923) 35;
US troops arrive 143
Yokosuka 113, 114, 116, 119, 121, 137, 155; US
troops arrive 143, 147
Yomiuri Hōchi 114, 115, 124, 125, 146
Yoneyama Saburō 139–40
Yongdo 40
Yōpan 165
Yosano Hikaru, Dr 156
Yoshimoto Teiichi, Lt-Gen. 21
Yoshiura 136
Young, Iris 181
Young Women's Corps 12
Yun Chung Ok, Prof. xv
Yun Kumi 178, 181

Zamami Island 112
Zhenjiang 15
Zushi 113